GUADALCANAL

GUADALCANAL

EDWIN
P.
HOYT

STEIN AND DAY/*PUBLISHERS*/New York

Published in the United States of America in 1981.
Copyright © 1981 by Edwin P. Hoyt
All rights reserved.
Designed by Judith E. Dalzell
Printed in the United States of America
Stein and Day/*Publishers*
Scarborough House
Briarcliff Manor, N.Y. 10510

CONTENTS

All photographs not otherwise attributed are from the National Archives. The maps captioned "Battle of Savo Island," "Battle of the Eastern Solomons," "Battle of Cape Esperance," and "Battle of Guadalcanal; air attacks on the Japanese" are reprinted by courtesy of the U.S. Navy. The maps captioned "The Solomons and the southern approaches," "Landing Objectives in the Tulago-Gavutu Area," "The Solomon Islands," and "Guadalcanal-Tulagi" are from *A Battle History of the Imperial Japanese Navy* by Paul S. Dull and are reprinted courtesy of The Naval Institute Press. The map captioned "The Pacific" is from Mark Arnold-Forster's *The World at War*, and is reprinted by courtesy of Stein and Day Publishers.

LIST OF ILLUSTRATIONS AND MAPS

Flooded marine camp
Japanese barges sunk in the Lunga River
Japanese troopship beached on Guadalcanal
The U.S.S. *San Francisco*
The U.S.S. *Pensacola* showing torpedo damage
Japanese transports burning
A B-17 bomber
Flaming Japanese plane falling during night attack
The sinking U.S.S. *Chicago*

Maps

THE BEST LAID PLANS . . .

ON the 5th of January, 1942, as exultant shouts of victory
resounded in the streets of Tokyo, Admiral Isoroku Yamamoto instructed the staff of the Imperial Combined Fleet to begin preparing
for the second stage of operations in the Pacific War. His study of
the situation reports on the Philippines, Malaya, and points south indicated that Japanese troops in a few months would be in control of
East Asia and the other areas they had attacked in December. So
Yamamoto told his chief of staff, Matome Ugaki, that he wanted the
plans to be completed by the middle of February.

The speed with which the Japanese had conquered the western
Pacific astounded the planners in Tokyo and brought about sharp
disagreement within the Imperial General Staff. The ardent military
nationalists wanted to press on as long as Japan was victorious, no
matter how far afield such planning led. Another group, represented
by Admiral Yamamoto, had been less than enthusiastic about the
opening of war with the United States and Britain, and worried
about the future. One reason Yamamoto was at sea aboard the Combined Fleet flagship *Yamato* was that friends on the Imperial General Staff had worried that if he remained in Tokyo he would be assassinated because of his public opposition to unlimited war. Even
now his opinions were no secret from those around him. His chief of

staff, Admiral Ugaki, wrote in his diary about the need for "far-sighted statesmanship" following this first month of glorious victory; those were words that Yamamoto often used in warning that Japan could not war on the Western Powers and hope to win in the long run.

Yamamoto's open criticism of the politicians was aimed at Prince Konoye and others who did not seem to know what sort of war Japan should wage in the Pacific. Three months before Pearl Harbor, Yamamoto had met with a friend, Ryoichi Sasakawa, president of the ultra-nationalist Kokusuei Domei organization at the Imperial Navy Club in Shiba. Yamamoto, warning his friend that war was inevitable because of decisions taken by the politicians, said that "at first we'll have everything our own way, stretching out like an octopus spreading its tentacles." And now, just a month after the war had begun, the octopus was spread almost flat.

Yamamoto, however, had also warned his old friend that the euphoria could not last. The time, he said, for political action was the moment that Singapore fell. That disaster would unsettle the British in India, and they would undoubtedly be willing to listen to talk of peace. Yamamoto knew the British well; he had been a member of the delegations to the London Naval Conferences of 1930 and 1934. He also knew the Americans. He had been Japanese naval attaché in Washington from 1926 to 1928. He agreed that once war was started by the politicians a major victory must be won quickly. But when that victory was achieved, he believed Japan would have only a year and a half to bask in glory. "We must get a peace agreement by then," he told Sasakawa, and he looked to this old friend to carry the word among the right-wing political leaders who were in power.

On January 5 the victory seemed close at hand. The American battleship fleet had been put out of action at Pearl Harbor on December 7. The British battleships *Repulse* and *Prince of Wales* had been sunk off the Malay coast. In the Philippines, Manila and the U.S. naval base at Cavite had been captured. The British had surrendered at Hong Kong, and Japanese forces were on their way to new landings in the Dutch East Indies, at Rabaul, on New Ireland, Amboina, and in the Solomon Islands.

The attack at Pearl Harbor, however, had not accomplished all Yamamoto had hoped for: the destruction of the major elements of the U.S. fleet. The aircraft carriers, which had been at sea, were

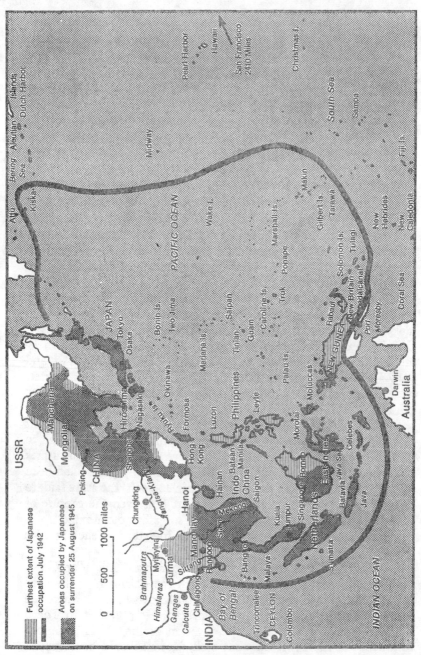

The Pacific

unharmed and represented a constant threat. What was needed was a spectacular achievement. Yamamoto did not expect the fall of Singapore for five or six months. (It came on February 15.) He believed that if he was to achieve his goal of setting up the stage for negotiation he must move in another direction.

The question before his planners was where to strike next. The army vetoed Yamamoto's suggestion for an attack on the Soviet Union; such a war would be fought almost entirely on land, and the army was heavily occupied in China and Southeast Asia.

Three other ideas were offered. Yamamoto's favorite was to attack in the Indian Ocean, invade Ceylon, draw out the British Far Eastern Fleet and destroy it as Yamamoto had destroyed the American ships at Pearl Harbor, and then push into the Middle East to link up with the Germans, who were driving toward the Soviet oil fields in the Caucasus. Thus the Japanese Navy would be assured of all the oil it needed.

The army refused to consider a Middle Eastern operation, so only two plans were left. One, advocated by the Naval General Staff in Tokyo, called for an attack on Australia to deprive the Americans of that forward base of operations. After moving into the Solomon Islands, the navy would take New Guinea, New Caledonia, Fiji, and Samoa. Advocates of this plan at Imperial General Headquarters were already setting up occupation systems for Australia and New Zealand.

But Yamamoto did not like the Australia plan, because he thought it would take too long and still would not be spectacular enough to halt the Americans. Yamamoto also knew the Pearl Harbor attack had aroused the spirit of vengeance in people the Japanese had been learning to detest as soft and incompetent, too soft, the army said, to fight a war to the finish. It was apparent that even the capture of Singapore would not stop the Americans. Yamamoto wanted a victory that would make it possible for Japan to extend a generous olive branch.

In January, Yamamoto ordered another plan drawn and, two months later, sent officers to Tokyo with the document, designated the MI plan, which envisaged a battle off Midway Island, where the American carrier force would be destroyed. He also sent to Tokyo the AL plan, which detailed the invasion of the North American continent via Alaska. If all went well, Hawaii would be occupied, and later perhaps, the West Coast. At least, victories at Midway and in the Aleutians would give the politicians a base for negotiating the sort of peace that Yamamoto hoped to achieve.

In Tokyo the admirals quarreled around the conference table in the Navy Ministry, but in the end Yamamoto had his way. Forgotten was the potential significance of the fall of Singapore in February, and the impending collapse of Bataan and Corregidor, either of which might have served Yamamoto's purpose. The reason they were no longer important lay in the April raid of Lt. Col. Jimmy Doolittle's B-25 bomber squadron on Tokyo. The Doolittle raid had shocked the Japanese into a realization that the Americans were only beginning to fight.

In June, after the Midway operation flamed into disaster for Japan, there was no time for recrimination; indeed, the army did not even know the full extent of the defeat. The news of the destruction of four big fleet carriers was carefully suppressed so that it was known only at the highest levels of the navy.

While Yamamoto had been off on his Midway excursion, the Naval General Staff in Tokyo had moved the navy and its air forces steadily southward to set up the forthcoming attempt to cut off Australia. Naval forces had taken Rabaul on January 23. From that time onward they had conducted constant air reconnaissance and bombing raids against other islands and New Guinea. It was apparent to the Australians, who communicated their concerns to General Douglas MacArthur after his arrival in March, that the Japanese would soon move against New Guinea. If they were successful it would be very nearly a walkover for the Japanese to take northern Australia. In February, the Japanese had already bombed Darwin. In March, when they invaded Salamaua, New Guinea, the pace stepped up.

In May, just before the Midway battle, the Japanese sent an occupation force toward Port Moresby, but it was turned back by the fierce defense of the Americans and Australians in the carrier Battle of the Coral Sea. The Japanese did occupy Tulagi, north of Guadalcanal, and built a seaplane base there.

The Battle of the Coral Sea convinced planners in Washington and Australia that they had to prepare for a Japanese move in the south. MacArthur told the Australian government it must be ready for an attack before a Japanese thrust that was generally expected to be made against India. He cabled General Marshall for two carriers and a thousand planes. But in Washington that May, Admiral Ernest J. King, Chief of Naval Operations, informed General Marshall that until the end of June he would have only two working carriers in the entire Pacific, while (on the eve of Midway) the Japanese had ten. And Pacific Fleet Commander Chester W. Nimitz had already given advance warning about the big move he expected the Japanese to make, which turned out to be the Midway battle.

While events were taking their course at Midway, the Japanese were establishing their forces in the New Guinea-Solomons area. Major General Tomitaro Horii landed the South Seas Force at Salamaua. Naval troops occupied Lae, and began to build up an air base there.

Independently of Admiral Yamamoto, the Imperial General Staff had planned the Port Moresby operation, and Lieutenant General Harukichi Hyukatake was ordered to press on toward New Caledonia, Fiji, and Samoa and to be ready to resume the advance against Port Moresby by July. That would be after the Midway battle, when Admiral Yamamoto could be expected to have returned with his Combined Fleet. That big carrier force was expected to protect this new move.

In spite of the defeat at Midway, which was reported as a victory to the forces in the field, Imperial General Headquarters did not alter its plans. A few days after Midway the Australians informed General MacArthur that the Japanese were ready to move. In view of the Midway victory, MacArthur suggested that the Allies make a preemptive attack on the New Britain-New Ireland area and then an assault on Rabaul, the main Japanese naval and air base in the area. With the two carriers and the 1,000 planes and an amphibious division, MacArthur would force the Japanese back to Truk.

On June 12, General Marshall offered the MacArthur plan to Admiral King with some modification: He wanted three carriers instead of two, and one marine division and three army divisions to make the assaults.

Admiral King opposed the idea, because it would put MacArthur in command of the fighting. King's other reasons were supplementary: The carriers would be subject to land-based attack, and they would not have enough protection. (As it turned out, the Navy had to cope with both of these tactical problems at Guadalcanal.)

King devised his own plan, a drive from the New Hebrides by forces under Navy command. MacArthur objected to having his Army forces serve under the Navy, but nobody could deny the necessity of stopping the Japanese before they took New Guinea and were poised to attack Australia. The problem for the Joint Chiefs of Staff was who was going to command the operation. They gave "phase one"—the primary task of taking the Santa Cruz Islands, Tulagi, and "adjacent positions"—to Admiral King. (Guadalcanal was just a spot

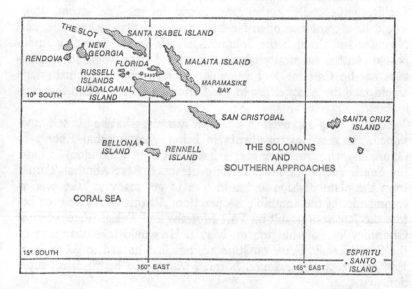

The Solomons and southern approaches

on the map with no known tactical or strategic value; it did not even merit a name in this JCS plan.) General MacArthur was thrown a sop: after "phase one" he was to take over and mop up the Japanese in the rest of the Solomons, Rabaul, and New Guinea.

Admiral King was given his way because the Joint Chiefs of Staff recognized that King had already planned a defense line down the Pacific to protect Australia, and his plan would need relatively less force than MacArthur's. Thousands of troops were training in New Caledonia, and King had wheedled General Arnold into sending several squadrons of U.S. Army Air Force planes there. He had reinforced Samoa and Efate in the New Hebrides. He planned to put a base in Tonga. Admiral Wilson Brown, whose indecisiveness at the time of the Wake Island crisis had aroused King's annoyance, was shipped off to a newly established unit called the Amphibious Training Command. At San Diego, he and Marine Major General Holland Smith were told to develop new techniques for island warfare. Rear Admiral Richmond Kelly Turner, King's chief plans officer, suggested that the first effort must be to hold the line in the South Pacific, while training the amphibious forces. The second stage would be a combined offensive by the United States, Australia, and New Zealand through the Solomon Islands, to the Bismarck Archipelago and the Admiralty Islands. The third stage would involve seizure of the Caroline and Marshall Islands, and the fourth stage would take the Allies either to the Dutch East Indies or to the Philippines.

Admiral King approved this plan; it was just what he himself envisioned. He made arrangements to bring Vice Admiral Robert L. Ghormley, who was serving as a naval observer in London, to head the South Pacific Command. King detached Rear Admiral Turner from the plans division and told him to get ready to take over as commander of the amphibious operation. All this was done even before the Japanese assault on Port Moresby and Tulagi. Vice Admiral Ghormley left Washington on May 1. He would take command of the South Pacific Force on June 19, but first he had to go to Pearl Harbor to report to Admiral Nimitz, who would be his direct superior.

By the time Ghormley got to Pearl Harbor the Japanese offensive was already beginning in the South Pacific. On May 22 an army plane saw a Japanese photo reconnaissance aircraft taking pictures of Guadalcanal. Army Intelligence suggested that the Japanese were preparing to build an airfield there. On June 25, Army Intelligence reported that the grass on the island's central plain had been burned off, and tents had gone up in the area. A wharf was under construction at Lunga. Six days later an Australian coastwatcher on Guadalcanal reported that construction of an airfield was only awaiting the arrival of Japanese construction units. He even knew the names: the 11th and 13th Pioneer Forces, which were the equivalent of American Seabee units.

This information was confirmed in a radio interception made by

Nimitz's intelligence officers at Pearl Harbor. The Pacific Fleet's radio intelligence group, which had broken parts of the Japanese naval code, picked up a message saying that the 11th and 13th Pioneer Forces would arrive at their destination on July 4. Fleet intelligence put two and two together. Admiral Turner happened to be visiting Pearl Harbor that day on his way to prepare for the amphibious landing somewhere in the South Pacific; when Admiral Nimitz received the radio intelligence report, Admiral Turner knew where he was going: It could be no place but the Solomons. Within two weeks, Turner was in Wellington, where he boarded his flagship the U.S.S. *McCawley*, the former Grace Line passenger ship *Santa Barbara*. His task was to train a whole amphibious task force in one month.

As Turner began to move ships and men around, Admiral Ghormley was on his way to Melbourne to confer with General MacArthur. Ghormley left New Zealand with his head full of gloomy thoughts about the foolishness of trying to stage an amphibious operation when no one knew how to do it. MacArthur, who had his own reasons for disliking the plan, agreed with him entirely. They also agreed that with the planes at hand they could not guarantee the landings sufficient air coverage. After all, this meeting occurred on July 18, and the landings were to be made in three weeks. They sent a dispatch back to Washington recommending that the operation be "deferred."

King was not happy with that message. King had told his new commander that he was handing him a difficult job, and that he would not be able to give him the proper tools until perhaps the fall.

The answer was No. The invasion would proceed as planned.

Ghormley had left Washington convinced that the United States was not ready for aggressive action in the South Pacific. His gloom increased when he tried and failed to get Seabees and other units sent immediately to New Zealand.

From the beginning, the Guadalcanal invasion plan was notable for failures of intelligence. All concerned commands knew that an operation was in the offing, particularly after July 10, when Admiral Nimitz sent Admiral Ghormley his operations orders. The major Japanese air base was located at Rabaul; planes from those fields could stop at Guadalcanal, refuel, and then bomb Australia. There was no doubt that they could strike a deadly blow at the Allied buildup. But on July 10, the Allied intelligence services report reaching King contained only a casual comment about airfield construction at Guadalcanal, and a few days later, a report located the field on the wrong side of the island.

By the end of July the Japanese had completed the airfield, and back at Combined Fleet Headquarters in Japan Admiral Yamamoto gave orders that the first staged mission would leave Rabaul on August 14.

As commander of the overall U.S. operation, Admiral Ghormley tried desperately to get more help, to build advance bases, to bring in more planes. But everywhere he turned he learned the truth of Admiral King's assertion that he would not be able to provide Ghormley with proper tools. The supplies of the invasion forces, for example, were loaded hodgepodge aboard the transports. At Auckland there were plenty of docks, so that the ships could have been unloaded and reloaded with supplies in the order of their intended use. Instead, the ships were sent to Nouméa, which had no such facilities.

Admiral King had at least a general idea of the difficulties, but there was not time for delay. King knew better than any of his subordinates the absolute necessity of stopping the Japanese before they got to Australia. The timetable remained.

By late July the rush was on. Seventeen thousand marines were moving by troopship from California, Pearl Harbor, Nouméa, and Samoa. Admiral Ghormley was "too busy" to hold a conference of his commanders, but on July 28 Admiral Frank Jack Fletcher, who was supposed to be in tactical command, called a meeting aboard his flagship, the carrier *Saratoga*. For the first time the tactical unit commanders met to talk about the invasion. Admiral Fletcher was to protect the invasion with his task force. Admiral Turner was to deliver the troops of Marine General Alexander Vandegrift. Once the marines had taken the island, "garrison troops" would be brought in. But so hastily was this operation called that no one had made provision for any troops to be held in reserve. There were no more men available in the South Pacific.

The meeting on the *Saratoga* was not a happy one. Fletcher began by announcing that he would protect the landings at Guadalcanal for only two days. He insisted, and Ghormley's staff members at the meeting concurred, that the carriers must not be risked. Fletcher was gun-shy because he had lost the *Lexington* at Coral Sea and the *Yorktown* at Midway. His thinking went no further than that. In fact, Fletcher said at the meeting that the whole operation was cock-eyed, hasty, and doomed.

Admiral Turner, who had a better idea of the global military picture than any other man in the cabin that day, chided his superior. There was no point in that sort of argument, he said. The decision had been made to risk all. It was their job to carry out orders. Fletcher ought to have known all that; after Coral Sea, Admiral King had been so displeased with Fletcher's constant avoidance of action that he had insisted Admiral Nimitz ascertain the condition of Fletcher's "fighting spirit." Nimitz was a kindly man, and he liked Fletcher. He had given the carrier commander a pep talk, and then when the Battle of Midway was won, Fletcher, who was in command there, could hardly be faulted. But on the eve of the first American offensive operation, to warn the troops and the men of the support ships that he was going to desert them in 48 hours was a most inauspicious beginning.

The "rehearsal" for the Guadalcanal invasion was staged on July 28 and lasted three days. The scene was Koro Island near Fiji. Only a third of the assigned troops managed to get ashore, and when they did, they didn't know what to do. General Vandegrift regarded the mock-up as a "complete bust." But there was no time even to second-guess. On July 31 the marines were back aboard the transports, heading for Guadalcanal. On the afternoon of August 6, as the task force of 75 ships neared the Solomons, Admiral Fletcher nervously broke away with his carriers. He would have his planes over the landing force as promised, but the 26 ships of the carrier group were being taken as far from harm's way as possible.

2

THE LANDINGS

IF American intelligence was so faulty as to permit the Japanese buildup of the airfield at Guadalcanal, Japanese intelligence was faultier, for as the U.S. invasion fleet massed in the South Pacific, the Japanese had no inkling of a forthcoming attack.

In July 1942, the Japanese Army was preoccupied with trying to capture New Guinea as a staging point for its operations against Australia and New Zealand. Major General Tomitaro Horii's South Seas Force landed 2,000 troops near Buna. After capturing Buna, the Japanese planned to construct airfields there as a prelude to a new attack on Port Moresby, so in July Japanese air power was concentrated against Port Moresby. Bombers and fighters swept over the piers and airfields nearly every day. After the Japanese landings, the Japanese air forces were also called on to support the beachhead, and in the early days of August their attention was fixed on the new drive. The combined Australian and American air force responded with raids on the Japanese air bases at Lae.

During these preparations, Admiral Yamamoto's flagship *Yamato* was anchored at Hashirajima in Japanese waters. In a leisurely fashion, he was preparing for the forthcoming air operations over Australia. He would see then what action was to be taken next. In preparation, on August 3 the naval air groups stationed at Lae were brought back to Rabaul to be ready for the Guadalcanal operations that would begin the following week.

During the first week of August the South Pacific skies were cloudy, and only a handful of Japanese search planes took to the skies. None of them found the American armada that was steaming toward Guadalcanal. The Japanese airmen flying out of Rabaul were surprised to encounter American carrier aircraft in the skies around Buna; they had been told that the U.S. carriers were destroyed at Midway. The pilots assumed that the carriers were operating with Australian forces that had marched across the Owen Stanley mountains. Actually, they were training for the Guadalcanal invasion. No one in the Imperial High Command or in the field suspected a forthcoming invasion. After their eight months of continuous victories, it was hard for the Japanese to believe that the Allies could launch a seaborne invasion. Had the idea been suggested, they would have agreed with General MacArthur and Admiral Ghormley that such an invasion had almost no chance of success.

So as the American expeditionary force moved toward Guadalcanal, it enjoyed the element of surprise. On August 4 and 5 the 75 ships steamed on under an overcast sky. On August 6 the fleet moved through rainsqualls almost all day long, but as dawn rose on the morning of August 7 the sky cleared, which meant the carrier planes would have good visibility for their attacks.

The fleet went to General Quarters at 5:30 and at 6 o'clock the carriers launched their first strike. The planes from the *Wasp*, *Saratoga* and *Enterprise* were assigned targets on Guadalcanal Island, Tulagi, Gavutu, and Tanambogo. The Japanese had established a seaplane base on Gavutu and Tanambogo, which were connected by a causeway. The Japanese planes had been kept down the day before by bad weather. Admiral Fletcher's task force reported one unidentified aircraft during the day, but whether it was Japanese or a plane from General MacArthur's command was undetermined. In any event, the Japanese were not aroused until 6:12 when the communications headquarters at the Tulagi seaplane base sent a frantic message announcing the attack. The radio message went to the 4th, 6th, and 8th Fleets, Admiral Yamamoto, and Imperial Headquarters. It was simple and succinct: Enemy heavy bombardment in progress.

The weather had cleared, and the carrier planes flew off into scattered cumulus clouds in the light of a quarter moon. The fighters

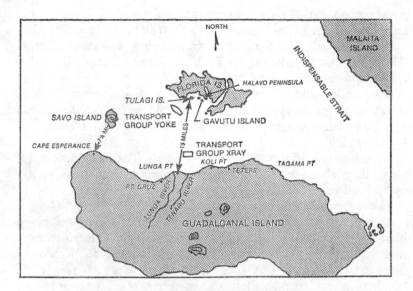

Guadalcanal-Tulagi

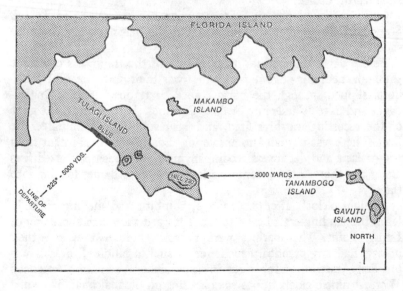

Landing objectives in Tulagi-Gavutu area

and bombers moved off on their appointed missions. Eight fighters led by Lt. L. H. Bauer took off from the *Enterprise* to attack Guadalcanal's aircraft, PT boats, troop installations, and supply dumps. They found no aircraft, and no PT boats. They did strafe the buildings on the airfield at Lunga Point.

Meanwhile another eight fighters from the *Enterprise* maintained a combat air patrol over the transports from six until eight o'clock, when they were replaced by others. Bombers began to hit Tulagi and the Lunga Point area.

No enemy air activity was seen all morning. The Americans had it all to themselves, and the only planes damaged were those hurt in operational accidents.

Planes from the other carriers struck the seaplane base at Gavutu. The surprise was complete. The American planes arrived and began bombing and strafing the seaplanes in the water. They destroyed nine float planes similar to the Zero, one four-engined Kawanishi flying boat, and eight seaplanes that doubled as search planes and bombers. A few Japanese pilots who tried to take off were shot down before they were airborne. Not a single Japanese plane at Gavutu survived the attack.

Other carrier planes hit Japanese troop concentrations on Tulagi. Some struck targets on the beaches that the marines would soon invade.

Before dawn the marines on the decks of the transports could see the high mountains of the island that was their objective. The transports slipped through the narrow neck that runs between Guadalcanal and Savo Islands into Sealark Channel. As dawn rose, the guns of the escorting warships fired, and flashes of light illuminated the fleet. There was virtually no answering fire. The bombardment from the cruisers and destroyers accompanying the troopships started fires along the shore. An oil dump exploded, sending flames leaping into the sky.

At eight o'clock, after two hours of bombing and shelling of the island, the landing craft began to move toward the north shore east of Lunga Point. The marines were nervous; neither they nor their officers had any practical experience in such a landing, for this was the first American amphibious invasion since the Spanish-American War. At nine o'clock, troops were landing on Guadalcanal. They met no resistance because the Japanese had fled into the hills.

The going was ridiculously easy. The marines soon saw how completely they had surprised the enemy. They came across wooden barracks that had never been slept in. They found a tent, with a breakfast table full of platters and bowls of meat, rice, and cooked plums. There were half-filled rice bowls scattered around, chopsticks hastily dropped on the table or on the straw mats of the floor. The tents themselves told why the Japanese had left so rapidly: They were torn by shrapnel, and some were knocked flat by the shelling of the naval vessels before the landing.

But any marine who felt like celebrating over the ease with which they had taken their early objectives had some shocks coming. It was true that the Japanese had been surprised on Guadalcanal. They had not dug in yet nor created permanent fortifications, because most of the men were construction troops, not fighting men. But over on Tulagi, Lieutenant Colonel Merritt Edson's 1st Marine Raider Battalion and the 5th Battalion of the Second Marines had encountered stout resistance. About 250 Japanese were located on this island. The Japanese were troops of the Yokohama Air Base detachment under Captain Hasike Miyazaki. They were experienced and dedicated fighters. Edson's 1st Raiders were the toughest American troops in the Pacific. They were all volunteers, chosen from the ranks of a force known for its fighting qualities. The Raider concept had come from Lt. Col. Evans Carlson's recommendation for creation of a commando force, and Carlson's experience had included a service tour of several months with the Chinese Communist Eighth Route Army in its guerilla struggles against the Japanese in North China. Edson's Raiders had trained for many months under Spartan conditions, and when they came to Guadalcanal they already had a powerful reputation. As it turned out, they would need every trick they had learned and would learn some new ones.

This invasion was the first contact between highly trained American troops and seasoned Japanese veterans since the war had begun in December. The Japanese had a reputation even more fearsome than that of the Raider battalions, gained through the phenomenally rapid march of their forces through the Philippines, Malaya, and the East Indies. For months, Tokyo had crowed over its victories, and half the world had come to believe the Japanese were invincible, a reputation the Imperial High Command was pleased to encourage.

Tulagi, then, was in a sense the first testing ground. Edson's troops

landed at 8:15 A.M. on the northwestern part of the island, and at
the beginning the going did not seem much harder than it was on
Guadalcanal. They encountered some resistance from a few outposts.
The northwest part of Tulagi was covered with thick jungle, small
trees, vines, and bougainvillea with its beautiful leaves and sharp
thorns. At first the terrain seemed to be the worst obstacle. Edson
lost only one man, and that one to a sniper as the marines hit the
beach. Edson planned to move inland to a ridge that ran the length
of the island and then work along the top of that ridge, clearing the
slopes as they moved south. But the terrain was so difficult that it
took three hours for the men to chop their way along a mile and a
half of rising ground. Having reached the ridge line, the marines
moved ahead, came out of the jungle, and ran straight into the central Japanese defenses, built on the hillside. The Japanese had constructed dugouts and rock embrasures and had placed their machine
guns carefully to create interlocking fields of fire. The Japanese defense was based on keeping the enemy below them, but the marines
found that by crawling up the cliffs they could drop charges of dynamite and grenades into the dugouts, and that was the method they
had to use to advance. Once a dugout was blown it still was not safe:
In one hole the Americans killed 17 Japanese with dynamite charges;
one marine spotted a radio inside, and went in to retrieve it; there
were still two Japanese soldiers alive, and they shot him and another
man who came after him before they were killed.

One section of marines took on this defense position in the center
of the island, while the center and left flank of Edson's force pushed
down the ridge. But even along the ridge line the going was not easy.
One company suffered 15 percent casualties that first afternoon.

The frontal resistance was stiff, but with the Japanese, frontal resistance was only half the battle. Snipers seemed to be everywhere,
tied in trees, in the tops of buildings, behind rocks. A favorite tactic
of the snipers was to let the forward element of a marine unit pass
and then begin shooting at the men from behind. This move almost
always meant death for the sniper, but usually not before he had
caused several casualties. And one thing the 1st Raiders learned that
day was that the small .25 caliber Japanese rifle and machine gun
slug were more apt to wound than to kill, which from the Japanese
point of view was satisfactory, since it took additional troops and resources to care for the wounded.

During the afternoon, the Raiders drove along the ridge until they ran into a three-sided ravine, whose floor was an old British cricket field. The Japanese had dug into the ravine walls and established the fields of fire that would become so familiar in later months. As the marines moved up they ran into crossfire, and Edson stopped because darkness was coming and this was no time to be probing unknown dangers.

That night the marines on Tulagi had another new experience. The Japanese, knowing they were outnumbered with no chance of survival, staged one of the desperate counterattacks for which they would become infamous. They waited until the marine perimeter was quiet, then at 10:30 they broke through between two companies and surrounded one of them. The marines fought in their foxholes and in the open, using guns, machine guns, grenades, and knives. The Japanese came along the ridge toward Colonel Edson's command post, and reached a point fifty yards from him. Finally, the marines overpowered the Japanese and threw them back, but not before one company had lost half its noncommissioned officers.

The next day, August 8, more troops were landed on Tulagi, until there were 7,500 on that side of Sealark Channel. Edson's Raiders and men of the 5th Battalion of the 2nd Marines began moving again toward the southeastern end of the island. One by one they attacked the dug-in machine gun positions on the steep sides of the old cricket ground. From one cave they removed 35 dead Japanese, some of them already rotting and stinking but some killed in the last moment of defense of the position. From this the Americans deduced properly that the Japanese tactic was to hold a position until the last unless ordered to retreat, proof of the discipline of the Japanese armed forces. Those troops who surrendered on Guadalcanal were mostly members of labor battalions, not combat troops.

The Raiders that second day encountered dozens of examples of a spirit they had not seen before. In one dugout they cornered three Japanese officers who at the end had only one loaded pistol among them. As the marines were ready to make the final assault they heard three shots. When they entered the dugout they discovered three bodies and an empty pistol. One officer had fired all but his last three rounds, then shot his two companions and himself.

In those first days this suicidal attitude surprised the marines. It was hard for an American to understand how cornered or wounded men with no hope of survival in their hole, knowing that the enemy had an enormous material and numerical advantage, would almost invariably choose death to surrender. It took some getting used to, but after a few Japanese had pretended to surrender, only to pull out guns or bayonets to attack their "captors" or to explode grenades to kill themselves and their enemies, the marines took the Japanese on their own terms. Thereafter, there was virtually no further attempt to persuade Japanese soldiers to surrender. Tulagi was brought under control on that second day, although not all the Japanese on the island had been killed. For days afterward Japanese snipers harassed the American troops, until the last sniper was killed.

One gets a feel for the stubbornness of the fighting on Tulagi in the experience of Gunnery Sergeant Angus Goss. He had gone ahead of his men to attack a cave near the cricket field. The Japanese had fired sporadically from that position. He moved up close enough to throw hand grenades into the cave. The marines had been trained to pull the ringpin of the egg-shaped grenade, throw, count slowly, and hear the explosion. Sergeant Goss pulled the pin, threw, and counted. On six, the grenade was lobbed back out of the cave, and he had to duck to escape the blast of his own weapon. After another identical experience he held the grenade for three seconds, then threw. Four, five, six, and out it came again. Sergeant Goss called for a satchel charge, a bag filled with dynamite, usually used to blow buildings. He thrust in the charge, primed it, and ran back a little. The Japanese thrust the charge out of the mouth of the cave; the dynamite exploded and drove a rock splinter into Goss's leg. The wound was not serious enough to fell him, but it hurt enough to infuriate him. He picked up his submachine gun, and dashed into the cave, spraying fire. He killed four Japanese soldiers and counted eight others who had died earlier.

If possible, the fighting on Gavutu and Tanambogo was worse than that on Tulagi. The landings there came in the middle of the morning. Not many troops were committed, because no one expected to find many Japanese there. But since the seaplane base was on these islands, the Japanese had fortified them, and the marines ran into trouble. The Japanese were surprised and had still not recovered from the bombardment and aerial attack that had destroyed their seaplanes, so the first troops ashore were met by rifle fire only. But when the second wave of marines reached the beach, the Japanese had organized about 500 yards back, and the fire was intense. The third wave came under fire before the landing craft reached shore, and the casualties were heavy.

Gavutu and Tanambogo were both dominated by small hills, not quite 150 feet high. But above the sea level landings, this height was enough. The Japanese had built their defenses along the slopes, and they were well supplied with machine guns, automatic rifles, and ammunition. As on Tulagi, each Japanese position had to be taken. They did not retreat.

The viciousness of the fighting on Tanambogo was almost unbelievable. In the early waves, the marines had landed tanks. The Japanese had come surging toward the Tanambogo dock, where the landings had been made. They had jammed crowbars under the treads, thrown grenades, and tried to set the tanks afire with rags soaked in gasoline. One tank commander had opened the hatch and employed the tank's machine gun to kill 23 Japanese soldiers before one scrambled up the side of the tank and stabbed him to death with a bayonet. Another Japanese then threw gasoline soaked rags inside the tank and it burned.

By midafternoon on this first day it was apparent that the marines could use reinforcements, and a unit that had landed earlier on Florida Island (where there were no Japanese) was called over to assist. Tanambogo had been taken, but the marines were unable to secure the causeway that linked the two small islands. The reinforcements were ordered to Tanambogo, and at dusk were given five minutes of preparatory bombardment from naval vessels. Unluckily, one of the last shells hit a fuel dump near the beach and lit up the shore as if it were noon. As the marines came up, the Japanese had them clearly silhouetted against the sea.

From the dugouts on the hills came a steady stream of machine gun and rifle fire. Two boatloads of marines reached the beach, but the coxswain of the third boat was killed at his tiller, and the boat slewed around and headed back out to sea. The following boats did the same, believing there had been some change in orders, so the men of the two boats were stranded ashore, and their only protection was the concrete pier. The Japanese were firing. As soon as the Americans returned the fire, the Japanese spotted the position by the tracers. Soon several men were down. One boat retired, taking the wounded, and it was some time before the confusion was eliminated and other boats began to land. Meanwhile, the Japanese launched a counterattack on the beach. Captain Crane, the leader of the unit, was cut off from his boat. He and five men hid in the brush, and in the darkness they escaped to return to the beach after the Japanese had drawn back to their hillside positions. Eventually they were extricated, but it was four o'clock on the morning of August 8 before another unit landed and was able to secure the causeway. When the fighting started there were 500 Japanese on the connecting islets of Gavutu and Tanambogo. When the fighting ended there were none.

Early on the morning of August 7, the Tulagi radio station flashed the first word of the U.S. assault to Rabaul. The astounding news reached the Rabaul airfield just as the pilots of the early morning missions were preparing to take off for another day's harassment of the Australians on New Guinea. The orders were immediately cancelled, and all available planes were dispatched to strike the American invasion force. Before the planes could take off, they received the unwelcome news from Tulagi that the entire flying boat flotilla had been destroyed. Then contact with Tulagi was broken, which could only mean that the base there had been overrun.

At 8:30 a flight of 27 twin-engined Betty bombers took off from Rabaul. They had been loaded for the strike against Australian forces on New Guinea, so they carried bombs instead of torpedoes. Eighteen Zero fighters accompanied them as they climbed to 13,000 feet, flew east to Buka Island and turned south along the Bougainville coast.

They were picked up by four *Enterprise* planes just after one o'clock in the afternoon. The *Enterprise* fighters were flying at 18,000 feet, when down below they spotted the large formation of Betty bombers, escorted by the Zeros, just above Florida Island. The F4Fs attacked, and Lt. V. P. DePoix shot down one bomber. Four others began to smoke and were listed as "probables." But after this initial run, the Zeros joined the fight, and the F4Fs broke off to take refuge in cloud cover, as they had been instructed to do. They had been hard hit: One of the F4Fs had been shot down, and Lieutenant DePoix's plane was so badly shot up he had to make an emergency landing on the *Wasp*.

Lieutenant G. E. Firebaugh led another flight of six fighters from the *Enterprise*, and they found the enemy off Santa Isabel Island. The Zeros came in fast, ten of them, and attacked three of the fighters. All three F4Fs were shot down. The other three American fighters attacked the bombers, and Ens. R. N. Disque shot down one Betty. The first kill of a Zero was made by Radio Electrician T. W. Rhodes. But the Zeros came after them in force, and the F4Fs ducked into clouds to hide. There were ten Zeros after them in two formations, and they came in, observing the Japanese rule: never let your wingman out of sight. They attacked the F4Fs from the starboard quarter and Lieutenant Firebaugh and enlisted pilot W. S. Stephenson, Jr., and Pilot Machinist W. H. Warden were shot down. One of the coastwatchers picked up Firebaugh from the water off Santa Isabel Island; a Guadalcanal coastwatcher sent a canoe to rescue Warden off that same island, but Stephenson was not found.

Aboard the other carriers the story was much the same. The bombers were much easier targets. Six fighters of Flight 323 ran into enemy bombers off Lunga Point, and shot down four of them. Machinist D. E. Runyon destroyed two singlehandedly, just after 2:30 in the afternoon.

When the Japanese Betty bombers and Zero fighters began their run over the islands, coastwatchers were on the alert. Paul Edward Mason, a copra planter in peacetime, was stationed on Malabita Hill on Bougainville, overlooking Buin. At nine o'clock in the morning he sent a message that 24 Japanese bombers were heading toward Guadalcanal. They were still four hundred miles, or two and a quarter hours away from the target when that message was broadcast back from Pearl Harbor to the fleet.

That message reached the invasion fleet in plenty of time for preparations. The reaction of H.M.A.S. *Canberra*, one of the Australian cruisers, was typical. When the word came, the bosun's mate piped the message:

"The ship will be attacked at noon by 24 torpedo bombers. All hands will pipe to dinner at 11 o'clock."

The torpedo bombers came in right on schedule.

The U.S. fighters climbed above them to 20,000 feet, as the bombers reached the north shore of Guadalcanal and looked down on the invasion fleet at noon. The American carrier fighters and the guns of the ships were ready for them. For the first time in the South Pacific the Japanese were feeling the results of counterattack.

The American fighter planes were quite effective against the twin-engined bombers. Of the 24 Bettys that finally arrived over Guadalcanal, all but one were shot down, and the only damage sustained in that first attack was to the destroyer *Mugford*, which was hit by a bomb.

Against the Zero fighters, however, it was a different story. Pilot officer Saburo Sakai, Japan's leading "ace," was among those 18 chosen for their skill to make this first long-range mission. Over the target, the Japanese force was "jumped" by F4F Wildcats from the carriers. They went in straight for the bombers, ignoring the Zeros. The Zeros protected the bombers as well as they could, but then turned to the American fighters. Sakai was puzzled by the American tactics: The navy pilots dived against the Zeros, but if they missed on the first pass, they scattered and evaded. They had been instructed well by their intelligence officers, who knew that the Zero was superior in turning and climbing ability, as well as faster.

After a grim and skillful battle, Sakai shot down one F4F and an SBD dive bomber that by itself jumped four Zeros. Several other Japanese pilots made "kills," while one Zero was lost. Pilot Sakai attacked a group of the SBD torpedo bombers, thinking they were fighters, and ran straight into four spitting machine guns manned by rear gunners who had him cold as he came in. His Zero was badly smashed and he was seriously wounded, yet he managed to fly the plane back to Rabaul and land it before collapsing.

In the air, the Japanese still had a temporary advantage in the quality of the Zero, but already the Americans in their F4Fs were beginning to learn to use the limitations of the enemy to their advantage. The matter of control of the air was obviously going to be hotly contested. At this particular moment the Americans had the advantage of propinquity with the carriers close offshore, but the Japanese had the advantage of numbers at Rabaul, and the American effort was seriously hampered by the superiority of the Japanese Zeros over the American fighters. The carrier pilots were flying the F4F Wildcat, which was not as fast or as maneuverable as the Zero, and the Japanese could fly rings around them. The one advantage of the F4F was its sturdy construction and armor protection—all that was needed to keep the ratio of lost planes as low as it was for the Americans.

At Rabaul, the Japanese recovered rapidly from the surprise of the American invasion. The problem for the Japanese fighters was the 1,100-mile round trip. For that reason on the first day Commander

Nakajima, the leader of the fighter squadron, had resisted demands by higher authority that all Zeros available be sent into the fight and had dispatched only his most experienced fliers. He was soon to be sending others, and the losses grew more serious, largely because of the vast distances to be traversed.

By nightfall of the first day, the U.S. invasion seemed secure. The American troops had moved up near the airfield and had not encountered any substantial resistance. One prisoner was captured, and he indicated that there were only about 600 combat troops on the island and 1,400 laborers and that they had fled to the opposite side. Admiral Turner had moved 11,000 marines ashore, and vast piles of ammunition, food, and other supplies crowded the beaches. General Vandegrift had noticed that the beach force was unable to assimilate the supplies, but fearing that the carriers would soon move out, he was glad to see the supplies still coming in. He did establish a second beachhead, but it was soon crowded as badly as the first.

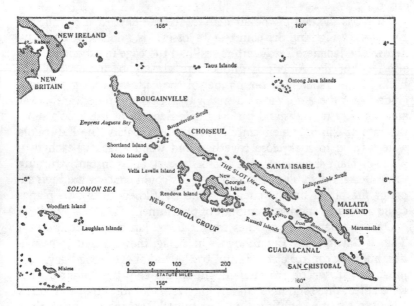

The Solomon Islands

At 8:40 on the morning of August 8, Coastwatcher Jack Read at Buka Passage spotted 45 Japanese dive bombers that had taken off from Kavieng. Thirty minutes later Pearl Harbor repeated the broadcast to the ships. The carrier planes attacked and destroyed many of the enemy bombers, but on this day the U.S. ships did not escape unscathed. A blazing bomber dived into the deck of the transport *George F. Elliott* and set it afire. One dive bomber sent a torpedo into the destroyer *Jarvis*, putting it out of action.

That morning the planes of the *Enterprise* and the other carriers took off on their missions and found the skies clear. They strafed and bombed troop concentrations along the Tenaru River, and they worked over the airfield again. At about 10 o'clock three fighters from the *Enterprise* discovered a group of Japanese torpedo bombers coming in low over the surface of the water to attack the transports. The Americans jumped them. Machinist Runyon shot down one bomber and one fighter, Ens. W. H. Rouse shot down two twin-engined torpedo bombers, and Ens. J. D. Shoemaker shot down another.

That was the end of the air activity for the day. At nightfall, the *Enterprise*'s Fighting Six counted its losses: six pilots shot down by Zeros. The Japanese Zero fighters still had the edge in experience and aircraft, but the American pilots were already beginning to learn tricks of the trade. The commander of the *Enterprise* air group concluded that the Zero had two major weaknesses—limited fire power and inability to withstand punishment. Because of the Zero's superior rate of climb, maneuverability, and fuel capacity, the F4F pilots were warned to stick close together, and when attacked, each two-plane element should set up a scissors movement, constantly turning toward each other. Thus the pair of F4Fs could concentrate their superior fire power on the enemy, while they knew their own planes could absorb an enormous amount of punishment.

On the ground, the marines fought fierce Japanese opposition on Tulagi, Gavutu, and Tanambogo. On Tulagi they suffered 90 casualties, but took control of the island by the end of the second day. The Japanese garrison of 250 men fought to the end; two hundred men were killed, three surrendered, and the rest swam the strait to Florida Island to continue fighting. On Gavutu and Tanambogo the marines suffered 250 casualties. The 500-man Japanese garrison was wiped out to the last man.

The fierceness of this fighting on Tulagi was in sharp contrast with the easy advance of the marines on Guadalcanal. There, on the morning of August 8, the marines reached the edge of the airport they would name Henderson Field, after a flier killed at Midway. They were beginning to develop a contempt for the enemy.

"I wish those fucking Japanese would come out and fight," one marine said within the hearing of Richard Tregaskis, the International News Service correspondent who had accompanied the invasion. "All they do is run into the jungle."

On the surface then, the marines couldn't ask for a finer war. But the officers were edgy that second afternoon; it was too easy.

At sea, the Americans apparently had no opposition either. A few Japanese patrol craft and tenders and one or two transports had been caught off the shore, and they had been destroyed in the first hours of the invasion by shelling and bombing.

Only in the air were the Japanese giving the Americans pause. Most of those first waves of bombers were destroyed, but the cost of meeting the Zeros was 21 of Admiral Fletcher's 99 carrier planes. That loss, not high by operational standards, convinced Fletcher that his decision to withdraw was sound. At six o'clock that evening Fletcher asked Admiral Ghormley to allow him to withdraw his carriers; he withdrew before he had a reply. When Admiral Turner intercepted Fletcher's dispatch he realized that the carrier withdrawal would leave him without any air cover. The number of Japanese planes could be expected to increase sharply as the enemy brought down more aircraft through the island chain. As Fletcher began to withdraw, the Japanese were moving in force.

When the word "invasion" had been flashed from Guadalcanal to Rabaul, Vice Admiral Gunichi Mikawa had reacted immediately. Admiral Mikawa was Commander of the Japanese 8th Fleet and the Outer South Seas Force, which meant he had the responsibility for the whole South Pacific operation. His first move was to load six small transports with troops and dispatch them with destroyer escort to reinforce the 2,000-man Guadalcanal garrison. But the convoy ran into the American submarine S-38, which was operating out of Australia following the fall of the Philippines. The S-38 sank the transport *Meiyo Maru* with 342 men aboard. The sinking, coupled with the reports of the "enormous" American invasion flotilla, persuaded

the admiral that it was too dangerous at the moment to try to reinforce the garrison, and he called back the other five transports.
By that time, Japanese naval assistance was already on the way to
Guadalcanal. Admiral Mikawa had been lucky in the matter of timing. Early on the morning of August 7, as the Tulagi garrison sent its
last message, five heavy cruisers left Kavieng on the northern tip of
New Ireland. Three of them were headed northeast for Manus Island in the Admiralty Group, and two were bound for Rabaul. Admiral Mikawa soon ordered all five cruisers to hasten to Rabaul.
Shortly after noon, the cruiser *Chokai*, accompanied by a destroyer,
moved into Simpson Harbor. The other four cruisers waited in St.
George's Channel between New Ireland and New Britain for the
Chokai to rejoin. When she came up late that afternoon, she was
carrying Admiral Mikawa himself and was accompanied by the light
cruisers *Tenryu* and *Yubari*. So the Japanese moved toward Guadalcanal with five heavy cruisers, two light cruisers, and a destroyer. As
they sped south, Admiral Mikawa composed his battle plan.

By cutting speed, they could delay their arrival until after midnight on August 8 and make a surprise night attack on the American
forces at the beachhead. The admiral knew that the Americans had
several carriers in that area, while he had none. A night attack was a
guarantee that he would not be harassed by American planes, since
the Americans had no record of proficiency in night aerial operations. In fact, the Americans had no record of competence in any
sort of night naval operations, while this aspect of tactics had become a Japanese specialty.

Mikawa's problem that afternoon was how to move close to Guadalcanal without coming in too soon, and still not give away the element of surprise. He had to attack to support the Guadalcanal defenders, but if he could surprise the enemy the effectiveness would
be enormous. The admiral did not know it just then, but the nature
of the divided command, the inferiority of the American air intelligence system, and the lack of clearly defined search methods would
all play directly into his hands.

For intelligence about Japanese ship movements, the Americans at
Guadalcanal had to depend on air search and submarine reports.
Only under the most special circumstances would the reports of
coastwatchers be of much use concerning naval ship operations.
Early in the day the cruisers were sighted by U.S. B-17 army

bombers as they moved down toward Rabaul. On the evening of August 7, the Mikawa force was sighted by the S-38 just as it came out of St. George's Channel. That night the commander of the S-38 reported the contact to Brisbane. But those two reports were not given much credence by American naval commanders because Rabaul had become the Japanese navy's forward base, and it was quite normal for ships to move in and out. The Americans saw no indication that the ships in question were steaming toward Guadalcanal.

Admiral Ghormley was responsible for the coordination of all elements of the American attack, but to secure air searches, he had to depend on several sources. First were the long-range B-17 bombers of General MacArthur's American Army Air Force and the Australian army air force, part of MacArthur's command, which operated independently. Second was Admiral McCain's land-based naval air force, which included a number of seaplane tenders and PBY patrol bombers. General MacArthur's planes were to take responsibility for the search of the Bismarck Islands, concentrating on the big naval and air base at Rabaul. McCain was to watch the northern approaches to the region, which meant Truk and the Marshalls. Admiral Fletcher's carrier planes were supposed to make short-range searches, but actually made none at all; Fletcher was bemused with his worries.

Admiral Turner had looked at his charts and seen that the Japanese had a marvelous approach to the island of Guadalcanal along the west coast of Bougainville, straight down between Choiseul Island and Vella Lavella, past Kolombangara, between New Georgia and Santa Isabel, and then between Florida Island and Guadalcanal's north coast. The lane was christened "The Slot." Soon it was to become infamous in American naval history.

On the morning of August 8, four PBYs were scheduled to fly from Nandi on a 700-mile long triangular pattern whose apex was the Fiji Islands. They would come up almost due west of Santa Cruz Island. Six PBYs would fly search patterns from Espiritu Santo, northeast over the Santa Cruz Islands and end at a point slightly above the Bismarcks, but far to the west of the Japanese task force. Six PBYs would spread out from Malaita across The Slot from Guadalcanal, to search an area north and west of The Slot. Three B-17s were to search north of Guadalcanal.

On the night of August 7, when Admiral Turner studied the

search plan for the following day he found The Slot was completely uncovered. He asked Admiral McCain for a special search there the next day, but somehow, between Admiral Turner's flagship, Admiral McCain's headquarters, and the seaplane tender *Mackinac* at Malaita, the message was lost. The search was never made. Thus, on August 8, the Americans had left uncovered the most obvious approach of any enemy naval force to Guadalcanal.

When the Japanese force was sighted by the S-38 coming out of St. George's Channel, the submarine was nearly six hundred miles from Guadalcanal. The fact that the cruisers were travelling fast was indicative of trouble, but the report was marred by the S-38's identification of a cruiser as a destroyer, thus downgrading the force.

At about 10:30 on the morning of August 8, an Australian Hudson bomber from New Guinea sighted the Japanese force. The pilots had been working under orders for radio silence, but in the invasion they were told to break silence if something urgent seemed to be in the offing. The pilot of this search plane did not radio; he noted the ships and their direction and then proceeded with his search mission, which took most of the afternoon. He returned to his base at Milne Bay, had tea, and then went in to the intelligence office to report the contact. It was about six o'clock in the evening before the report of ships travelling down The Slot was dispatched. The Australians reported to General MacArthur's headquarters, which reported to Pearl Harbor, which broadcast to the fleet, and that is how Admiral Turner got the word. But the report was fatally defective: the Hudson pilot identified the ships as three cruisers, two destroyers, and two seaplane tenders. When Admiral Turner read that message, he inferred that the enemy was moving to set up a seaplane base. The most likely spot was a protected harbor at Rekata Bay, about 175 miles from the landing beaches of Guadalcanal. So while the message indicated a Japanese response, it did not show the Americans what Admiral Mikawa had on his mind. Another Australian pilot, who correctly identified the Japanese force about half an hour after the first pilot, also delayed passing on the information, and his report did not arrive for many hours.

As darkness began to lower over Sealark Channel, Rear Admiral V. A. C. Crutchley (RN), Australian commander of the screen around the amphibious force, sent his cruisers and destroyers to their night dispositions. He and Turner had divided the landing area into three defensive sectors. In the south were the cruisers *Australia, Canberra,* and *Chicago* and the destroyers *Patterson* and *Bagley.* Crutchley took personal command of this group, which was to patrol south and west of Savo Island to prevent any enemy ships from coming through between the island and Cape Esperance on the northwest end of Guadalcanal. The northern sector ran from Savo Island to Florida Island, northeast of Guadalcanal. This area was to be patrolled by the cruisers *Vincennes, Astoria,* and *Quincy* and the destroyers *Helm* and *Wilson.* The officer in command of these ships was Captain Frederick L. Riefkohl of the *Vincennes.* The destroyers *Blue* and *Ralph Talbot* were given a special mission west of Savo Island to cover the large sea area west of the channel, because they carried modern radar.

The eastern sector ran from Lunga Point, where the marines had established the first beachhead, to the approaches to Lengo and Sealark Channels. Here, Rear Admiral Norman Scott was in command of the light cruisers *San Juan* and *Hobart* (Australian) and the destroyers *Monssen* and *Buchanan.*

Admiral Turner in the transport *McCawley* had personal command of the 19 transports and freighters. He planned to conduct unloading operations all night long, because Fletcher's abandonment persuaded him it was imperative to move the transports away from the beaches at dawn.

At 8:30 on the night of August 8, Turner called an urgent conference aboard his flagship. He had just learned that virtually no cargo had been unloaded from the transports at Tulagi, and he had to give General Vandegrift and Admiral Crutchley the bad news. Vandegrift had to be told that whatever supplies they did not get that night would be delayed, because the transports had to be taken away from the beach for protection. Crutchley had to be told that the surface forces would have no air protection for the next day or two. And Turner had to tell both commanders that he expected the Japanese to send bombers the next day from that seaplane base. They could also expect air attack from Rabaul and Kavieng.

It was nearly midnight before the three commanders assembled in Turner's cabin aboard the *McCawley.* They talked about the reports of the sighted Japanese vessels, and Turner said he was sure the force would head for Rekata Bay. The next morning, he said, Admiral McCain's land-based aircraft would bomb Rekata Bay.

The three commanders did discuss the possibility of a night attack by Japanese surface forces, but Admiral Turner was not seriously worried. In the first place, as far as he knew, the air search that day had covered every area. In the second place, with the radar destroyers out front and with the disposition of the cruisers, he was confident that the protective forces could meet any challenge.

At midnight Admiral Crutchley and General Vandegrift left the flagship. The weather was cloudy and rain hid the western horizon. It was too late for Crutchley to take the *Australia* south to his patrol area, so he ordered the captain to steam just west of the Guadalcanal transports. The clock said it was August 9. All was quiet.

3

LIKE WOLVES ON
THE FOLD . . .

REAR Admiral Mikawa and his staff had left Rabaul so rapidly that there had been no time to agree on a plan of attack against the invaders. Mikawa did not know the size or composition of the American force, and all these matters had to be ascertained. Early on the morning of August 8, Mikawa sent out float planes from each of his five heavy cruisers to conduct an air search. They were much more skillful and successful than the Americans, and two of them got a good look at the American invasion fleet between Tulagi and Guadalcanal. They came back to report having sighted a battleship, 6 cruisers, 19 destroyers, and 18 transports. The Japanese error was in slightly overestimating the strength by calling one cruiser a battleship, but that minor mistake did not have any effect on the planning or the outcome of Mikawa's operations.

Admiral Mikawa's plan for action had been approved by the 8th Fleet and sent by radio to Tokyo. At first the Naval General Staff considered the plans reckless, but after a few hours of discussion, it was approved, and no attempt was made to stop Mikawa. The planes reported sighting many American warships and transports around Guadalcanal.

When Admiral Mikawa sent his search planes out 250 miles, he kept his force in the area north of Choiseul Bay, between Bougainville and Choiseul Island. It was in this area that the first Australian Hudson search plane found the Japanese force. To keep the plane away, Mikawa's ships put up an antiaircraft barrage, and that was probably the reason for the pilot's faulty identification of "two seaplane tenders," which lulled Admiral Turner into a false sense of security that day.

Early in the afternoon the Japanese cruisers recovered their float planes, and the striking force began to steam south through Choiseul Bay. At 4:20 in the afternoon the ships were in the middle of The Slot, and there they turned to parallel Choiseul Island and pass Vella Lavella and Kolombangara. Since those two sightings by the Australian planes, the Japanese forces had remained undetected as they came straight down. The only ship they saw was the Japanese seaplane tender *Akitsushima* en route to do what Admiral Turner expected: establish a seaplane base, but on New Georgia, not Santa Isabel Island.

Admiral Mikawa had no time to dispatch couriers with formal battle plans to his captains. The flagship's signal blinkers began to work at dusk, sending the battle orders: All ships were to go in with guns and torpedoes to attack the ships at the Guadalcanal anchorage. They would dash in at high speed and dash out across Sealark Channel to Tulagi, strike the transports there, retire north of Savo Island, and steam back up The Slot. As one last check on the plans, Admiral Mikawa sent out two search planes from the cruisers, and they returned to report that all was as it had been in the morning.

The admiral called on one of his staff officers to compose an appropriate message to the fleet in the spirit of the Samurai: "Let us strike in certain victory in the traditional night attack of the Imperial Navy. Let each man do his best."

The message was sent to every ship. The men of seven Japanese cruisers and one destroyer made their final preparations for battle.

Shortly after 11 o'clock, Admiral Mikawa ordered two more seaplane scouts launched from the cruisers. They were to fly above the American ships, report on their night disposition, and remain over Guadalcanal to light up the sky at the proper time with flares. As the

planes came in through the intermittent rainsqualls, the burning
hulk of the transport *George F. Elliott* was as good as a beacon.

One of the Japanese scout planes was sighted by the U.S. destroyer
Ralph Talbot, the northern radar picket boat. The *Ralph Talbot's*
radio operator broke silence to give the alarm that a plane had been
seen over Savo Island, heading east, which would bring it across the
path of the American fleet. The warning was heard by the destroyer
Blue and a few other ships, but for some reason it failed to reach Admiral Turner. Other ship commanders, hearing or seeing a plane, assumed that if it was unfriendly Admiral Turner would have sent out
a general alarm. On Guadalcanal, a little before one o'clock, one
plane woke up a tentful of marines. It did not sound like an American aircraft; the engine had a high-pitched tone that was unfamiliar,
and it kept circling around the island, which seemed unusual. Suddenly, the marines knew the plane was Japanese, because it began
dropping flares in several sectors of the sky over Guadalcanal and
Sealark Channel. They glowed with a greenish white light.

For an hour and a half these float planes circled, broadcasting to
Admiral Mikawa the dispositions of the transports and the steaming
patterns of the cruisers and destroyers. The transports were the major
target of Admiral Mikawa's planned attack. Before midnight he ordered his force to assume a long battle column with his flagship the
Chokai at the head, followed by the heavy cruisers *Aoba, Kako, Kinugasa,* and *Furutake.* Behind came the light cruisers *Tenryu* and *Yubari* and the destroyer *Yunagi.*

At 12:30 Admiral Mikawa issued his battle warning and fifteen
minutes later the force was called to combat stations. Just before one
o'clock in the morning, the *Chokai* crossed the track of the American destroyer *Blue.* The squadron trained its guns on the U.S. destroyer. But the lookouts aboard *Blue* saw nothing in the murk, and
the destroyer steamed away to the southwest, as the Japanese ships
passed by.

Admiral Mikawa was nervous, believing the *Blue* had reported his
coming, and he changed course and then changed again when his
lookouts reported another destroyer. At one o'clock in the morning
the *Chokai* rounded Savo Island, and just after 1:30 the lookouts
saw the lines of an American destroyer two miles north. This ship
was the *Jarvis,* the destroyer damaged in the Japanese air attacks that

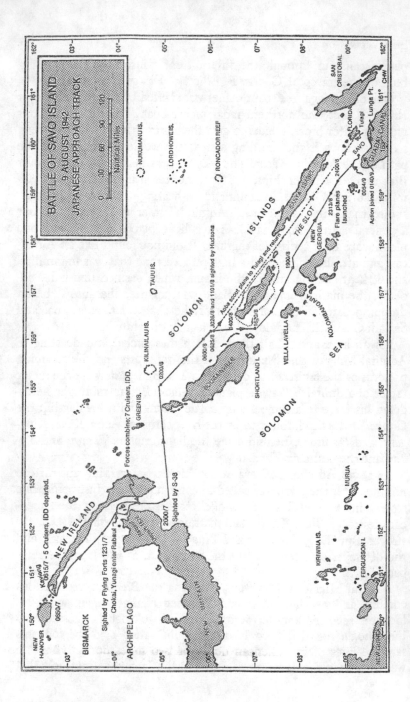

BATTLE OF SAVO ISLAND
9 AUGUST 1942
JAPANESE APPROACH TRACK

Nautical Miles
0 30 60 90 120

day. Her captain was taking the ship to Sydney for drydock repairs. If the men of the *Jarvis* saw the Japanese, they had no way of alarming the American fleet, because the destroyer's communications system was dead. The orders given by Admiral Mikawa before the battle had specified that ships should be prepared to fire torpedoes, and the cruisers fired several torpedoes at the *Jarvis*, but all missed. The Japanese ships did not open fire with their guns because this was the prerogative of the flagship. Thus the *Jarvis* escaped, and the Japanese went on toward the American fleet, still unheralded.

The Japanese continued to come at 26 knots. The lookouts spotted two American destroyers, and then two U.S. cruisers seven miles away. Still the Americans were asleep. Admiral Mikawa ordered the ships to begin firing torpedoes independently as they found targets. The first targets were the cruisers *Chicago* and *Canberra* and the destroyer *Bagley*. It was fully five minutes after the first torpedoes were launched before the destroyer U.S.S. *Patterson* finally saw a ship of strange configuration 5,000 yards ahead, where no ship should be. The *Patterson* broadcast the first alarm:

Warning: Strange ships entering harbor.

Even as the warning was issued it was overtaken by events. Those two Japanese float planes began dropping their greenish flares, and the *Chicago* and *Canberra* were silhouetted against the land. The *Chokai* opened fire from less than three miles' range. The *Aoba*, three-quarters of a mile further away, also began firing and so did the *Furutaka* from just under six miles. As the lookouts aboard the *Canberra* sighted the enemy through the gloom, two torpedoes struck her on the starboard side. She was hit by several eight-inch and five-inch shells from the Japanese cruisers, even as her general alarm bell was ringing. Captain F. E. Getting of the ship was wounded mortally, and the gunnery officer was killed instantly. The *Canberra* fired a few torpedoes and a few guns, but in five minutes her power failed, and she went dead in the water.

Strike one Allied cruiser.

Having warned the fleet with blinker signals as well as radio, the *Patterson* turned hard left to engage the enemy. The captain shouted "Fire torpedoes," but no one heard him. A Japanese shell hit aft near one five-inch gun and ignited the powder. The executive officer, who was off watch below, hurried up, but so swiftly did the Japanese pass by that he scarcely saw them. Now, at least he had time to organize damage control parties, which was his function in combat, and to put out the fires aft.

The destroyer U.S.S. *Bagley* saw the Japanese cruisers storming through, fired eight torpedoes from the tubes on her port side, and the enemy column disappeared without firing back. None of her torpedoes hit the Japanese ships.

The cruiser U.S.S. *Chicago* was the object of the second run of torpedoes fired by the Japanese cruisers. Captain H. D. Bode, who had been asleep in his bunk, was only half awake when a torpedo hit the *Chicago*'s bow and knocked part of it away. The *Chicago*'s gunners began firing, but the star shells they put up to illuminate the enemy didn't ignite. The men didn't know what to fire at until they saw a gray shape ahead, and they began shooting at it.

The shape was the destroyer *Yunagi*, which Admiral Mikawa had sent back to cover the rear of the Japanese attack, lest some American heavy ships slip through by Savo Island and hit his cruisers as they were attacking the transports. The *Yunagi*'s searchlight was sweeping ahead of her. The *Chicago* fired two dozen rounds of eight-inch shells and the searchlight went out. The *Chicago* then turned on her own light but found nothing.

In the confusion no one thought of informing the other U.S. cruisers of the attack. The Japanese steamed ahead, unreported to the transports even yet. At 1:45 Admiral Mikawa changed course and split his ships into two sections, the flagship leading three other cruisers on the west, and a second group of three cruisers led by the *Furutaka* on the east.

The two Japanese cruiser groups turned north, guided by the flares the seaplanes had dropped over the landing areas at Guadalcanal and Tulagi. The American northern defense force was steaming in a box pattern, with the cruiser *Vincennes* in the lead, the *Quincy* and the *Astoria* behind, and the destroyers *Wilson* and *Helm* on the flanks. It was only five minutes since the Japanese had gone into action, but the *Canberra* was wrecked and floundering, and the *Chicago* was out of the fight.

Strike two Allied cruisers.

The *Chokai* fired four torpedoes at the first cruiser her captain saw from a range of nearly six miles. The battle against the second American defense unit had begun.

That cruiser was the *Astoria*. When the *Chokai* came down, she was steaming along at 10 knots. Captain W. G. Greenman was asleep in his sea cabin just below the bridge. The watch officer, Lt. Comdr. J. R. Topper, was on the bridge devoting his attention to keeping in line, so as not to disturb the box pattern, and the ship had just completed her turn to the northwest to begin a new leg. On the bridge all was quiet. The officers and men watched tracers and heard gunfire on Tulagi Island and noted correctly that the marines were having their troubles over there. Topper noticed a slight tremor of the ship's hull at 1:45, which he identified as depth charges exploding. That was to be expected. Admiral Turner's messages had repeatedly warned of the danger of submarine attack. (The tremor was actually caused by the explosion of the spent torpedoes the *Chokai* had fired at the *Chicago*.) Topper had little time to worry about this oddity, however, because as he was speaking to the damage control watch over the intercommunications system, a lookout reported a plane overhead, and then a flare lit up the sky on the ship's port quarter. Soon it was not one star shell but an entire string of them.

The gunnery officer, Lt. Comdr. W. H. Truesdell, was the first man aboard the *Astoria* to sense the danger. He told the bridge to order General Quarters. As he did so the ship was lighted by searchlights, and in a few seconds the first salvo of Japanese shells bracketed the *Astoria*. Truesdell ordered his guns to begin firing, and the first *Astoria* salvo went out. As it was fired, the captain came stumbling sleepily up to the bridge and demanded that the ship cease firing. He feared they were shooting at their own ships. Perhaps the junior officers had acted hastily.

This stoppage threw the ship into confusion. A minute passed. Truesdell pleaded to the talker. "Tell the captain: Sir, for God's sake give the word *Commence Firing*." The captain realized there might be a battle on, and gave the order, but the debate had given the *Chokai*'s gunners time to get the range, and as Captain Greenman gave the order, an eight-inch shell ripped into the *Astoria*, starting fires amidships. By the light of these flames the *Chokai* poured shells into the American cruiser. The *Astoria* was firing, but not accurately. She fired 11 salvos, but managed to hit the *Chokai* only once, a shell that smashed into the admiral's chart room, but did not slow down the Japanese flagship.

The *Astoria* was rapidly becoming a hulk. Both forward eight-inch gun turrets were destroyed. The float plane amidships caught fire and burned. The five-inch guns were wrecked. A shell hit the bridge and killed the quartermaster at the wheel and several others. The fires created such terrific heat in the engine rooms that the black gang had to abandon their stations. From stem to stern the ship seemed to be ablaze. After fifteen minutes only No. 2 turret was still operating. Lieutenant Commander W. B. Davidson aimed its guns at a searchlight and fired the ship's last salvo. A shell hit the *Chokai's* forward turret. But the big Japanese warship swept past.

Strike three Allied cruisers.

The American cruiser column's next ship in line, the *Quincy*, was the new target of the Japanese. As the *Chokai* devoted her attention to the destruction of the *Astoria*, the *Aoba* began firing on the *Quincy*. Like the *Canberra*, the *Chicago*, and the *Astoria*, the *Quincy* was unprepared for action. As the *Aoba* came up, she opened her searchlights on the *Quincy*, and in the bright light the Japanese on the bridge could see with wonder that the American ship's guns were still trained fore and aft. It was like shooting ducks in Tokyo Bay. Captain S. N. Moore had refused to listen to junior officers' assertions that the aircraft overhead for the past hour were enemy. When the searchlights came on he ordered the guns to fire on them, then had second thoughts—what if they were friendly ships?—and ordered his recognition lights turned on. Then he turned to starboard, precisely the wrong way with an enemy shooting at him from the port quarter, and the *Quincy* could not fire her forward guns. That was the last error. The Japanese shells began to hit. One struck the seaplane in its catapult and sent up a glow of flame that was as good as a beacon. The *Quincy* then came under fire from the *Furutaka* cruiser column, and after the *Astoria* began to sink, the *Chokai* also turned its attention to the *Quincy*. Station after station was wiped out by shells. The bridge went, and the captain was mortally wounded. The engine rooms were sealed off by flame, with no chance for the black gang to escape. The turrets were hit, and the small guns destroyed. The sick bay disappeared in a shell blast. The ship was abandoned just after 2:30 in the morning, and she sank almost immediately.

Strike four Allied cruisers.

At least aboard the *Vincennes* the Americans were alert. At 11:45 the officers on the bridge had heard the warning from the destroyer *Ralph Talbot* that an enemy plane had been sighted. Captain Riefkohl had instructed them then to exercise extreme vigilance. The warning from the *Patterson* that the wolves were in the fold did not reach them, but when the Japanese flares went up, Captain Riefkohl lost no time in getting to the bridge and no time in worrying whether or not this was the enemy. General Quarters was sounding, and he did not question it. As he was going to the bridge he felt two underwater explosions, torpedoes going off nearby, and saw gun flashes and heard gunfire. But even then, Captain Riefkohl and his officers believed they were under air attack only.

At 1:50 Captain Riefkohl saw the searchlights reaching for the American cruisers. He assumed they were American searchlights and asked by voice radio that they be shut off, but his gunnery officer, Lt. Comdr. R. L. Adams, trained his guns on the nearest searchlight. A salvo fell and splashed a quarter of a mile short of the *Vincennes*. She fired back, and on her second salvo hit the *Kinugasa*. But almost at that moment enemy shells began landing on the *Vincennes*; at least three of the Japanese cruisers were attacking her. The port side of the *Vincennes'* bridge was destroyed by a shell. A dozen shells knocked out most of the small guns. Captain Riefkohl turned hard right, and ran into three torpedoes from the *Chokai*. The fire rooms and the engine rooms were filled with smoke, and steam began to plume up from ruptured pipes and valves. A torpedo struck the No. 1 fire room and killed every man. Communications went out as the power failed. The captain, seeing two searchlights on the starboard side, mistakenly assumed they were friendly and ran up the American colors. The Japanese cruisers, mistaking the flag for that of a U.S. admiral, redoubled their shelling.

By 2:10 the *Vincennes'* guns were all silent; none remained that could be fired. The *Vincennes* was listing to port, and Captain Riefkohl was wondering if the moment had come when he should give the order to abandon ship, when the Japanese suddenly ceased firing and moved off. But the *Vincennes* was finished. She lingered awhile, dead in the water; most of the living got off, and began to swim, paddle, or float clinging to jetsam. Then the *Vincennes* sank.

Strike five Allied cruisers.

The destroyers of the American northern group milled about, not able to ascertain the pattern of movements of the American cruisers, and therefore unable to help much. The *Wilson* saw the flares and was alerted and then watched the Japanese column illuminate and

attack the American cruisers. She opened fire, shooting at the searchlight five miles away. The shells did not hit anything. The Japanese
threw a few shells at the *Wilson* but were too busy with the destruction of the cruisers to pay much attention to her. She nearly was
wrecked in a collision with the destroyer *Helm*, which suddenly appeared out of the darkness. The captain of the *Wilson* rang up full
speed, turned hard left, and barely passed clear.

The *Helm*'s captain did not realize an action was in progress, until
he saw the American cruisers illuminated by the Japanese searchlights and burning. At two o'clock the *Helm* went rushing off in pur-
suit of a ship, and discovered it was the U.S. destroyer *Bagley*.

The Japanese were crowing over their victory, and they grew careless. The *Chokai* turned, but the others did not follow, and Admiral
Mikawa had to run after them like a small boy chasing his peers. Just
then, the burning *Quincy*, very near the point of sinking, hit the
flagship with two shells; one wiped out the chart room, and the other
smashed the deck near the aviation crane. A third shell only bounced
off the forward turret but still gave the admiral something to worry
about. Mikawa did not like taking punishment, so he ordered his
captains to withdraw. The *Chokai* column formed up again and
sped off at 35 knots. The *Furutaka* column headed homeward and
crossed the path of the destroyer *Ralph Talbot*.

When the Japanese came down around Savo Island, the *Ralph
Talbot* was on the other side of the sound, near Florida Island, and
thus missed out on the original action. Her bridge watch heard the
Patterson's first warning call (unlike the other ships), and she went
steaming southwest at 25 knots to try to catch the invaders. The captain and crew could see the flashing lights of battle, but they did not
know what was happening until, on the way out, the retiring *Tenryu*
put a searchlight on the *Ralph Talbot* and began firing at her. Soon
the *Furutaka*, *Yubari*, and *Tenryu* were all firing at the destroyer, but
she made an elusive target, and in several salvoes the Japanese ships
hit her only once, knocking out some of the torpedo tubes. The
Ralph Talbot's captain, Lt. Comdr. J. W. Callaghan made a mistake
that was very common that night: He assumed that the ships were
American, called them up on voice radio, and turned on his recognition lights. But the call was answered by the Japanese cruiser *Yubari*,
which turned its searchlight on the *Ralph Talbot*'s bridge and began
firing more rapidly. On the third salvo, the *Yubari* got the ship's

range, and the shells began to cause damage. The chart room, gun control system, the wardroom, and a five-inch gun were all destroyed or partly destroyed. The *Ralph Talbot* launched four torpedoes that did no damage and then ducked into a rainsquall. The ship was burning and listed 20 degrees to starboard.

By this time, Admiral Mikawa's column had reached a point north of Savo Island. Until now, the admiral could be forgiven for not accomplishing his primary mission, which was to destroy the transports off the beaches. He had, to understate the case, been a busy man. But he was heading away from the transports, and the decision had to be made: Should he move back in and destroy them, or should he go home to report a phenomenal naval victory? His staff estimated that they had sunk seven cruisers and five destroyers. He decided to retire, and the U.S. transports were saved.

Off Guadalcanal the Allied defense force was in shambles. The American and Australian Navies had lost more than 1,000 men killed and 700 wounded. The *Canberra* was dead in the water. Her crew fought fires that blazed fiercely in spite of a heavy rain. Ammunition was exploding aft, which kept the destroyer *Patterson*, which had rushed to her aid, from coming in to assist her. After an hour, the *Patterson* managed to get alongside and pass over hoses and a pump for the survivors, but it was too late. Admiral Turner ordered the ship either to join up with the transports or be destroyed. He was already planning to move out before the expected air and sea attacks of the daylight hours began. Since the *Canberra* could not move, she had to be destroyed, and the destroyer *Ellet* torpedoed her.

The crew of the *Canberra* was rescued by the destroyers *Patterson* and *Blue*. The *Patterson* then went off and was nearly sunk by the *Chicago*, whose nervous captain at this point opened fire on anything that moved, but the destroyer and the battered cruiser managed to identify one another before the matter became serious. Luckily their gunnery was not accurate, so neither was hurt by the other.

Before daybreak, the *Quincy* and the *Vincennes* sank. The *Astoria* lingered on until noon of August 9, and then, despite heroic measures to save her by fighting fires and plugging holes, a magazine exploded and she sank. The *Ralph Talbot*, although sorely damaged, managed to limp into Tulagi.

The Japanese retired from the scene at high speed because Admiral Mikawa was certain that as dawn came so would the carrier planes, searching for him. But he did not reckon with the timidity of the American air commanders. Admiral Fletcher had retired before getting permission from Admiral Ghormley. But twelve hours later, when he still did not have permission to quit, he apparently decided there were worse dangers than the enemy, and he headed back toward Guadalcanal. At 3 A.M. he received a report of surface activity in the Guadalcanal area, but he was too far away to do anything about it even if he had wished. Captain Forrest Sherman of the carrier Wasp asked Rear Admiral Leigh Noyes, the flag officer aboard his carrier and commander of the task unit, for permission to steam northwest at high speed until he reached launching distance. The Wasp's air group was one of the few in the naval air force that had been trained in night operations. Admiral Noyes refused.

A few minutes later, Captain Sherman asked permission again, and again it was denied. And still one more time Sherman pleaded, but Admiral Noyes, knowing Fletcher's state of mind, would not even forward the request for his decision. At 3:30 the long-delayed permission for Fletcher to retire came from Admiral Ghormley, and Fletcher turned the force around again and fled south, away from the enemy.

On the morning of August 9, Admiral Turner had all the bad news. Earlier, in the conference with General Vandegrift and Admiral Crutchley aboard the flagship McCawley, Turner had indicated that, since Fletcher had deserted them, he must get the transports out of the dangerous Guadalcanal waters before the next day's expected air attacks began. But on the morning of the 9th, surveying the carnage and wondering why the Japanese had left the transports untouched, Turner made the bold decision to remain in place at least for the day, so they could unload more supplies. General Vandegrift came aboard the flagship again, and they agreed that the transports would have to move out later that day. In the interim, a message came from Admiral Ghormley ordering all surface ships out of what the sailors now called Iron Bottom Sound. Admiral Ghormley also warned that the marines would have to be prepared to repel Japanese reinforcements that were on the way.

When General Vandegrift had that information, knowing that his men were likely to be short of supplies before the transports could return from Nouméa, he ordered the marines to go on the defensive.

They would restrict their activity to patrols and shoring up defenses against attack from the sea.

So, on the evening of August 11, as the transports pulled away from the shore, 11,000 marines on Guadalcanal and 6,000 on Tulagi were stranded. They had enough ammunition to last perhaps a week of heavy fighting. They had food for 37 days. They had no air cover, no supply train, and no naval protection. The men ashore knew that a naval battle had occurred that night, but it was two days before they had the rumor that it had been a stunning defeat for the Allies. The fact that they were ordered to hold, place the main line of resistance on the beach and keep the reserve forces inland, indicated that Vandegrift expected attack from the sea, but that is all the men really knew. Around the perimeter they flushed a few Japanese. Some snipers inflicted casualties, but were usually hunted down and shot. As of August 10, the marines began to "sweat out" a counterinvasion by the enemy, and the tension grew.

But the Japanese were not ready to follow up immediately on their victory. There were no air attacks. No enemy reinforcements appeared. No warships except submarines moved in The Slot, and these contented themselves with shelling small groups of Americans and small boats crossing from Guadalcanal to Tulagi.

On the morning of August 9, Admiral Mikawa was worried enough about probable attack by American carrier planes that he ordered his cruisers into the rough circle of antiaircraft disposition. The damage reports showed that the *Chokai* had only the chart room damaged, the *Aoba* had lost a set of torpedo tubes, the *Kinugasa* had a storeroom flooded when a shell went through the hull and had suffered steering damage, and the *Kako* had lost a float plane and its crew. All the ships had shrapnel and machine gun damage, but only 58 men had been killed and 53 wounded.

When Admiral Mikawa reached Bougainville, the four heavy cruisers *Furutaka, Kinugasa, Aoba,* and *Kako* were sent to Kavieng for repairs. The *Chokai, Tenryu, Yubari,* and the destroyer *Yunagi* went to Rabaul. The groups parted company.

On the afternoon of August 9, an Australian Hudson scout plane found and followed the *Furutaka* group but stayed out of gunshot. The pilot's report brought no Allied action on the surface, because the Japanese ships were too close to their own bases, but the next morning the American submarine *S-44* discovered the squadron. The four cruisers were steaming in the box formation, protected by a single aircraft. The captain of the submarine, Lt. Comdr. John R. Moore, decided to attack, closed in despite the patrol plane, and fired four torpedoes. *Kako* was hit and sank within a few minutes, carrying down many of her crew.

When Admiral Mikawa stepped ashore at Rabaul he was greeted by a special message from Admiral Yamamoto, congratulating him on his victory, but reminding him that he must make every effort to support the land forces of the Imperial Army "which are now engaged in a desperate struggle."

Mikawa may have gotten the hidden message. Privately, Yamamoto was furious with his subordinate for failing to carry out his primary mission of destroying the transports off Guadalcanal.

Until Admiral Mikawa made his report, Admiral Yamamoto had not known the strength of the enemy in the area, and Mikawa exaggerated. But his story was an antidote for a more ridiculous tale. The Japanese military attaché in Moscow had told Tokyo there was nothing to worry about in the American invasion; the Americans had only 2,000 troops on the island, and their plan was to destroy the airfield and then withdraw.

Even at this late date the Japanese Army had very little interest in the trouble at Guadalcanal. Lieutenant General Hyukatake, the commander of the 17th Army, was interested only in the Port Moresby invasion. Hyukatake said he could not help. He had no orders from Tokyo. On August 10 the fleet hastily organized a very small force of 300 navy riflemen and 100 troops of the 5th Sasebo Special Naval Landing Force and sent them to Guadalcanal.

On August 11, Admiral Yamamoto detached Vice Admiral Nobutake Kondo's 2nd Fleet from the Combined Fleet in Japan, and sent Kondo toward Guadalcanal. At the same time Yamamoto made preparations to move his flagship and Combined Fleet headquarters to Truk.

The naval battle that the Americans called the Battle of Savo Island and the Japanese called the First Battle of the Solomons had ended. The Japanese had scored an impressive tactical victory but had missed their great opportunity to wipe out the supply ships of the invading forces. The American defenses were decimated, the American carriers were frightened away, and General Vandegrift was persuaded not to move ahead to capture all of Guadalcanal Island, which, if he had been given supplies, he could have done in a day or two with his 17,000 men against the few hundred Japanese naval troops and the 2,000 laborers who remained on the island.

The result of the lost opportunities for both sides was that there would be no "lightning-like" victory, but a long, desperate slugging contest.

4

COUNTERATTACK

THE reinforcement of the Japanese garrison at Guadalcanal was a full week in coming, and its composition was an indication of a major Japanese military weakness. A week after the American invasion, General Hyukatake still refused to take it seriously as a threat to his Port Moresby plan. Admiral Mikawa had asked for army help, but all he could get was the Ichiki Detachment, which had been scheduled to land and occupy Midway. After the Midway battle, this detachment had been taken to Guam and retained as a special unit not under 17th Army control.

On August 15, Admiral Yamamoto ordered the creation of a Guadalcanal Reinforcement Force, and chose Rear Admiral Raizo Tanaka and his Destroyer Squadron Two for the task. For the moment, the ships were loading supplies at Truk. Tanaka was told to pick up 900 officers and men of the Ichiki Detachment who had been brought there and to take them to Guadalcanal. From the first, Tanaka was indignant. He could not understand how Combined Fleet could expect to do anything with fewer than a thousand riflemen and no heavy equipment. "Bamboo spear tactics," he called them.

Admiral Yamamoto and the navy in general knew a good deal about the United States and Americans, but the reverse was true of the Imperial Japanese Army, particularly in the South Pacific. In all those years between wars, the navy had been studying American methods and American psychology, but the army had been deeply immersed in the Asian continent. If you asked a Japanese general a question about the Russians, he was likely to know the answer, but if you asked him about Americans, he was not.

The extent of this ignorance was indicated at Rabaul when Comdr. Keisuke Matsunaga, who had once been Yamamoto's aide, was asked by a Southern Area Army staff officer to describe the United States Marines. Just what sort of an organization was this? the staff officer demanded. When told that the marines were the "soldiers of the navy," the army officer scoffed. Americans! They could be expected to quail at an attack and flee a Banzai charge, abandoning equipment and comrades.

Thus the Imperial Japanese Army entered the Guadalcanal conflict. The navy's flights over Guadalcanal and Tulagi had indicated the size of the American invasion operation. Navy pilot Saburo Sakai, looking down on the American flotilla off Guadalcanal on August 7, had said, "it was almost unbelievable; I saw at least 70 ships pushing toward the beaches, a dozen destroyers cutting white swathes through the water, around them. And there were other ships on the horizon, too far distant to make out in detail or to count."

This view would certainly dispel any belief that the American invasion effort amounted to the 2,000 troops reported by the Japanese naval attaché in Moscow, but Sakai was a navy pilot, and his observations did not reach the enemy. The error persisted at army headquarters, and when General Hyukatake decided to send reinforcements to Guadalcanal, he estimated that about a thousand men could do the job, given the superior Japanese fighting spirit.

Quite unaware of the developments in Tokyo and Rabaul, the marines on Guadalcanal waited. On August 10 they stayed within their perimeter and cleared Japanese away from the north shore of the island. There was some shooting, but altogether it was a quiet day. So was August 11. Several times, lookouts on the shore reported submarines. Whether it was one submarine or more was not ascertained, but there was no shelling and the marines' sleep was undisturbed. It was the same on August 12, except for an incident that was to color the whole Guadalcanal campaign. While the island was quiet, General Vandegrift was eager to learn the disposition of the Japanese troops, and on August 10 he sent patrols through the jungle west of the Lunga River. They were forced back at the Matanikau River by heavy Japanese rifle and machine gun fire. The Japanese headquarters was located here. When a Japanese naval warrant officer surrendered, he told the Americans that the majority of the Japanese on the island were west of the Matanikau River. Furthermore, he said, he thought they might all surrender. One of the marines said he had seen a white flag in the area during a patrol, and Col. Frank B. Goettge, the 1st Division intelligence officer, decided to take a reconnaissance party in. The Goettge party went by boat to a point west of the Matanikau and then began to move inland. Within a few minutes of landing, the Americans ran into a Japanese ambush. Colonel Goettge was killed, and only three Americans escaped. The flag they had seen earlier had been an ordinary Japanese military flag, white background with a red rising sun in the center. Folded, the red sun was concealed, and it had appeared to be a white flag of surrender. The Japanese had not intended treachery; they had never offered to surrender, but the marines back at Lunga Point would never believe that. From the moment of Colonel Goettge's death, it was almost impossible to persuade the marines in the line to accept surrenders on the rare occasions when the Japanese offered them.

The marines expected an attack at any time, and they prepared their defenses as best they could without 70 percent of their supplies. The expedition had brought large guns for coastal defense, but they were still on the ships that had sailed for the safety of Nouméa. The largest weapons available for the coast were a few 75-mm guns mounted on half-tracked vehicles, 37-mm antitank guns, and one captured 3-inch Japanese gun. The marines were better prepared against air attack. The ships had landed a number of 90-mm antiaircraft batteries on the first day. In fact, the Japanese pilots flying over the landing beaches on August 7 were astounded to see the antiaircraft guns in place so quickly. In Japanese amphibious operations it took a whole week to get antiaircraft guns ashore, because more vital supplies came first. (They did not know about the helter-skelter loading of the U.S. transports.)

From the beginning, supply was on American minds. On August 10 the ration was reduced to two meals a day, and Japanese rice began to supplement American foodstuffs.

On August 14 the marines used their antiaircraft guns for the first

time. Japanese bombers came over the island at noon, eighteen of
them, and the dinner bell that served as an air raid alarm at General
Vandegrift's headquarters began to jangle. Above, the marines saw
slender, silvery planes, flying at 27,000 feet to avoid the antiaircraft
fire. Their bombing was not very accurate, and most of the bombs of
this raid fell into the sea. Only three Japanese planes came the next
day at noon, but this time they were bombers and messengers. Commander Matsunaga had been ordered by Captain Masao Kanazawa,
the commander of the 8th Base Unit at Rabaul, to fly over the Japanese positions on Guadalcanal and drop messages telling the men
that help was coming.

Kanazawa's three land-based Betty or Nakajima 96 bombers
bombed near the airfield, wounding one marine, and then dropped
messages and food parcels for the Japanese defenders. The messages,
attached to red tassels with long white cloth streamers, informed
troops that they had dropped supplies and that help was coming.
The marines brought several copies of the message to Vandegrift's
headquarters after an interpreter translated it. Later, marines went
out after the air drop and recovered fourteen packages that Kanazawa's planes had dropped. They were cushioned wicker baskets con-
taining cans of meat, bags of biscuits, boxes of rice candy, and .25
caliber ammunition.

The message began: The enemy before your eyes are collapsing. . . . friendly troops, a landing party. . . . relief is near. . . .

The packages also contained copies of the Japanese forces special
South Pacific area newspaper. This edition reported on the Savo Island naval battle that had occurred in The Slot earlier that week.
Tokyo claimed the sinking of 1 battleship, 2 heavy cruisers, 3 light
cruisers, 3 destroyers, 10 transports, and the serious damaging of 2
heavy cruisers, 2 destroyers, and 1 transport. The Japanese also
claimed that they had shot down 32 U.S. fighter planes and 9 fighter-
bombers (dive bombers and torpedo bombers).

General Vandegrift, who knew what had happened on the sea, recognized the overstatement, but the Japanese on Guadalcanal could
not be expected to do so. The Imperial General Headquarters was
continuing the policy so lamented by Admiral Yamamoto—de-
liberate exaggeration and outright lying. For the moment, the
"news" cheered the Japanese naval troops on the northwest end of
the island and gave them renewed courage to await the rein-

forcement promised from Rabaul. That night of August 14 the "scuttlebutt" (rumor) started its rounds among the marines: The enemy was winding up to deliver a smashing counterattack. The tension among the marines grew by the hour, until night ended, and another day began.

On August 15 the Americans had their first resupply since Admiral Turner's transports had left them five days earlier. The destroyer transports *Colhoun, Gregory, Little,* and *McKean* brought in loads of aviation gas, bombs, and ammunition. Admiral Turner was trying to make Henderson Field ready for aircraft. The passengers included Maj. Charles H. Hayes, who would be operations officer for the field, and Ens. George W. Polk and 120 mechanics to service the planes that were expected at any moment. The marines then set to work to lengthen the field by 1,000 feet, but there was nothing they could do about the mud. What mud it was!—viscous, clinging stuff—gray-brown—that clung to the men's boots and swallowed trucks up to the hoods. On August 12 an amphibious Catalina flying boat had made the first landing, and there were many pointed remarks about the nature of the plane it took to land on Henderson Field, but General Vandegrift insisted that the field was ready for use as long as the weather was dry.

The Americans were not the only ones using destroyers for transportation.

On the night of August 15, 1,000 soldiers of the Imperial Japanese Army boarded 6 destroyer transports at Truk and headed for Guadalcanal. The unescorted destroyers came down quietly on the night of August 18, past Savo Island and Lunga Roads and through Lengo Channel to land at Taivu Point, about 20 miles east of the American position. Colonel Kiyonao Ichiki, the commander of the unit, still believed there were only 2,000 Americans on the island. With the 5th Sasebo Special Naval Landing Force troops (Japanese marines) who had landed at Tassafaronga and the existing garrison bivouacked in the Matanikau River basin, Ichiki expected to work a pincers movement. He would move westward toward Lunga Point, and they would squeeze the Americans between them.

The Japanese destroyers were so contemptuous of the American defenses that they stopped to bombard Guadalcanal and Tulagi Harbor after landing the troops. They shelled the airfield without effect.

They destroyed a landing craft that was running between Tulagi and Lunga Point. They bombarded the Tulagi docks. By the time they began to move in leisurely fashion up The Slot it was daybreak, and the Army's B-17s from Espiritu Santo had been informed of their presence. The big bombers attacked and scored one hit on the destroyer *Hagikaze*. She and the other ships moved leisurely no more but dashed back to Rabaul.

The Americans first became aware of the Japanese reinforcements on Guadalcanal when Maj. Martin Clemens, the Guadalcanal District Officer, showed up at Vandegrift's headquarters with 60 members of the Solomon Islands Defense Force. The islanders proved invaluable to the marines in tracking, and on August 19 led a patrol under Captain Charles Brush to one of Colonel Ichiki's units. The Japanese were moving west, in a column, without regard to patrol vigilance. The marines ambushed them and killed 31 of the 34 men. Examination of their equipment and belongings showed that they had landed recently. They had maps of the marine positions, although they did not seem to have any conception of the marine strength on the island.

The marines dug in along the bank of the Tenaru River, which ended at the mouth in a dry sandbar. They dug in along the west side of the bar, and set trip wires and barbed wire on the other side at a place they called Hell Point, and put a 37-mm gun to cover the bar.

On the evening of August 20, the Japanese began moving from the east toward the Tenaru. They gathered in the thick jungle and waited. As the hours drifted by, the marines waited on the west bank of the river. Midnight came, and the jungle was still silent. One o'clock came on the morning of August 21, and still no action. But at 1:30 the Japanese launched an attack. Two hundred Japanese came storming up to the trip wire, the soldiers with their bayonets fixed, hurling grenades ahead of them, the officers swinging their long Samurai swords. This sort of attack had paralyzed Allied troops in the jungles of Malaya and Burma, but the marines turned their rifles and machine guns on the wire, and the Japanese began to fall. The 37-mm gun began firing canister shot, which spread out like big shotgun pellets. The Japanese went over, around, and through the wire, and began to overrun the marine positions, but the marines stood their ground, swivelling in their foxholes to fire and coming out to slug with the Japanese toe to toe, bayonet to bayonet. By the time daylight arrived, all the Japanese who had forded the Tenaru were dead, and Colonel Ichiki's force was totally disorganized. His whole strategy had been based on a surprise attack that would demoralize and destroy a small number of American troops. The tenacity and numbers of the marines had turned the tables. The marines sent a battalion upstream along the Tenaru, crossed the river, and flanked the Japanese on the east. They squeezed the Japanese into a pocket in a coconut grove on the shore of the island. From the position beyond the Tenaru, field guns and machine guns kept the Japanese from crossing the river. As the marines pushed westward, the Japanese fought back with a bayonet charge, but they did not get through. The marines responded with a bayonet charge, and disrupted the Japanese defense. Some Japanese soldiers took to the sea, and a few swam eastward along the coast to safety, but most drowned. Some managed to squeeze through the marine line to the east and escape. But the majority of the 900 Japanese troops died in the palm grove. That evening, as the marines brought up tanks and began knocking down the trees to eliminate snipers, Colonel Ichiki and several of his officers committed suicide, and the organized defense was ended. The Ichiki force of nearly 1,000 men had lasted just three days on Guadalcanal. The marines had taken only 15 prisoners; they remembered the fate of Colonel Goettge. They had lost 35 marines killed and 75 wounded in this bloodletting. The Japanese reinforcement effort had failed completely, and the Americans had established a new confidence in their ability to stand up against troops who had been touted as the fiercest jungle fighters in the world.

5

THE LOST OPPORTUNITY

THE successful Japanese attack in the waters off Savo Island made it very clear that the entire Guadalcanal expedition was in serious danger. For the moment, the island was isolated, and General Vandegrift and his 17,000 marines might be in danger of annihilation unless help was brought before the enemy could stage a major landing. Had the Japanese been prepared to move 15,000 to 20,000 troops immediately, the outcome for the Americans would have been disastrous. So far, by August 20, General Vandegrift had been extremely lucky, because the Japanese had first misread American intentions and then moved too slowly. The Japanese had not really understood that there was no reason to maintain strongpoints in New Guinea unless the Guadalcanal threat was removed.

Admiral Nimitz was under the mistaken impression that at least Vandegrift's troops and the transport force were protected by Fletcher's carriers. With the announcement of the defeat at Savo, Nimitz hurried to dispatch two marine fighter squadrons from Pearl Harbor, but they could not sail until August 15. He still thought there would be no gap, not knowing that Fletcher was miles away.

One of the major problems at this difficult period was communication. The "shoestring" nature of the operation was nowhere more apparent. Admiral Ghormley had located his headquarters at

Nouméa in New Caledonia, not realizing that due to weather conditions at this time of year, he could not communicate with Guadalcanal much of the day. Messages were routed to Auckland and then back up to Vandegrift. Also communication between Nouméa, Guadalcanal, and Espiritu Santo, where Admiral McCain's land-based air force was located, were equally bad, which accounted in part for the American failure to spot the Japanese cruisers as they had come charging down The Slot.

As soon as word of the disaster at Guadalcanal was known, Admiral Ghormley had asked General MacArthur to detail submarines of the Southwest Pacific Command from other areas to Guadalcanal, but MacArthur replied that to do so would leave Rabaul and Kavieng uncovered. It was better to sink the Japanese ships as they headed south than to wait until they arrived on the scene. Ghormley agreed, and so in the difficult days of mid-August the only submarine the marines saw off Guadalcanal was Japanese. So were the aircraft that hovered above the green island in the second ten days of August. The Japanese had been hit hard by the antiaircraft guns and the fighters from the carriers during the initial landings on Guadalcanal. When Admiral Yamamoto had realized the Americans were on the island in force, he had sent Vice Admiral Nishizo Tsukahara, commander of the 11th Air Fleet, down to Rabaul to take direct charge of operations. On August 10 the admiral discovered that he had only 22 bombers and 17 fighters in operational condition. Those first two days of raiding from distances that were too great for effective operations had cost the command heavily in planes and experienced pilots. Pilot officer Sakai, for example, who was one of Japan's greatest fliers at that point, was so badly hurt in that first day's operation that he was invalided back to Japan for many months. But since the Americans had absolutely *no* planes in the sky above Guadalcanal, Admiral Tsukahara's force was significant and useful.

On August 11, half a dozen Zero fighters flew over the island, looking for American planes. They found none, but they did get a good look at the work the marines were doing below to lengthen the airfield, and they interrupted construction with a series of strafing runs. They went back to Rabaul to report on the activity. The next day three twin-engined Betty bombers flew over to take pictures. On August 13 the weather was too foul for flying, and Henderson Field became a soggy morass of mud, a matter of concern to the marines, who wondered how any planes could ever operate here.

On August 14 a flight of three Bettys photographed the field. They had a good respect for the marines' 90-mm antiaircraft guns, and they stayed high, out of range. On August 16 Commander Matsunaga came over with his food drop and leaflets to cheer up the Japanese soldiers on the ground.

Since there was no opposition, and a few planes were coming in to Rabaul every day from Truk, Admiral Tsukahara ordered a bombing raid on August 18. Eight Bettys came in to bomb, and were so determined that they risked the fire from the 90-mm guns. They did bomb and created huge craters in the field, but the marines had the satisfaction of damaging five of the bombers.

The true import of the debacle at Savo was slower in moving up the U.S. chain of command than the news of the landings was among the Japanese. Admiral Turner did not arrive at Nouméa with the transports until August 14, when he gave Ghormley his report, which was sent on to Nimitz. So when Ghormley turned about after his rejection by MacArthur to ask Nimitz for submarines, Pearl Harbor was not fully aware of the need for desperate measures, and Nimitz refused.

On August 12, Admiral McCain reported that one of his pilots had managed to land a PBY amphibian on the Henderson Field runway, which had been lengthened to 3,600 feet. He suggested that planes could be moved in. But Ghormley had no planes. From MacArthur he might have borrowed a few B-17s, but the runway was too short for them, or some P-40 fighters, but their maximum operational altitude was 15,000 feet, and the Japanese had been bombing from 17,000 feet.

The escort carrier *Long Island* was en route to Guadalcanal, carrying marine pilots and planes, but the captain of the *Long Island* informed Admiral Ghormley that many of the marine pilots were so badly trained that it would be murder to send them into combat.

No one could blame them. Their unit, Marine Air Group 23, had been organized on May 1 at Ewa Field west of Pearl Harbor, and the two squadrons of fighter pilots had been given Brewster "Buffaloes," slow, old-fashioned aircraft that had not been able to stand up to anything the Japanese had put in the air in the past six months. The two bomber squadrons were slightly better off, flying SBD-2s, but these were already obsolete by two generations. This unit had been selected for the Guadalcanal air mission in July, the Buffaloes had been replaced by Grumman F4Fs, but there had been little time for training. Many of the pilots brought in to fill up the squadrons were fresh from flying school, and the "hottest" aircraft they had flown were advanced trainers. This was scarcely adequate training for pilots who were going to meet some of the most experienced fliers in the Japanese Navy. There were, however a few survivors of VMF 221, the squadron assigned to Midway, which was virtually wiped out before the carrier battle. A dozen of them were sent ashore at Efate, and their planes were taken by experienced pilots from VMF 212.

Fletcher continued to stay outside the danger zone, thereby tying up the carriers, cruisers, and destroyers that could be useful in defending Guadalcanal. Ghormley had word that the Japanese were bringing motor torpedo boats into the waters of the island, and directed Fletcher to be ready to move the task force in at night to destroy the Japanese surface ships that had occasionally bombarded the American positions. Fletcher balked. So the confusion continued, and until August 20 General Vandegrift received no help at all. On that day, the *Long Island* catapulted 19 F4F fighters and 12 Douglas SBD dive bombers from a point southeast of the San Cristobal Islands. The little carrier then steamed away from the combat zone, because her planes would not return. They landed at Henderson Field to become the nucleus of the "Cactus Air Force," the small group of fighters and bombers that would try to protect the marines from air and sea attack. That same day Admiral Nimitz sent as strong a message as he could: He instructed Ghormley that carrier planes must be used to defend Guadalcanal from enemy landings.

The message fell on ears that were generally unreceptive. Having opposed the Guadalcanal landings from the beginning, Admiral Ghormley looked gloomily at the future, and suggested that there was doubt whether or not they could hold the area. No one had more doubts than General Vandegrift at that point, his troops virtually alone on a tiny island surrounded by his country's enemies, but no one heard that sort of complaint from him.

The pilots of the Marine Air Group 23 landed at Henderson Field. The first plane to land was that of Major R. C. Mangrum, commander of Scout Bombing Squadron 232. No one had ever been greeted more joyfully. As the planes came in over the island the marines in their defensive positions looked up, and for the first time in ten days saw above them American planes rather than Japanese. They began to cheer. When Major Mangrum stepped down from the wing of his bomber, he was met by General Vandegrift with a hearty handshake, and as the other pilots came down, one by one, they too were cheered and treated as conquering heroes instead of as the untested fliers they were.

They had come just in time. The next day the Japanese resumed serious air operations. On August 21 the newly arrived American planes were in the air flying support missions for the ground troops who were mopping up Colonel Ichiki's shattered force, and flying air patrol over the island. Captain John L. Smith, the commander of Fighting 223, was flying a patrol mission with 3 other pilots when they encountered 6 Zero fighters. Smith saw them first, about 500 feet above the marines' 14,000-foot level, and just as he identified them from his memory of silhouettes in training days, the Zeros turned into them and began an attack. From that point on the 10 planes turned and dodged and fired, each seeking advantage. The Zeros, as Smith had known, were faster and more maneuverable than his own craft, and the Zero pilots got in many bursts against the four F4Fs. But unlike the Allied fighters that usually faced the Japanese, the strong construction of the Grummans kept them flying when badly shot up, and the armor behind the seat back saved the pilots. That day Captain Smith shot down his first Zero, without knowing it until later.

He had been firing at one Zero, when suddenly he found two more Zeros on his tail, and took sharp evasive action. The first Zero zoomed away, and Smith found it difficult to disengage from the other. After he had, he looked around and found that one of his pilots was missing. He turned back, north towards Savo Island, and found that pilot, Sgt. John Lindley, beset by several Zeros. The four American fighters attacked again, the Zeros shot them up, but soon the Zero pilots realized they were running low on fuel for their long flight back to Rabaul, and they disengaged. The Americans limped home, and Captain Smith discovered when he tried to land that his hydraulic system had been shot out, and the wheels would not come down. The oil system failed, and the engine quit. He glided in on a dead stick landing, and the F4F ground across the gravel of the Henderson Field runway to a crunching stop. Captain Smith walked away from the landing, but his plane was a total loss.

The Japanese resumed serious air operations against Guadalcanal on August 21, sending over surface bombers escorted by Zero fighters. The F4F fighters had their disadvantage in mixing with the Zeros, which were faster, but the F4Fs had the major advantage of armor to protect the pilot. On the second day, Capt. John Smith, leader of the group fighter squadron, shot down a Zero. But many of the F4Fs were also shot down. These eager but green pilots were facing some of the cream of the Japanese Naval Air Force, fliers who had flown hundreds of combat hours.

Two days after the arrival of the marine fliers, General Millard Harmon, the South Pacific air commander, arranged to bring in a part of the Army Air Corps 67th Fighter Squadron. These pilots were equipped with P-400 fighters, an advanced version of the P-39, but a plane that was incapable of attaining 20,000 feet, the height at which the Japanese liked to come in and drop down out of the sun. They could be used as flying artillery, for each carried a 37-mm cannon in its nose, plus six machine guns. Part of their problem was the heavy armament that bogged them down.

From the beginning, the airmen were beset with the most vexing difficulties. Ensign Polk and his navy mechanics had been able to bring up the gasoline drums brought in by the destroyer transports to supply the planes with aviation gas, but every gallon had to be pumped out of a drum by hand and decanted into the airplane fuel tanks. The bombers had to be loaded by manpower for there were not even any handhoists on the island, and the machine gun ammunition belts had to be manhandled and carried by truck or jeep.

Captain Dale Brannon's 67th Army Air Force Fighter Squadron was supposed to arrive in force, but the condition of the field was so bad after a few landings and a few rains, that two-thirds of the squadron was delayed at Espiritu Santo for several days. Captain Smith's Marine F4Fs found themselves in difficulty almost immediately, because the planes had exhausted their oxygen bottles, and none had been brought in during the first slender supply effort. The F4F pilots had to get up high to fight the Zeros, and they could not go up to 20,000 without oxygen. On August 22, General Vandegrift informed Admiral McCain that he had been forced to suspend fighter patrols until more oxygen arrived.

Admiral Fletcher was still operating far from Guadalcanal, which he justified by claiming that it was essential to conceal the presence of the carriers until necessary. But on August 20 a Japanese Kawanishi flying boat on long patrol spotted the carrier force and reported its presence 500 miles west of Bougainville. Admiral Yamamoto had that information and the news that Colonel Ichiki's force had been wiped out. Japanese headquarters on Guadalcanal also made it very clear for the first time that the American force was not to be numbered in the hundreds but in the many thousands.

These reports caused Admiral Yamamoto to reconsider his plans. Admiral Kondo's force was scheduled to stop over at Truk for fuel and supplies, and to make a more or less leisurely attack on Guadalcanal. The presence of the carriers and the new knowledge that the American invasion was a major operation caused an immediate change. From that point on Japanese planes shadowed the U.S. carrier force. Admiral Yamamoto ordered the Combined Fleet to fuel at sea. There was no time for leisure. Refueling at sea was just as difficult for the Japanese as it was for the Americans—the ships had to slow to six knots and became prime targets for submarine or air attack—but it was done. Early on the morning of August 23, Admiral Kondo's ships were 400 miles north of Guadalcanal. Ahead of them were two transports carrying 1,500 Japanese troop reinforcements, escorted by a cruiser and 6 destroyers.

In the hiatus of August 10–20 it became obvious to the American air search planes that the Japanese at Rabaul were building for attack. Admiral Nimitz dispatched the carrier *Hornet* to the South Pacific on August 17 to join the *Enterprise, Saratoga,* and *Wasp.* Admiral Ghormley had concurred in Admiral Fletcher's decision to hold the carriers out of action until the Japanese launched their major naval attack, expected at any moment. For that reason, during those long ten days the Japanese had complete control of the seas around Guadalcanal, and their destroyers ranged in and out. On August 21, the supply transports *Fomalhaut* and *Alhena* were on their way to Guadalcanal to deliver some desperately needed supplies. The marines were on short rations, and those made available largely through captured Japanese supplies. The airfield had to have gasoline, and as yet, in spite of McCain's pleas, no transport planes had been provided. So the surface convoy was the only answer, dangerous as it was. That night the destroyer *Blue,* one of the transport escorts, was torpedoed by the Japanese destroyer *Kawakaze*, and damaged so badly that later she had to be scuttled. Once more the Japanese had shown their superiority in night fighting.

The Japanese also showed their greater aggressiveness in air operations. Admiral Yamamoto had not hesitated to order his 58-ship force descending on the Solomons to fuel at sea. Admiral Fletcher, however, worried about fueling in the face of the enemy. And on August 23 the fuel problem was much on his mind, since his carriers were less than half filled with oil.

On that morning, one of Admiral McCain's PBYs from the tender *Mackinac* in the Santa Cruz Islands, "spooked" the transports and warship escort that was 50 miles out ahead of the Japanese fleet. The pilot had made a minor error; he identified the escort as 2 cruisers and 3 destroyers; actually it was 1 cruiser and 6 destroyers; but the import was clear: The Japanese were moving to reinforce the garrison on Guadalcanal with two shiploads of troops. With the Japanese naval superiority in the area, it might be expected that this small force would not be the last reinforcement.

Admiral Fletcher had the word that morning, and the *Saratoga* air group was ordered to attack the Japanese. By 2:45 that afternoon the planes were in the air, 32 bombers and 6 fighters. Fletcher had other indications of Japanese activity: At 7:30 that morning the search planes of the carrier *Enterprise* had encountered a Japanese submarine traveling fast on the surface, heading south. They attacked unsuccessfully. An hour later another plane sighted a second submarine also speeding south on the surface. It attacked, also unsuccessfully. It was known throughout the fleet that the Japanese always sent a scouting line of submarines ahead of a war fleet, so this should have been warning to Fletcher by midmorning that he faced much more than transports and their escort vessels. But Fletcher did not regard the presence of the submarines as "positive" indication of the presence of a fleet.

The report from that PBY about the reinforcements reached General Vandegrift at about the same time that Fletcher received it. Vandegrift was vitally concerned lest the Japanese bring in strong reinforcements when he had so little food and ammunition on Guadalcanal. He was also worried about the obvious weakness of his tiny Cactus Air Force with its handful of F4F fighters, one of them already reduced to scavenger parts, his P-400s which were really only equipped for troop support, and the handful of bombers. The absence of the oxygen bottles meant that any pilot who tried to attain altitude above 10,000 feet was potentially in trouble. But by this time Vandegrift had no confidence in Fletcher, so he decided that even if it was suicidal for the pilots, he would have to launch an attack on the Japanese transport force.

The Japanese reinforcement unit actually consisted of one big transport, the *Kinryu Maru*, and four destroyers converted for fast transport work. The escort was commanded by Rear Admiral Raizo Tanaka, and in his cruiser he led Destroyer Squadron Two in escort. Tanaka's lookouts saw the PBY that reported them to the Americans, and in turn, he reported the contact. When Admiral Yamamoto had the word, he abruptly revised his attack plan. Admiral Tanaka was to reverse his course to avoid attack, and he did so. Thus the 37 planes from the *Saratoga* and the 23 planes from Henderson Field found nothing when they reached the probable point of interception, given the speed and course of the Japanese force seen by the PBY. The American planes then fanned out to search for the enemy, but the weather was spotty that afternoon, heavy with cloud interspersed with rainsqualls, and they found nothing. Actually, the original PBY had continued to shadow Tanaka after he changed course, until the Japanese were lost in the bad weather. But so poor was the American air intelligence reporting system that the search planes never got the word. A relief plane that was supposed to cover the area crashed on takeoff, and the original PBY did not get back to its base until late. That pilot's message about the course change was sent again for relay to Vandegrift and Fletcher. By this time all the planes from Henderson Field and the *Saratoga* had landed at Henderson Field. Not knowing what had happened to the Tanaka force, General Vandegrift spent the hours until midnight worrying about the enemy transports. From the early report, they should be arriving at Guadalcanal at midnight.

Late in the afternoon, Admiral Fletcher concluded that there was no immediate threat from the enemy and that there would be no battle for several days, so he cut his force by a third, sending Admiral Noyes's *Wasp* group south to fuel. This was the difference between the Japanese and the Americans: The Japanese took the chance of discovery rather than lose the initiative; the Americans did not.

As of the late afternoon of August 23, the American carrier air force outweighed the Japanese considerably; Fletcher had 259 planes available on his three carriers, while Yamamoto had only 177 planes. But with the dispatch of *Wasp* out of the area, Fletcher reduced his force to 176 planes.

Admiral Yamamoto had two ends in mind for the Combined Fleet in this operation. The 10,000-ton carrier *Ryujo*, the smallest with him, was to move 190 miles east of Guadalcanal to support Admiral Tanaka's landing. She was accompanied by the heavy cruiser *Tone*, the newest in Japan's fleet, and the destroyers *Tokitsukaze* and *Amatsukaze*. Meanwhile Admiral Chuichi Nagumo's carrier striking force, with the 40,000-ton carriers *Shokaku* and *Zuikaku*, would attack any American fleet units in the area, including carriers. Once the carriers were destroyed, the battleships and cruisers would proceed at leisure to the waters off Guadalcanal to destroy Henderson Field and give support to the Japanese land forces.

By this time, Admiral Yamamoto knew that the Americans had a large military establishment on Guadalcanal, and if Yamamoto considered the undertaking important enough to employ the Combined Fleet, it seems odd that the Japanese did not move in many thousands of troops, for they were available at Rabaul, Truk, and New Guinea. But such reasoning did not take into account the enormous difference between American and Japanese command organization. Admiral Yamamoto had no control over the army's reinforcement of Guadalcanal, since Imperial Headquarters had given the army the task of retaking the island. The army had one way of moving: First it landed a battalion (that of Lt. Col. Ichiki) and then the rest of the regiment, and then the remainder of the brigade. The force that was coming in the transports was the rest of the Ichiki regiment.

During the evening hours of August 23, the Japanese main force also turned back. So that night the Japanese were north of the Solomons, and the American task force was south of the islands.

All night long the mechanics at Henderson Field gassed and armed the *Saratoga*'s planes that had spent the night ashore. The work was interrupted briefly at about two o'clock in the morning when the destroyer *Kagero*, landing supplies on Guadalcanal, bombarded the island. But the work resumed. By dawn the planes were ready to fly. They were held at the field until General Vandegrift received a long-delayed report that Admiral Tanaka's force had turned back. Then he released the planes and they flew back to the *Sara-*

toga. They left behind 2 dive bombers that had engine trouble, and 27 1,000-pound bombs for the Cactus Air Force.

That morning of August 24, Admiral Fletcher was badly hampered by his unfortunate decision to release one carrier on the eve of battle. With the *Saratoga's* air group on Guadalcanal, all he had to send out for search, combat air patrol, and any missions were the 87 planes of the *Enterprise.* The dawn search used 23 bombers, and they discovered nothing but another surfaced submarine, whose presence still did not seem to mean anything to Admiral Fletcher. But even if the Japanese had been found that morning, Admiral Fletcher had only 28 bombers with which to attack, until the *Saratoga* planes could land on their carrier, and be refueled and rearmed.

At four o'clock in the morning the *Ryujo* and her escort were detached from the main force for their mission. U.S. Navy historian Samuel Eliot Morison said that *Ryujo* was sent out as "bait" for the American carriers. Captain Tameichi Hara, commander of that force's destroyer *Amatsukaze,* indicated that the decision was a hasty one, but historian Paul S. Dull, a student of the Japanese Navy, found no indication that the decision was a hasty one or that Yamamoto expected to sacrifice the *Ryujo.*

But some of the Japanese officers in this detachment were more than a little worried. *Ryujo's* pilots were mostly replacements.

The Japanese and American search planes were out early on the morning of August 24. The Americans made the first sighting. At 9:35 a PBY reported a carrier, two cruisers, and a destroyer about 150 miles northwest of Guadalcanal. The report, again, was inaccurate in describing the ships, but that was unimportant; the plane had spotted a carrier and placed it correctly. Admiral Fletcher had been annoyed with the failures of McCain's air search planes in the past, and he was still angry about the poor reporting by the PBY on the 23rd which had caused him to launch a mission that never made contact. So he ignored the PBY report. But this particular PBY continued to shadow the *Ryujo* and her escort and reported again to the *Mackinac* on the sighting. Admiral Fletcher had the second report but still refused to believe. Then, at noon, another PBY reported on the *Ryujo* detachment, and finally, Fletcher reluctantly ordered a search.

Meanwhile, the usual morning search launched by the *Saratoga* had turned back at the end of 200 miles, since that was the optimum range for carrier bombers. Here again was an illustration of the inferiority of the American search patterns: The searchers missed the Nagumo carriers by about 100 miles.

The *Saratoga* air group began to arrive around the carrier at 11:30, and twenty miles out four fighter pilots spotted a Japanese Kawanishi four-engined flying boat, and shot it down. But the American force had been discovered.

Just after noon, as the *Saratoga* planes were refueling, the remaining bombers were launched for the search to the northwest. Each of the 23 planes was assigned a narrow pie-shaped section of ocean, extending out 250 miles from the carrier.

Aboard the *Ryujo* the lookouts spotted the PBY that discovered them, and watched helplessly as the big plane trailed along. Admiral Tadaichi Hara could have sent up fighters to shoot down the PBY, but it would not have solved the problem: It was certain from the first few minutes that a report had been sent out. At one o'clock in the afternoon, just as the planes from the *Enterprise* were taking to the air, the *Ryujo* launched 15 Zero fighters and 6 Betty bombers to attack Henderson Field. As the Americans moved toward the carrier, ships' radar spotted the planes as radar blips, and at last Admiral Fletcher was convinced. He ordered *Saratoga*'s air group to attack, and although the pilots were red-eyed from lack of sleep and had already flown five hours that morning, they manned their planes.

The marines on Guadalcanal were alerted by a coastwatcher that enemy planes were coming in from Malaita, and at 2:20 the 14 F4Fs of the Cactus Air Force were in the air, although they did not have oxygen bottles. Luckily they didn't need them that day, for the Japanese bombers came in at 9,000 feet and from above the F4Fs dived down and caught them. One after another the torpedo planes fell into the sea as the F4Fs and the Zeros cartwheeled in the sky. Captain Marion Carl shot down 2 torpedo planes and 1 Zero that day, but 3 of the F4F pilots fell beneath the guns of the Zeros. A few of the bombers got through, bombed Henderson Field, and then formed up again under the protection of the Zeros and headed back to the *Ryujo*.

For some reason, Adm. Chuichi Hara had not ordered up a combat air patrol that day. At about 2:30 the Guadalcanal raiders reported back that they had bombed Henderson Field and were returning. Then there was nothing, for just after sending the message, the flight leader's plane was shot down, and since he had the only long-range radio, the remaining planes lost communication with their carrier.

At about three o'clock in the afternoon, lookouts with the Japanese task unit discovered several B-17s above them. The guns of the escort ships opened fire, although the range was extreme, and the B-17s droned on high above, until finally, the *Ryujo* sent up two fighters. Then the B-17s moved off, and when they had gone the Zeros remained in the air as combat air patrol.

Still, the carrier did not launch any more planes until four o'clock in the afternoon. Just as the captain of the carrier was turning her into the wind to launch planes, the bombers from the *Saratoga* arrived. They were a combination of dive bombers and torpedo planes. Commander Harry D. Felt led them in, then the dive bombers peeled off first and headed down to the sea from 14,000 feet.

As the Japanese ships saw the American planes, the escorts moved out into a 5,000-yard circle around the *Ryujo*, in order to make better use of their antiaircraft guns to protect her. The bombers screamed down through a sky dotted with smoke puffs, released their bombs, and straightened out to fly over the carrier and strafe the ships. Fighters came down strafing too and struck at the Zeros. Then the torpedo bombers came in, using a technique the Japanese had employed so successfully in the Battle of the Coral Sea: A pair of torpedo planes attacked simultaneously, one from each bow, so that no matter which way the carrier turned, it was likely to run into one of the torpedoes.

The bombers scored several hits on the *Ryujo* near the stern, and the 1,000-pound armor-piercing bombs went through the flight deck. Then more bombs came in, and great clouds of smoke rose, punctuated by columns of fire. From his perch on the bridge of the *Amatsukaze*, Captain Hara could see the smoke and sense that the carrier's fuel tanks had caught fire. He did not see any torpedo hits, but the Americans claimed some. Whether torpedoes struck or not, the *Ryujo* was in her death throes ten minutes after the bombers arrived. The fires were uncontrollable, and they got to the aviation gasoline supply and the magazines. She began to list to starboard and her red coat of antifouling paint was exposed. The flight deck dipped down until it nearly touched the waves. A few of the American planes had saved bombs and torpedoes for the *Tone* and the de-

stroyers, and other planes came over low to strafe, but neither these
Japanese ships nor the American aircraft were damaged in this attack. Commander Felt gave the signal, and the American planes
turned back toward their carrier.

As dusk came, the Japanese destroyers rallied to begin rescue operations. The captain of the *Ryujo* had sent messages warning the returning planes from the Guadalcanal strike to head for Buka, since
he could not land them. But the planes came in anyway, circled their
carrier, and then ditched alongside. The pilots were rescued by the
destroyers. At about 6:30 that night a pair of B-17s appeared in the
gloom and bombed the sinking carrier and the rescuers, but all the
bombs missed by a wide margin.

The *Ryujo* was dead in the water. The destroyers moved alongside
even though the carrier had a 40-degree list and could not last more
than a few minutes longer. The *Amatsukaze* came up so close that
the superstructure of the carrier brushed the destroyer's bridge, and
sailors with long poles had to stand by to hold the little ship off the
carrier. Planks were set between the decks, and more than 300 men
poured across. Captain Tadao Kato was the last man off his ship,
and after he stepped across, the destroyer engines speeded, and she
gunned away from the side of the carrier.

The *Tone* and the *Tokitsukaze* were both picking up crewmen
who had gone overboard. More *Ryujo* planes arrived and circled
overhead in the growing darkness. Fourteen planes then ditched in
the sea, and the ships picked up the aircrews. The ships turned away
as *Ryujo* sank.

It was not three minutes since Captain Kato had stepped across
the planks. He turned to Commander Hara of the *Amatsukaze*, his
voice quavering: "Commander Hara. . . . I don't know how to
thank you. . . ." And it was then that Commander Hara learned
that his dear friend, Hisakichi Kishi, executive officer of the *Ryujo*,
was one of those who did not make it. The war seemed suddenly
very real and very deadly.

During the afternoon, as Admiral Fletcher worried aboard the
Saratoga, the combat air patrol shot down three Japanese
"snoopers." The last of these was destroyed just after two o'clock,
and although Fletcher did not know it, the plane was from the
cruiser *Chikuma* of the Combined Fleet, and its crew managed to

send off a position report on the American carriers just before the plane crashed into the sea.

Admiral Nagumo, the commander of the 3rd Fleet and of the carrier striking force, was still smarting from Admiral Yamamoto's obvious dissatisfaction with the conduct of the Midway operation. Privately, Yamamoto held Nagumo responsible for the defeat because of his failure to find the Americans in time, and Nagumo was well aware of the attitude of his superior. When he learned that the Americans had two carriers south of Guadalcanal, and that they had just flown a strike, his lined, square face broke into a smile. Here was the chance to avenge the misfortune of Midway. In less than an hour the first attack wave rolled along the decks of *Zuikaku* and *Shokaku*, 27 bombers and 10 Zero fighters from the 2 carriers.

Ten minutes after that first wave left the decks, two of the *Enterprise* search planes discovered the *Shokaku* and attacked her with the 500-pound bombs they carried on search missions. The search planes claimed a hit and a near miss. Lieutenant Roy Davis dropped his bomb just off the starboard side, and Ensign Robert C. Shaw's hit off the starboard quarter. A Zero of the combat air patrol came after the SBDs, but in one of those accidents of war, the Zero fighter was shot down by antiaircraft fire from his own ships before he could attack. The carriers were unscathed, and within half an hour were launching their second strike against the American carriers.

Admiral Fletcher learned of the whereabouts of the two big Japanese carriers early in the afternoon, but he was very short of planes, having sent the *Wasp* off to refuel and having launched the *Enterprise* search and the *Saratoga* attack on the *Ryujo*. So he did not send an attack against the Japanese carriers. Instead, he concentrated on the defense of his own. Extra combat air patrol fighters were put in the air, and more fighters sat on deck, armed and full of fuel, ready to take off in a hurry.

The two carriers separated. Each moved into the center of a circle on whose perimeter, about two miles away, were ranged the cruisers, destroyers, and battleships to help screen the carrier from air attack with their antiaircraft barrages.

At 4:25 the first Japanese attack wave found a group of American planes winging home from search missions and followed them back to the American carriers. Then, just before 4:30 in the afternoon, the Japanese flight commander saw the American carriers and split his planes into several small groups, better to avoid the antiaircraft fire.

The Americans, who had seen them on radar twenty minutes earlier, had their maximum fighter strength in the air. Fifty-three planes
headed out from the carriers to attack the Japanese bombers before
they could strike. At the same time, the *Enterprise* sent off her last
11 bombers and 7 torpedo bombers to strike the enemy ships. *Saratoga* sent off five torpedo bombers and two dive bombers, even
though the pilots had just gotten into the planes to taxi them out of
the way for landing of the combat air patrol. The pilots had not
been briefed, nor did they have any navigation equipment aboard.
But they were told to join up with the *Enterprise* group and find the
enemy. The order had to come from the admiral; no one else would
have given it; it was further proof that carrier operations ought to be
run by aviators and not by battleship men who wear observers'
wings.

The fighters from the two American carriers scattered to offer the
most protection. Some of them circled the carriers at various altitudes between 10,000 and 15,000 feet. Nine were 40 miles north of
the ship at 15,000 feet. The remainder were sent out to meet the Japanese as they came in.

An *Enterprise* fighter made the first contact 33 miles out. The
pilot reported 36 bombers at 12,000 feet, with many other planes
above and below. But aboard the *Enterprise*, Lt. Comdr. Dow, the
fighter director, was overwhelmed by the senseless chatter of the
fighter circuit between pilots.

"I'm in high blower. . . ."

"Where are you Bill?"

"Let's go get 'em. . . ."

It was good theater but bad radio discipline, and Dow was unable
to make much sense of what the pilots were seeing, or to give information from one group to the other. All he could do was remind the
fighters that they were to concentrate on the enemy bombers and
torpedo planes and leave the fighters alone.

Because of this poor radio discipline, several of the Japanese units
managed to sneak through the American fighter net and approach
the carriers.

So the Japanese bombers came bearing in, the F4Fs trying to get
at them and the Zero fighters rising to meet the Americans. The

weather was superb, ceiling and visibility unlimited, and the wind was about 14 knots.

Aboard the *Enterprise* the radar units lost track of the enemy bombers as they came within minimum range, but just after five o'clock, the crew of one 20-mm antiaircraft gun spotted the first Japanese plane at 12,000 feet, already in its dive. The gun began firing, although there was no chance of hitting the target at this range, but the 20-mm fire attracted the bigger guns of the ships around the carrier, and they began to fire.

The Japanese chose their targets. Most of them selected the *Enterprise*, but a number went after the battleship *North Carolina*, which was 2,500 yards off the starboard bow of the carrier. The dive bombers came down one after the other, with no hesitation, dropping to 2,000 feet or less, bombing, and pulling out low over the target. The volume of antiaircraft fire from the American ships was tremendous, the five-inch guns were so effective that several bombers broke off their dives and several others were set afire. The 20-mm guns and the 1.1-inch guns were most effective on planes that had made their drops and were zooming over or alongside the carrier.

In this, the American destroyers were extremely successful. The crew of the *Grayson*, 1,800 yards to port of the *Enterprise*, saw the first bomber pulling out and coming up along the *Grayson's* starboard quarter at 300 feet above the sea, strafing the destroyer it passed. The strafing injured several members of the crew of No. 3 gun and of the nearby 20-mm antiaircraft gun. But as the plane moved over the ship, the after 20-mm guns trained on it and poured in a concentration of fire. The plane staggered and crashed off the port beam.

The fire from the *North Carolina* was also devastating, but in spite of it and heavy fire from every one of the other seven ships in the screen, the Japanese did not hesitate. Ten of the bombers were seen to splash around the carrier, but a dozen carried out their attack with various degrees of success. The attack had been in progress for three minutes, and the carrier had managed to avoid damage, when a near hit in the water under the ship's fantail blew the after end of the flight deck up a foot, buckling the plates and shattering the wooden deck. One 20-mm gunner was thrown into the air and 15 feet across the flight deck to land in another gun position on the port quarter. Miraculously, he was scarcely hurt.

But the same could not be said after the next strike. A large bomb struck the forward edge of the No. 3 elevator and penetrated to the third deck below before blowing up. The explosion was devastating on the second and third decks. Fires began to blaze. Decks bulged out, and holes appeared in the plating of the ship so that men could look out at the sea. When the smoke cleared it appeared that 35 men had been killed in this explosion. The bomb also knocked out the power for the five-inch guns aft, which meant they had to be fired by hand, and this cut their efficiency in half. The ship began to list, about 3 degrees.

Almost immediately the *Enterprise* was hit by another bomb, about 20 feet from the first one. The blast set off powder, killed 38 men at the two five-inch guns at No. 3 gun gallery and knocked out both guns. Then came the third bomb, which hit just aft of the island. Luckily it blew up as it penetrated the flight deck and so the damage was not serious below, although No. 2 elevator was put out of use. Several other near misses started fires, ruptured plating, and damaged gasoline piping and water systems.

In his efforts to escape the Japanese attackers, Captain Arthur C. Davis increased the speed of the *Enterprise* to 30 knots, and thus outran his screen. The *North Carolina*, with her immense fire power, could not keep up, and dropped about two miles behind, rendering her antiaircraft support negligible.

Captain George H. Fort of the *North Carolina* estimated that 16 dive bombers, 12 level bombers, and 8 torpedo planes attacked his ship. Only three of them got through the antiaircraft barrage, and they dropped bombs that nearly hit the ship, but not quite. *North Carolina* was shaken, some gunners were knocked down, and water spewed over the ship, but there was no real damage nor any casualties.

Before those bombers had attacked the *Enterprise* task group, they had run the gauntlet of American fighters sent out ahead to intercept them. The F4Fs followed the instructions of their fighter director and went after the bombers, Aichi 99 dive bombers and Nakajima 97 torpedo bombers, but each time they attacked a bomber, they found a Zero or two attacking them, and in turning to avoid the guns of the Zeros, they had to let the bombers through the screen. Machinist Runyan, who had scored so well in the early hours of the invasion, was again in the forefront of the defenders. He was flying at 18,000 feet, five miles north of the carrier, when he saw a dive bomber that had escaped through the first screen of fighters. He came down out of the sun and began firing. The bomber exploded before him. He turned back up into the sun, waited a moment, and when another dive bomber came through, he set it afire too. He was attacked by a Zero whose pilot overshot on his first run and let Runyon get onto his tail. Runyon began firing his .50 caliber machine guns and the Zero blew up. Then he shot down a fourth bomber, and damaged a fifth so that it turned back toward its carrier.

The Japanese attack on the *Enterprise* was over in four minutes. As the enemy turned back toward the *Zuikaku* and the *Shokaku*, they passed the returning squadron of 10 dive bombers, coming back from the strike on the *Ryujo*. Just after five o'clock, Lt. Comdr. L. J. Kirn spotted four dive bombers a few feet above the water, heading home. The American bombers dived underneath the Japanese planes, fired a few bursts from the pilot's guns, and then let the free gunners in the back have a chance. The technique was effective; three of the Japanese bombers were shot down and the fourth escaped smoking.

The Americans believed they had shot down nearly all the Japanese planes that had attacked, but it wasn't so. The second Japanese attack never found the American carriers because of an error in the leader's navigation, but four of these bombers were shot down by American fighters. Of the first attack's 10 fighters and 27 bombers, 6 fighters and 18 bombers were lost, although the *Enterprise* group claimed to have been attacked by 70 planes and to have shot down more than 40 of them.

The planes that had been ordered off the decks of the *Enterprise* when the enemy appeared now went looking for the Japanese carriers, but they did not find them. They prepared to attack what appeared to be a group of speeding ships, only to discover that it was a reef. At least they had not wasted their bombs. The torpedo planes managed to make it back to the carrier that night, but the dive bombers nearly ran out of gas and finally landed safely on Henderson Field.

The *Saratoga*'s group of two dive bombers and five torpedo bombers, sent out to find the enemy without any specific information, was luckier. Lieutenant Harold H. Larsen spotted Admiral

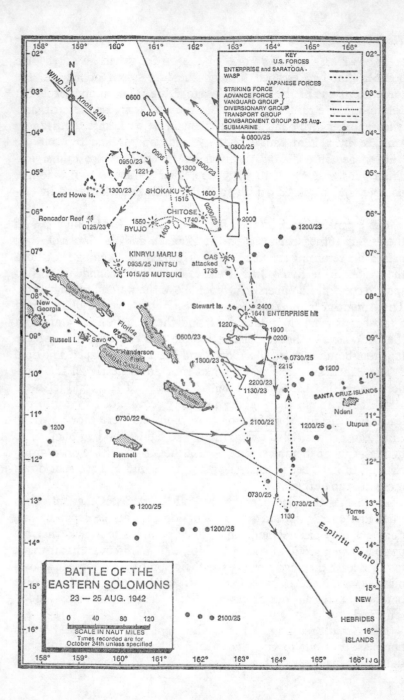

BATTLE OF THE
EASTERN SOLOMONS
23 — 25 AUG. 1942

0   40   80   120

SCALE IN NAUT MILES
Times recorded are for
October 24th unless specified

Kondo's main group of surface ships north of the Stewart Islands. The five torpedo bombers attacked first, but the ships managed to evade their "fish." The two dive bombers attacked a ship, the seaplane tender *Chitose*, and neatly bracketed it with near misses that destroyed several of her seaplanes and put her port engine out of action. She had to limp back to Truk, and thence was sent to Japan for repairs.

As darkness closed in, the Americans counted their air losses. They had lost 20 planes but not that many pilots; the crews of 7 planes were rescued.

That was the end of the action on August 24. That night Admiral Kondo went searching to the south, hoping for a night surface engagement, but when he had found nothing by 11:30, he turned about and headed north again.

Not all the pilots and crews of the opposing air forces made it back to their carriers. One *Saratoga* bomber ditched off the beach of San Cristobal Island, and the crew swam to shore to await rescue. Another, coming home late and low on gas, ditched near a small island, and the crew took to the life raft. A number of the *Ryujo*'s planes landed or crash landed on Japanese-held islands to the north. The destroyer *Amatsukaze* rescued two Japanese air crewmen who were floating in a raft about 50 miles from the American task force.

During the afternoon, the damage control parties aboard the *Enterprise* put out the fires and began to put the flight deck as much to rights as they could. Within an hour after the bombing, the ship was steaming again at 24 knots and landing aircraft. Seventy-four men had been killed and another 95 wounded, but otherwise the ship was functioning almost normally. Then, at seven o'clock that night the ship's rudder suddenly jammed as she was turning hard right, and she very nearly ran down the destroyer *Balch*. Water used in the firefighting had seeped into the steering engine room and shorted out the controls. The ship had to slow to 10 knots as the repairs were made, but in less than 40 minutes the steering was rerigged.

That afternoon, too, Fletcher learned of the sighting of Admiral Nagumo's force, but it was too late and he had too few planes to launch a new attack. The fueling of the *Wasp* probably cost the Americans the chance of a major victory.

On the night of the 24th, Fletcher retired to the south, still worrying about fuel, and on the 25th he began fueling. The *Enterprise* was sent back to Pearl Harbor for repair, with the cruiser *Portland* and four destroyers as escort. The *North Carolina*, the cruiser *Atlantia*, and the destroyers *Grayson* and *Monssen* joined the *Saratoga* group, which soon met up with the *Wasp*. Fletcher still had two carriers and a strong surface force.

On the next morning, August 25, the two carrier forces had retired, almost as though both had forgotten the reason for the mission: the need of the Japanese to protect the convoy bringing 1,500 reinforcing troops to Guadalcanal and the need for the Americans to destroy the convoy. The task was left to the 12 dive bombers and 18 pilots of Marine Air Group 223 and 10 pilots of Scouting Five, the force from the *Enterprise* that had landed on Guadalcanal on the night of August 24 and was directed to remain when the carrier was sent back to Pearl Harbor.

Just after midnight on August 25, the Japanese sent four destroyers down The Slot to bombard Henderson Field. They shelled for two hours. At 2:30 in the morning, Major Mangrum and two other pilots took off to bomb the enemy ships, but they missed them. An hour and a half later three more pilots took off, and again their bombs fell astray. One SBD was lost when its pilot became confused about direction, ran low on gas, and ditched.

In those predawn hours, a PBY located the Tanaka reinforcement convoy and reported on it. At six o'clock Henderson Field put up eight SBDs to attack.

Admiral Tanaka's group arrived, led by the cruiser *Jintsu*; the *Kagero*, *Isokaze*, *Kawakaze*, and *Yayoi*, had headed back toward the Shortlands after keeping the marines awake that night. The four destroyers turned around to join Tanaka's force, and they all began the run for Guadalcanal. Just then, at 8:30, the American dive bombers began to peel off above them. Five of the planes attacked the cruiser *Jintsu*, and Lieutenant Lawrence put a bomb into the ship between her A and B turrets. The bomb knocked out the ship's radio communications, which meant the admiral could no longer direct the battle by radio. It took him some time to direct the battle at all, because he had been knocked senseless by the concussion. The bomb had gone below the deck and started fires so near the magazines that the officers feared they would blow up. The captain flooded them, and the fires were soon brought under control, but *Jintsu*'s fighting ability was sorely hurt. She turned and headed back to Truk, leaving the destroyers to guard the convoy.

Three American bombers headed down at the transport *Kinryu Maru*. Lieutenant Chris Fink's bomb struck amidships and set the transport afire. She began to burn fiercely, ammunition took fire and began to pop off, the ship went dead in the water, and the destroyer *Mutsuki* came alongside to take off the 1,000 men of the Yokosuka 5th Special Naval Landing Force. Just then a flight of B-17 bombers came overhead, and saw the sitting ducks in the water below.

Admiral Tanaka, conscious again, directed the *Yayoi* and two patrol craft to help the rescue operations, but they had not arrived alongside when the B-17s dropped their bombs. Three of them struck squarely on the *Mutsuki*, and soon she was as dead as the transport beside her, her engine room knocked out. Seeing this, Admiral Tanaka ordered the other two transports, *Boston Maru* and *Taifuku Maru*, to retire back toward the Shortland Islands and await orders. They were escorted by the destroyers *Kawakaze* and *Umikazae* and two patrol craft.

The survivors of *Mutsuki* and *Kinryu Maru* were picked up by a destroyer, and a submarine sunk the *Mutsuki* rather than let it fall into American hands. The *Jintsu* and her ships then headed north, to protect the remains of the reinforcements until they could get out of American air range. The reinforcements did not land, and Admiral Yamamoto instructed Tanaka to transfer his flag to the destroyer *Suzukaze* and send the *Jintsu* to Truk for repairs. The survivors of the Yokosuka 5th Special Naval Landing Force were directed to transfer into smaller ships at the Shortlands so they could be brought back posthaste to reinforce Guadalcanal.

The last act of the battle was the attack by 22 twin-engined Betty bombers and 13 Zeros that night. They came in high at 27,000 feet and dropped 40 bombs around the Pagoda, as the Americans called the oriental-style operations building the Japanese had erected in July. Most of the American planes had been sent into the air to try to meet the enemy so the damage inflicted by the bombing was confined to the runways.

And that was the end of what the Japanese called the Second Battle of the Solomon Sea and the Americans called the Battle of the Eastern Solomons. It had not been definitive in any way. The Ameri-

cans had sunk the old carrier *Ryujo,* but the *Enterprise* had been
damaged and was out of action. Neither side had lost desperately in
aircraft. The Japanese had failed to reinforce Guadalcanal, and Admiral Fletcher had lost a great chance to strike a major blow at the
Combined Fleet.

Admiral Yamamoto was furious with Admiral Nagumo for retiring
on the night of the 24th without having struck a mortal blow at the
enemy. Nagumo still had his 2 carriers intact, with 41 fighters, 25
bombers, and 34 torpedo planes available for a strike, plus the land-
based air forces that could be brought into play from Rabaul. It was
Admiral Nagumo's timidity that prevented him from seeking the further engagement, and Yamamoto did not like it.

Timidity was the problem, but the Japanese had no monopoly on
it. Admiral Fletcher's constant avoidance of battle had begun to get
on the nerves of even the phlegmatic Nimitz. When he learned that
Fletcher had sent the *Wasp* off to fuel on the eve of battle, he was
short and to the point: "There is plenty of fuel in the vicinity of his
force," he said. But by August 25 it did not matter. An opportunity
had been missed, and the result was going to be a long battle of attrition.

THE SLUGGING MATCH

GUADALCANAL was quiet after the noon air raid of August 25. The Japanese effort to reinforce the garrison having failed, the troops had been taken back to Shortland Island to re-group and try again. The Slot was still quiet that night, so General Vandegrift could take time to assess his situation. Until the Americans could achieve at least parity in the air, it was unlikely that supplies could be brought in on a regular basis. So the primary need was to strengthen the Cactus Air Force, which had suffered enormously in the battles of the last five days. Of the 19 F4Fs flown in from the *Long Island*, 5 had been destroyed and 3 were inoperable and waiting for parts. Of the 12 dive bombers, only 9 were operational. Vandegrift did have the addition of the 10 *Enterprise* bombers, but the net gain was minor. On August 23, about ten minutes after the F4Fs had taken off to intercept the *Ryujo* bombers, Admiral McCain's personal PBY had shown up at the field crammed with all the oxygen bottles that could be found on short notice at Espiritu Santo. But that was no way to support an air force; what was needed was real supply, and that meant the dispatch to Guadalcanal of the transport *William Ward Burroughs*, which was carrying the ground crews and supplies for the Marine Air Group 23.

Admiral Yamamoto decided that, pending a major naval action, he would continue the resupply of the Japanese garrison by destroyer, and from the air he would keep the pressure on Henderson Field to prevent a buildup. On August 26, the Rabaul air force sent 16 Bettys over to bomb. They arrived over the island at 11:24 A.M. announced as usual by the coastwatchers, and every available U.S. aircraft was in the air to meet them. Most of the pilots were too green to be effective, but Captain Smith, Capt. Rivers Morrell, and two other pilots shot down 3 bombers and damaged a number of others. Captain Marion Carl shot down 2 Zeros. One F4F was shot down, and its pilot, Lt. R. A. Corry, was killed. Despite the harassment, the Japanese dropped their bombs, damaging several planes and setting fire to a dump of precious aviation gasoline. By the end of the day the Cactus Air Force was down to 11 F4Fs and 9 SBDs plus the *Enterprise* contingent.

Meanwhile, on August 26, Admiral Yamamoto arrived at Truk in the flagship *Yamato,* and he was assembling the reports of the inconclusive battle that had just ended. Yamamoto was at the big Truk naval base. General Hyukatake was at Rabaul. And while Yamamoto understood the importance of Guadalcanal, the army was still laboring with the dream of conquering New Guinea. The significance of the unwelcome intrusion in the Solomons had not struck home.

On August 27 the Rabaul air base launched attacks, but the two bombing raids failed to get through because of bad weather. A B-17 and 14 Army Air Force P-400s landed to augment the Cactus Air Force.

At Shortland, the Japanese relief troops were once more divided among destroyer transports, and now escorted by Destroyer Division 20, they again set out for Guadalcanal on August 28.

The Japanese ships were to be covered from the air by a bombing raid of 18 twin-engined Bettys, escorted by Zero fighters. Just before dusk on August 28, the coastwatchers announced the Japanese convoy coming down The Slot. The Japanese bomber force was not in evidence, and it never did appear that day, again held back by bad weather between Kavieng and Guadalcanal. The American evening air patrol of two dive bombers discovered the Japanese flotilla and bombed, but did not score any hits. These scouts, however, did arouse Henderson Field and before six o'clock 11 dive bombers took off.

When the Japanese commander of the destroyers came under that

Admiral Isoroko Yamamoto, commander of the Imperial Fleet, had warned that Japan lacked the resources to carry out a prolonged war. He counted one quick decisive victory to force the Americans to the peace table. (top photo, *U.S. Navy)*

南太平洋の最前線基地にて、
艦隊参謀に出動する海鷲を見送
る山本五十六師匠たり、日の勇
委（岡本西南報道班員撮影）

Rear Admiral Gunichi Mikawa scored an impressive tactical victory at the Battle of Savo Island. *(U.S. Navy)*

Vice Admiral Nobutake Kondo's force inflicted damage on the *Enterprise* in the Battle of the Eastern Solomons. *(U.S. Navy)*

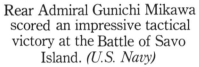

Rear Admiral Richard K. Turner withdrew his carriers in the face of Mikawa's approach.

Rear Admiral Norman Scott won a tactical victory at the Battle of Cape Esperance but failed to stop the landing of Japanese reinforcements. *(U.S. Navy)*

Rear Admiral Daniel Callaghan's delay in opening fire in the Naval Battle of Guadalcanal resulted in terrible damage to the American fleet. Admiral Callaghan lost his life in the battle, too. *(U.S. Navy)*

Rear Admiral Raizo Tanaka's destroyermen played a crucial role in the Japanese naval victories. His bluntness in expressing his opinion about the problems of resupplying the Japanese troops on Guadalcanal, however, led to his eventual transfer. *(U.S. Navy)*

The *Enterprise* launches dive bombers against the Solomons on August 7, 1942.

Fire sweeps Tulagi after attack by dive bombers from the *Enterprise* on August 7, 1942.

HMAS *Hobart* and HMAS *Australia* off Guadalcanal.

Task Force 16 leaves Tulagi on August 10, 1942, after battle. HMAS *Canberra* burns before sinking after the night engagement.

Henderson Field was the focus of the battle for Guadalcanal.

The "Pagoda" served as headquarters for Henderson Field.

"Ace" K.A. Walsh in cockpit.

Marine sniper climbs a palm tree.

A marine field gun emplacement. This position was captured from Japanese in the early stages of the battle.

attack, he radioed Combined Fleet for help, and Admiral Yamamoto sent a force of bombers and fighters to protect the ships. But the American planes were much closer and got there first. Just before dark, the dive bombers began to peel off. Lieutenant Chris Fink dropped a 1,000-pound bomb directly amidships of the destroyer *Asagiri;* the bomb drove through the deck to the ship's magazine, and the *Asagiri* blew up. Lieutenant Turner Caldwell of the *Enterprise* put a bomb into the destroyer *Shirakumo* and damaged her badly. The Americans lost one dive bomber to the destroyers' antiaircraft fire. The other destroyers came to the assistance of the survivors of the *Asagiri,* but among those lost was Capt. Yuzo Arita, the divisional commander, which left the force without its leader. The *Amagiri* and the *Yugiri* were both damaged. The *Amagiri* was able to tow the *Shirakumo* back to Shortland, and the *Yugiri* made it under her own power. But once again the reinforcements had been turned back.

From Rabaul, the Japanese saw that unless they could keep Henderson Field neutralized, it would be virtually impossible for them to land reinforcements. As of August 25, Rabaul's 11th Air Fleet was seriously short of planes, following the almost constant activity of the previous week and the heavy losses occasioned by the 500-mile distance from Guadalcanal, which damaged planes could hardly negotiate. The Japanese force was down to 29 bombers and 19 Zeros. More were in the pipeline, but the reaction in Tokyo had not been as swift as anticipated, and the shortage persisted.

Still, Admiral Yamamoto was determined that the reinforcements would be landed. On August 29, the 11th Air Fleet sent two bombing attacks. The first was staged at four o'clock in the morning by float planes from New Georgia, and the three bombers did no serious damage. The second appeared at the usual hour, just before noon, which represented the five-hour flight between a dawn takeoff at Rabaul and arrival at Guadalcanal. Twenty-two twin-engined Bettys came in escorted by 22 Zeros. The marines again had plenty of warning from the coastwatchers. The Americans had 10 F4Fs and 14 P-400s in the air. But when the Japanese arrived at high altitude as usual, the P-400s were useless—they could not climb to reach the bombers. It took the F4Fs a little time to get altitude, and by then the Japanese had already bombed the airfield, damaging two more F4Fs, and tearing more holes in the runway. The fighters took after

them and claimed to have shot down four bombers and four Zeros.
The figure was probably much lower, but at least one Betty, the pilot
apparently killed at the controls, went into the ground at a speed of
600 miles an hour, to erupt in a blaze of flame.

In its way, the raid was a success. At the end of it, General Vandegrift counted his aerial resources: Only eight F4Fs were operational, and the P-400s might as well not have been there; they were
of no use at all in protecting the airfield.

Admiral Tanaka at Shortland had learned from the experience of
August 28 that it was dangerous to move the destroyers carrying reinforcements into the waters of Guadalcanal in the daylight hours, so
on August 29 he delayed the sailing of the six destroyers that would
make the run with 1,000 reinforcements. The force was spotted by a
PBY patrol plane in midvoyage, but there was nothing for General
Vandegrift to do but wait until the Japanese approached the island.
That day the marines on the ground were busier than usual. For the
past few days they had been engaged in small firefights with the Japanese in the Matanikau area. Every day they waited for something
to happen. With General Vandegrift's order to assume a defensive
stance, the marines had drawn up in a perimeter seven miles wide
and four miles deep around Henderson Field from Lunga Point on
the channel. Since the island of Guadalcanal is 90 miles long and 30
miles wide, this disposition gave the Japanese almost unlimited area
in which to land and move troops.

Just before noon the transport *William Ward Burroughs* arrived
off Lunga Point showing that Admiral Ghormley had reacted to
General Vandegrift's pleas as quickly as he could. This meant Marine Air Group 23 would have its own mechanics and spare parts.
After a week and a half of operations the planes needed serious attention. The dust and mud of the airstrip plus the damages sustained
in combat affected every plane. After the Japanese air raid that day,
the unloading continued until late afternoon, when a report of the
new Japanese destroyer force en route from the Shortlands caused
General Vandegrift to have the transport moved over to the protected harbor on the Tulagi side of the sound, where there was less
likelihood of an attack. The *Burroughs* moved and promptly ran
aground at Tulagi.

On August 29, when the seven Japanese destroyers were warned
that American ships, a cruiser, two transports, and two destroyers,

were off Guadalcanal, Admiral Tanaka opted to go ahead anyway. After some hesitation, Admiral Mikawa, the commander of the 8th Fleet, agreed. That evening, when the destroyers were sighted again, General Vandegrift feared they would not only land troops, but sink the stranded *Burroughs*. The pilots at Henderson Field were warned that they must be prepared to make a late night attack, and all operational dive bombers were launched just after midnight, as the seven Japanese destroyers came in to Taivu Point to land troops. The American planes did not find the Japanese ships, but they served a useful purpose just the same. Admiral Tanaka had ordered the destroyer commander to land the troops and then shell the American ships in the sound. But when the commander saw the American bombers, he landed the 1,000 troops quickly, then hauled out at high speed and hurried out of the danger zone back to the Shortlands. Admiral Tanaka was so enraged by this timidity that he relieved the destroyer divisional commander on the spot.

However belatedly, the Japanese air and manpower pipelines in the South Pacific were beginning to flow. This had occurred when General Hyukatake had finally been convinced that there were many more Americans on Guadalcanal than anyone had earlier believed, and then he had convinced Tokyo. The quickest way to bring troops was to deliver small detachments via destroyer transport. Particularly as long as the Americans maintained their air control of Henderson Field, night delivery of troops seemed to be the solution. Admiral Yamamoto felt sure that if the Japanese interdicted supplies to the Americans, and resupplied their own men, the American effort would fail as they ran out of ships. So the Tokyo Express, as the Americans called these nightly forays, or the Rat Patrol, as the Japanese called them, became a major factor in Japanese naval policy in the South Pacific. It was not that Admiral Yamamoto did not have the naval power at hand to risk a battle; it was his decision that a battle was not necessary.

A week earlier, General Hyukatake had reluctantly decided that Major General Seiken Kawaguchi's brigade, which had been intended for Papua, New Guinea, must be diverted to stop the nuisance on Guadalcanal. When General Kawaguchi learned of the Rat Patrol system, he was appalled. He had been very successful in moving troops around the Dutch East Indies by landing barges and insisted that this method be employed. Admiral Tanaka disagreed, but the barges began collecting on Santa Isabel Island. In the meantime, however, even Kawaguchi recognized that the destroyer run was essential.

With the shortage of fighters and pilots in the 11th Air Fleet, Admiral Yamamoto decided he would have to employ the pilots of the carriers *Shokaku* and *Zuikaku* to fly cover for the bombers, and their first mission came on August 30. As usual the coastwatchers had the word and passed it along before the men at Henderson heard any planes. All 19 flyable fighters were put into the air, and that included 7 of the P-400s. Earlier, 4 P-400s had taken to the air, on the theory that their real value might be to circle above the *William Ward Burroughs* perhaps to prevent torpedo and low-level bombing attacks. When the fighters got up that day, the 7 army planes suddenly peeled off and went screaming down on Tulagi. The pilots in the F4Fs who were climbing for altitude, then saw the reason; the grounded *Burroughs* was indeed under Japanese attack by stub-winged Zeros from the carriers (the Americans called them "Hamps"). The P-400s and F4Fs came out of the sun and caught the Japanese by surprise. In the first pass, they shot down 8 Japanese fighters. Then the Japanese recovered, and the air was filled with dogfights. The sky was cloudy, a front that rose to 40,000 feet was standing between Guadalcanal and Florida Island, and American and Japanese planes ducked in and out of the clouds, attacking, as they went around and around. The whole engagement lasted less than five minutes, and when it was over, the Americans had lost 4 of the P-400s, although 2 pilots came back, and none of the F4Fs, although 3 were put out of action pending repair. Captain Smith shot down 4 Hamps himself, that day, and Capt. Marion Carl shot down 3.

But, as of noon on August 30, there were only five operational F4F fighters on the ground at Henderson Field.

That day, the fighter mission against the *Burroughs* was followed by a bomber mission to soften up the airfield in preparation for a landing again that night. Just after three o'clock, 18 Bettys appeared high overhead. The five F4Fs were not yet refueled by the laborious hand operation needed, nor rearmed, so they could not take off. For once, the Bettys were not interested in the airfield but in the ships in the sound. The *Burroughs* was on the far side, and the destroyer transport *Colhoun* was on the Guadalcanal side, with the destroyer transport *Little* and the auxiliary *Kopara* delivering a load of supplies to the badly depleted dumps of the marines. The Bettys came in high and bombed precisely. The *Colhoun* was surrounded by near misses and some hits, and within two minutes she sank with 51 of her crew.

That night the Tokyo Express ran again, and the first of General Kawaguchi's troops were landed, a battalion carried by three destroyers. What General Vandegrift feared—the successful buildup of Japanese land forces on Guadalcanal—had begun, and thereafter for the next two weeks almost nightly the Rat Patrol sneaked in under cover of darkness to land troops in the Japanese zones of the island. For the moment, the Japanese were not moving, but when they had brought in enough men, Vandegrift could expect the land battle to begin.

In the last few days of August, wheels began to move that would bring Vandegrift's desperate situation to the attention of higher commands in a most positive way. A short, wiry man, with the look of a retired prize fighter, showed up dressed in khakis at Nouméa and insisted on going forward to investigate the situation in the South Pacific. Ghormley, who had never bothered to do this himself, sent the man along with sufficient escort, and that is how Undersecretary of the Navy James V. Forrestal came to learn the grim facts of the Guadalcanal undertaking. At the beginning of September, he flew back to Pearl Harbor to report with horror on the desperate conditions he had found and then went on to Washington to begin stirring up the political animals who controlled the flow of supplies to Europe and the Pacific.

Immediately after Forrestal's visit, promises of assistance came from Pearl Harbor and from army commands across the Pacific. But help was to come quickly in a manner not quite envisaged by any of the high command.

On August 29, Rear Admiral George D. Murray arrived to join Admiral Fletcher, and his task force built around the *Hornet* brought the American carrier contingent back to three. As usual, Admiral Fletcher was talking about the need to refuel, so Ghormley ordered him to send one task force to Nouméa for oil and resupply.

On Guadalcanal, the situation on August 30 nearly warranted panic. As General Vandegrift contemplated the five working fighters on the field, and the sinking of the *Colhoun* without an American

plane getting into the air to try to defend it, the feeling of desperation was strong. But that very afternoon small craft brought across
from Tulagi several loads of parts for the planes from the grounded
Burroughs. In the next few hours more parts could have been unloaded, but in the sense of urgency, many were jettisoned over the
side in the belief that the ship had to be lightened and gotten off the
reef before the Japanese came back to do to her what they had done
to *Colhoun*.

Scarcely had the *Colhoun* settled to the floor of Iron Bottom
Sound when the sound of engines was heard over the island again.
The marines were ready to wince, but then began to shout when
above them they saw the familiar blue and white stars and the gray
wings of the F4Fs. Nineteen new F4Fs and 12 SBDs landed on Henderson Field to be surrounded by grateful well-wishers. These planes
represented the other two squadrons of Marine Air Group 23, and
one of them carried the commander of the group, Colonel William
Wallace.

Among the greeters was Rear Admiral McCain, the commander of
land-based air forces in the South Pacific, on a fact finding trip of his
own. Three weeks had gone by since the invasion, and neither Admiral Ghormley nor Admiral Turner had recognized the full extent of
the danger, although both were aware of the precarious foothold of
the marines and the supply problem. But after one look at the situation and a talk with Vandegrift, Admiral McCain sent Nimitz a
blunt message. The enemy had planned Guadalcanal as a major air
base, and they seemed to be determined to get it back, he said. The
Americans could expect a major effort, and already daily bombings
indicated the pattern. Guadalcanal needed at least 40 fighter aircraft
capable of taking to the air at all times and that meant two full
squadrons with the best planes, F4Fs or P-38s. Also a constant line
of replacement pilots and planes must be established to counteract
an attrition rate of three or four fighters per day. If Nimitz wanted
Guadalcanal to be held, then the air reinforcements must be delivered without delay. If not, Guadalcanal could not be supplied, and it
would fall to the Japanese.

For weeks Nimitz had been reading Admiral Ghormley's muddy
messages about difficulties, but Ghormley, who had still not visited
Guadalcanal, obviously did not understand the real problem, so con-

vinced was he that the whole Guadalcanal adventure was a ghastly mistake.

McCain's strident message came on top of the visit from Undersecretary of the Navy Forrestal. If the American people knew what a dreadful mess existed down in the South Pacific, Forrestal had said, there would be a revolution at home. The marines on Guadalcanal must have planes, and they must have them fast. By the time McCain reached Guadalcanal, Forrestal was already hurrying back to Washington, where he started buttonholing admirals and Army Air Corps generals to secure the aid.

Ironically, Admiral Fletcher provided the needed planes within a matter of hours.

Since the battle of August 23–24 the Japanese had kept a constant submarine presence in the area south of Guadalcanal where Admiral Fletcher was operating. Thirteen Japanese submarines were deployed in the Solomons and nine of them cruised south. During the battle Lt. Turner Caldwell had bombed the *I-17* but without effect, and Lt. Stockton Strong and Ens. John Richey had bombed the *I-19* with the same results. From the Japanese point of view it was a bad scare, but from the American viewpoint "close meant no cigar." The antisubmarine technique of Fletcher's task force left something to be desired.

After the battle, there were several reported sightings of submarines, and one definite one in which two planes from the *Wasp* unsuccessfully attacked a submarine. In the predawn hours of August 31 a radar man aboard the carrier *Saratoga* saw a blip on his screen. Then it disappeared, as the reflected signal of a submarine travelling on the surface would do when the vessel dived. The destroyer *Farragut* was sent to the contact point but her crew saw nothing and the sonar heard nothing.

Actually the blip was the Japanese submarine *I-26*. Commander Minoru Yokota had taken her here from Yokosuka naval base when the Combined Fleet came south, and he had been scouting for the fleet during the battle a few days before. Now he was hunting.

At six o'clock in the morning the crew of the *Saratoga* was aroused after a quiet night, and the men went to battle stations. Admiral Fletcher was patrolling at 13 knots in a rectangle 150 miles long and 60 miles wide south of Guadalcanal, really just staying in the area, since there was nothing there to be done. About an hour after sunrise, the carrier changed course from northwest to southeast, which took her back across that early morning contact. For some reasons no one thought to check out that area with destroyers before the heavy ships moved in.

The day's routine began. The men went to breakfast and looked forward to another dull day, since the task force was not involved in the desperate struggle to keep the Guadalcanal lifeline open.

As the men of the *Saratoga* ate, Commander Yokota raised the periscope of *I-26* and looked around. He had been sitting quietly in the same area since that early morning scare when the destroyer had come over. Now before his eyes appeared a carrier and a battleship escorted by several cruisers and destroyers. He snapped the handles of the periscope, the shears went down, and the *I-26* began working carefully into position for a shot just below the surface. It took Commander Yokota many sightings; first he had to estimate the zigzag pattern of the task force, and then he had to get into position.

He worked up to a position on the edge of the destroyer screen and fired six torpedoes at the carrier. Just as Yokota fired, the destroyer *MacDonough* made contact with the *I-26* and came charging up to attack. Lookouts sighted the periscope 30 feet off the bow. Commander Yokota dropped the periscope and dived, and the destroyer's keel scraped the superstructure of *I-26* as the I-boat went down. *MacDonough* made the submarine warning signal and dropped two depth charges, but the excitement was so intense that no one remembered to arm them, so they went tumbling down into the deep to explode uselessly at the critical pressure point hundreds of fathoms below.

Aboard the *Saratoga*, Captain Dewitt Ramsey received the submarine alarm just as a lookout sighted a porpoising torpedo. He turned hard right and rang up full speed. But Commander Yokota had fired a full spread of six torpedoes, fanning out to catch the carrier in a turn, and two minutes later one struck, just below the island. The explosion wounded a dozen men, including Admiral Fletcher, but none of them seriously. One fireroom was flooded, and the ship developed a slight list, but that was soon corrected. The real problem was in the carrier's electrical system. The explosion had shorted out the ship's two main electrical generators, and the *Saratoga* was virtually dead in the water in a few moments. It took a full eight hours before the electricians could repair the damage enough to give the carrier about a third of her normal speed.

In the meantime there was no more carelessness about submarines. The destroyers *Phelps, MacDonough,* and *Monssen* were detailed to go after the submarine. They dropped many depth charges, but the *I-26* was lying low, engines stopped. The *Monssen* was left behind to continue the harassment, and the cruiser *Minneapolis* took the carrier in tow. The carrier *Saratoga,* which had been hit by a torpedo seven months before, was out of action in the South Pacific, which left the Americans with two carriers once again.

Captain Ramsey worried about his aircraft, since the carrier was a prime target for any passing submarine, and he secured permission from Fletcher to fly them off to Espiritu Santo for safety. There, they were dispatched without delay to Henderson Field, and that is how General Vandegrift got another 20 fighters and 9 dive bombers. His prayers were answered that day. Three of the new F4F pilots of Marine Air Group 23 were lost on their first mission, because their oxygen masks leaked and they fell unconscious and crashed into the sea. On September 1, as the Japanese prepared for a major effort to retake Guadalcanal, there were only 26 fighters and 30 dive bombers on Henderson Field. The attrition rate was growing because of enemy action, equipment shortages, and lack of training.

7

SWEATING IT OUT

IN those early days at Guadalcanal the tiny air force was greatly assisted—possibly even made viable—by the Australian coast-watching network. By August 15 the system was working effectively. Watchers Read and Mason picked up the Japanese when they passed over Bougainville shortly after they had taken off. D. G. Kennedy caught them as they approached New Georgia, forty-five minutes out from Henderson Field. Three other coastwatchers sat on a 4,000-foot mountain on Guadalcanal and on a clear day could see them coming down The Slot. Watchers on Savo, Malaita, Vella Lavella, Kolombangara, and Rendova were also ready to report.

Australian Navy Lieutenant Hugh Mackenzie arrived at Lunga Point a week after the marines with his assistant radio operator and two islanders, Eodie, a radio operator, and Rayman, a New Irelander. This Australian group quickly gained the confidence of the Guadalcanal islanders, particularly because the Japanese had made the error of mistreating several highly respected men, including Jacob Vouza, a retired policeman. When Vouza refused to guide for the Japanese, they had tortured him and left him for dead, but he managed to make his way to the marine lines, where he was treated and brought to health. That sort of story made friends for the marines, and it was not uncommon. But the element of cruelty worked both ways, and some villages mistreated by allied troops were firm friends of the Japanese.

As soon as General Vandegrift learned how vital the coastwatching service was, Mackenzie's operation was augmented by four marine radio operators. Mackenzie established his radio station in a Japanese dugout on the northwest side of Henderson Field, where radio interference was minimal, and here his men monitored the coastwatcher network twenty-four hours a day. The word of an incoming raid or anything else of importance was given to the marines by field telephone.

On August 31, the hold of the *Burroughs* yielded up an air search radar set that could detect high altitude bombers 125 miles from the field. At this period, making use of both the radar and the coastwatchers, the men of Henderson Field had the enormous advantage of usually knowing when the enemy would strike. When word of an incoming attack was received, the men in the operations office, or Pagoda, would run up a rising sun flag, and the pilots would know it was time to man their planes. Since any planes on the field were more likely to be hit than those scattered about in the rude revetments, the ground crews took advantage of the warning time to move aircraft about for maximum protection.

The Japanese air raids had already become much more than a nuisance, but the early warning system prevented them from crippling the field. Yet nearly every raid brought its casualties; two or three men killed, half a dozen wounded by bomb blasts, and at least one or two aircraft damaged or destroyed.

On the last day of August help had come, and as September began, it was suddenly apparent that Admiral McCain's judgment had been accepted by the highest U.S. authorities. Everything was being done to speed the reinforcement of Henderson Field, including the assignment of a general officer, Brigadier General Roy Stanley Geiger, commander of Marine Air Wing One. He was on his way to take over command of the air defense of the island.

For the next few days the Japanese had the best of it in the air battle. Each night the Tokyo Express arrived off Guadalcanal, and each night several hundred more Japanese troops landed, until the whole Kawaguchi detachment of 5,000 men was ashore. General Kawaguchi himself came on the first night of September to supervise the new assault on the American foothold on the island. On September 1 and 2 the bombers came over and the fighters went up to meet them but without effect.

Admiral Fletcher arrived at Nouméa to announce that he must take the *Saratoga* back to Pearl Harbor. He was overruled, and the carrier was repaired in the South Pacific. By early September, the full results of the disastrous battle off Savo Island were available to Nimitz and Admiral King in Washington.

Since the earliest days of the war Admiral Fletcher had been sinking in Admiral King's esteem, and on at least two occasions Nimitz had protected Fletcher from King's wrath after questionable operations. King and Nimitz met in one of the regular meetings they held at San Francisco. They talked about the need for aircraft in the Pacific. They talked about mistakes that had been made and the responsibilities involved. King told Nimitz he wanted Fletcher back in Washington for a few weeks of temporary duty, which meant he wanted to look Fletcher over. As both men knew by this time, the central reason for the American surprise at Savo was the failure of the air search system, and in this the finger pointed directly at Admiral McCain. Turner was strong in his defense of McCain, but Turner's neck might well be next on the block, and King was obdurate; he wanted a change in command. So Rear Admiral Aubrey Fitch, commander of the *Lexington* task group at the Battle of the Coral Sea, was sent down to run the land-based air program, and Admiral McCain was sent back to Washington to become chief of the Bureau of Aeronautics, which would give Admiral King a good chance to look him over, too, before deciding whether to send him out to pasture or back to battle.

Back on Guadalcanal, the marines were lucky: The weather was stormy during the first few days of September. The bad weather helped the Japanese at night, as they brought up their troop reinforcements by destroyer and landing barge, but it helped the Americans by day, because the Japanese could not launch the usual bombing raids.

On September 4 the admirals and generals met aboard Admiral Ghormley's flagship in Nouméa harbor. Admiral Ghormley gave a gloomy prediction for the future, and General MacArthur's aides suggested that it would be much smarter to abandon Guadalcanal and throw U.S. might (MacArthur's) against New Guinea. From Pearl Harbor the Pacific Fleet let it be known that the prospects of getting more ships and even more planes were slim at that moment. So the American conference ended without solving any problems, and General Vandegrift was left with his troops on the island not knowing how much help to expect or when. General Geiger did not know when his handful of planes would be augmented. Admiral Turner, apologizing for failing to give Vandegrift adequate support, could not promise when he was going to get supplies in or where he would find the ships to protect his supply operations.

At the same time, the Japanese were holding similar conferences aboard Admiral Yamamoto's flagship in Truk harbor. Out of them came a combined operational plan for the seizure of Guadalcanal and the destruction of the American forces. On the ground, General Kawaguchi's force was to strike against the marines. Kawaguchi then had a total of 8,000 men on the island against the 17,000 marines, but the Japanese were still very hazy about the size of the American force, because the Americans occupied so small an area. It would have seemed obvious to the Japanese (not knowing the desperate supply situation) that if the U.S. commander had many troops he would long since have taken every point of the island against the tiny garrison that existed on August 7.

The Japanese attack was planned as a combined land, air, and naval assault on the island. General Kawaguchi intended to seize the air field on September 12. The 11th Air Fleet would put up every plane and the Combined Fleet would make an all out assault on the waters around Guadalcanal to wipe out any U.S. naval forces that might be in the area.

In these early days of September, the daylight hours on Guadalcanal definitely belonged to the Americans. During the day the marines patrolled their perimeter. American small craft moved back and forth across the sound, carrying troops, messages, and supplies from Tulagi to Guadalcanal. The Cactus Air Force held control of the sky. But at night Guadalcanal became a different island. Japanese troops moved around the edges of the American perimeter and engaged in fights just often enough to keep the marines on their toes. Japanese destroyers and barges came down The Slot and deposited their reinforcements, and then the destroyers usually lobbed a few shells into Henderson Field or against one of the marine strong points. Japanese submarines came along the shore to shell. One night the marine beach watchers claimed to have seen three different Japanese submarines off Savo Island.

The repeated presence of the enemy submarines convinced General Vandegrift that Japanese troops on Savo Island were sending them signals. He decided to send a "reconnaissance in force," which meant a large patrol to discover the enemy and, if possible, wipe them out. To do this job, Vandegrift selected part of Col. "Red Mike" Edson's 1st Raider Battalion. Lieutenant Colonel Samuel Griffith would lead the troops. They embarked in the destroyer transports *Little* and *Gregory* on the afternoon of September 3. The plan was to land on the northern end of Savo Island, one group going east and the other west until they met at the southern tip of the island. That meant a long hike, because the island was nine miles from its northern to southern extremity. They expected to finish the job by midafternoon—if they did not encounter any Japanese.

The ships reached Savo Island on the morning of September 4 and landed the marines. They came in by landing craft, half expecting to be greeted by the popping of Japanese machine guns. But there was no sound, and when they hit the beach and moved up they found no Japanese. They came to a village of bamboo and thatch huts amid a palm grove, and they found the villagers there, the men in loin cloths and most of them with red hair, which they created with lime juice dye. Were there any Japanese on the island? their Australian guide asked the head man in pidgin:

"Me fella lookum Japanese man"—Australian guide.

"No Japnee man island"—head man.

From time to time, there had been Japanese on the island, the head man said, most recently five days earlier, but they had gone. So the Raiders, each unit with a native guide, set out to circle the island and find out for themselves about the Japanese. They passed through several villages. On the beach they found masses of flotsam, the debris of the Battle of Savo Island: life belts, oil drums, and life rafts cluttered along the oil-stained high tide line. They found a notebook that had belonged to an officer on the *Astoria*, crates marked *Australia*, and a life raft marked *Quincy*. They heard engines and looked up: The planes were American for a change, bombers heading toward the Japanese base at Bougainville.

Finally, the two groups of marines met at the southern tip of Savo Island. There was no sign of Japanese here either. They got into the boats that had come down to meet them and then the ships, the *Little* and the *Gregory*, took them to Guadalcanal. They arrived at Lunga Point late in the afternoon, and by the time the marines were ashore it was dark. Usually under such circumstances, the two destroyer transports would move across to the sheltered harbor of Tulagi, but the weather had grown foul and the night was dark. Commander Hugh Hadley, the commander of the two destroyers, decided to patrol off Lunga Point that night.

Again on the night of September 4 the Japanese ran the Tokyo Express to land troops. This time the barges were accompanied by the destroyers *Yudachi*, *Murakamo*, and *Hatsuyaki*, which as usual were also ordered to shell Henderson Field and Lunga Point.

The *Little* and the *Gregory* were off the Guadalcanal shore just after midnight when the Japanese came through the channel. The Japanese ships opened fire on the Guadalcanal beach to create a diversion behind which the landing barges could put their troops ashore at Taivu Point. The *Little* and the *Gregory* came to action stations and moved up for battle. On their radar screens they saw several distinct blips.

But just as they moved, a PBY pilot flying over the sound saw the gun flashes from the Japanese destroyers and assumed that another submarine was harrying the beachhead, as the submarines had been doing for a week. He decided to show up the enemy vessel and dropped a string of five flares half a mile ahead of the American destroyers. The light made the American ships perfect targets for the Japanese. The two American destroyer transports had been selected for their particular task because they were old and underarmed by modern standards. The *Little* had one four-inch gun, some 20-mm guns, and machine guns. The *Gregory*'s armament was similar. The Japanese destroyers were armed with five-inch guns mounted in dual batteries. After a few aiming shots, the Japanese salvoes began to strike the American ships. One shell knocked out the *Little*'s one four-inch gun. Another hit a fuel tank and the ship burst into flame. Soon she was in desperate shape and Lt. Comdr. G. B. Lofberg, her captain, decided to beach her. But another Japanese shell caused the steering to jam, and one struck the bridge and killed Divisional Commander Hadley and Captain Lofberg. The ship was ablaze, and her steam lines were ruptured as the men abandoned ship.

The Japanese destroyers turned their attention to the *Gregory*. She took one five-inch salvo after another until the bridge was gone, the after stack fell, a boiler burst, and the ship was afire from one end to the other. The captain, Lt. Comdr. Harry Bauer, was wounded. He gave the order to abandon ship and was assisted into the water, but when he heard a sailor crying for help, he sent his rescuers to find the man, and he drowned.

For half an hour the Japanese continued to fire on the floating, blazing hulks, and then, sure that they had finished the job, they retired at high speed, leaving many men and corpses floating in the water. It was not until daybreak that any sort of organized rescue could be started.

Here again was proof that the night belonged to the Japanese.

Every day that the weather permitted the Betty bombers came over from Rabaul at high altitude and bombed Henderson Field. The American fighters, warned by the coastwatchers, were there to meet them and their Zero escorts. The Americans exacted a toll from the bombers and Zeros, and the Japanese shot down some American planes. It was a war of constant, deadly attrition, and had grown grating on the nerves of both sides. Admiral Ugaki, Yamamoto's chief of staff, wrote in exasperation in his diary: "It's infuriating—we shoot them down and we shoot them down, but they only send in more."

At midnight on September 3 the Japanese shelled the island, and the marines retaliated with an air strike that strafed boats and barges off Taivu Point.

On September 4 the Cactus Air Force spotted nearly 50 boats and landing craft off Santa Isabel Island and attacked. But the Japanese kept pouring into Guadalcanal every night by the hundreds and thousands. By September 6 the Japanese had caught on to the American naval patrol habits and were starting their barge runs in late afternoon, just after the last American patrol headed homeward. At night they operated "with impunity," Admiral Ghormley wrote in despair, and he called for more help to bomb the Japanese in the Buin area. But Admiral McCain replied that he could not use the TBFs at Espiritu Santo as Ghormley wished, because they had to be kept loaded with torpedos in case the Japanese fleet came down again. Otherwise the whole northern sector was left defenseless.

On September 5 two B-17s attacked the retiring *Yudachi, Hatsuyaki,* and *Murakumo* as they headed back to the Shortlands, but without effect. That day the Cactus Air Force patrol sighted 15 large enemy landing boats, each carrying 75 men, as the boats approached the northwest corner of Guadalcanal. The Japanese had made the mistake of trying once more to operate during the hours of daylight. The U.S. planes gave the landing boats a thorough working over; they came down strafing and sank three boats. The P-400s were in their element that day, strafing and bombing along the beach, and they killed scores of Japanese soldiers and sank most of the twelve remaining boats.

At noon that day came the daily Japanese air raid, this time 26 bombers and 20 Zero fighters. Many of the American planes were still busy attacking the landing craft, so the F4F response was slighter than usual, but 18 planes rose in the air to meet the Japanese. They shot down 2 bombers and a Zero, but 2 F4Fs were lost, one had been destroyed on the beach, and 3 more were badly damaged. That day a PBY shot down a Kawanishi flying boat near Guadalcanal. Attrition again.

Every day the Japanese soldiers came in their landing barges, 1,000 or 2,000 at a time. General Vandegrift could see that the enemy was building successfully for a counterattack. It was impossible for the marines to estimate the number of Japanese who had come in. Counting landing barges was not accurate, because some came in by destroyer, and some landing barges returned during the night to Thousand Ships Bay on Santa Isabel Island for new loads. All General Vandegrift could do was increase the vigilance of the marines. Vandegrift had asked for reinforcement, and, by juggling, Ghormley and Turner had been able to increase his force slightly. General Kawaguchi and Admiral Yamamoto were blissfully unaware of the size of this American force even now, although the Japanese troops on the island knew that there were a great many Americans, and that if the Japanese stirred past their perimeter, they were ambushed nearly every time.

As September moved into its second week, both sides were growing nervous. General Hyukatake was prepared to move an entire division into Guadalcanal, but General Kawaguchi, who had been on hand for a week, assured headquarters that he had enough troops at the end of the first week in September to retake the airfield, and that was the important point. Once Henderson Field was restored to Japanese control, it would make no difference how many Americans lurked in the jungle—they could be routed out one by one and exterminated.

Since his arrival at the end of August, General Kawaguchi had been preparing for the great attack on Henderson Field. He planned to send troops against all three sides of the marine perimeter around the airfield and cap the attack with an amphibious assault that would be led in by the warships on the day of battle.

The jungle around Henderson Field was virtually impenetrable, which meant that, except for the established trails (which the Americans held in ambush), the Japanese had to hack their own roads through the jungle. Kawaguchi's engineers did this in the first few days of September.

Oddly enough, despite the daily reports of landings, General Vandegrift was as uncertain about the real strength of the Japanese as General Kawaguchi was about the Americans. Solomon Islander scouts reported to the allies that there were "several thousand" Japanese in the main body, but until the coming of the war, Solomon Islanders' counting had been notable for its brevity—very seldom was there occasion to count anything larger than could be done on two hands. So while the Melanesians were correct in their estimate, the marines discounted it and operated on the principle that the Japanese reinforcements could not number more than 500. To deal with this group that was heading for a point south of Henderson Field, General Vandegrift brought Colonel Edson's 1st Raider Battalion and the remains of the 1st Parachute Battalion that had borne the brunt of the fierce fighting on Gavutu. They were assigned to make a raid behind the Japanese lines and eliminate the Japanese threat.

On September 7 these troops boarded the destroyer transports *McKean* and *Manley* and two landing craft, and at dawn the next morning were taken east of Taivu Point into the Japanese territory. They landed and began moving toward the village of Tasimboko. As they started, they discovered a new 37-mm gun with ammunition almost on the edge of the beach, and could not understand why it had been left there. The fact was that the Japanese had just landed another contingent of troops and weapons the night before the marines arrived, and at the time that the marines came in toward shore, a small convoy of American supply ships were moving toward Lunga Point. The Japanese got the idea that the Americans were launching a major invasion from the sea, panicked, and fled into the interior.

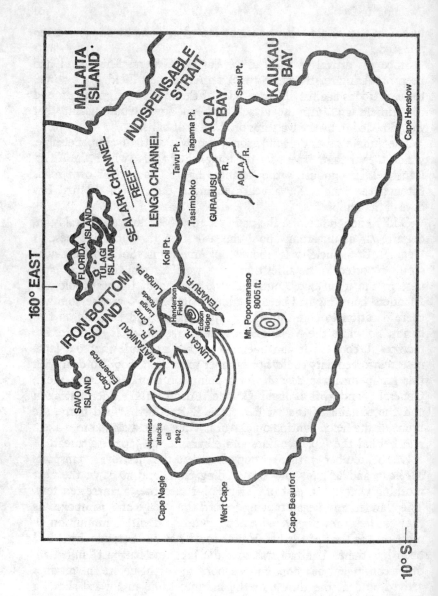

Guadalcanal

For the moment this seemed to be a godsend, but in fact Kawaguchi was in touch with Yamamoto's headquarters, and the result of this misapprehension was to step up the Japanese time schedule for the assault on Guadalcanal. The first Japanese effort was to launch a major air strike that morning.

The marines moved ahead up the trail. They found another new 37-mm gun and more supplies scattered along the trail, evidence of hurried evacuation. As usual, the Japanese bomber parade arrived, but it was not really so usual, for this was one of the largest raids yet staged, and a direct reaction from Rabaul to the news of the Edson raid. But luckily for the marines, the Japanese were turned away from Henderson Field by bad weather.

The Raiders moved around the perimeter of what was obviously an old Japanese camp. On the beach they encountered one group of soldiers still at their landing boats, and the Americans opened fire. By nine o'clock in the morning the marines were engaged at several points, and it soon became clear that there were more Japanese and better armed Japanese than Vandegrift's headquarters had anticipated; the Americans were under fire from 90-mm mortars and 74-mm field guns.

The marines called for and got help from overhead. The Cactus Air Force put up a succession of dive bombers and P-400s, and they bombed and strafed to relieve the pressure on the Raiders.

At noon it began to rain, which churned the dusty airstrip at Henderson Field into a platter of mud. The planes continued to shuttle back and forth, however, gassing, arming, and taking off again to bomb and strafe around Taivu Point and Tasimboko, where the marines were in trouble. That afternoon the mud caused 6 plane casualties. No pilots were injured, but at the end of the day, 6 of the 16 fighters had been lost and 2 others damaged.

The Japanese did all they could to support their men in the Tasimboko fight. They sent 12 seaplanes from their base at New Georgia to bomb Henderson Field, but they were stopped by the weather and bombed Tulagi instead, which was hard on the supply system but did not affect the day's operations.

After some heavy fighting, in which the marines captured a number of 75-mm guns, they moved into Tasimboko and discovered they had come upon a Japanese headquarters. They found a radio station there, which they destroyed, and dumps of ammunition and food. It was apparent that the enemy had been landing supplies as well as men for the past ten days. The Raiders burned the supplies they found and moved back to the beach. They reembarked in their destroyer transports and went back to Guadalcanal to report. They had suffered 2 men killed and 4 wounded in the raid and had killed 30 Japanese. That night the Japanese sent a cruiser and eight destroyers down The Slot to wipe out the ships that had brought the marines to Tasimboko. They did not find them, but they bombarded Tulagi Harbor and destroyed one patrol boat and wounded several men.

Studying the documents Edson had captured at Tasimboko and the terrain from Lunga Point back beyond the airstrip, General Vandegrift noted a grassy ridge south of Henderson Field that could command the field. It ran at right angles to Henderson Field, and could serve as a point of assault. Vandegrift decided this place must be defended, and he assigned Colonel Edson's combined unit of Raiders and parachute troops to the task. They moved up and dug in along the ridge.

The 3rd Battalion of the 1st Marine Regiment was sent to defend the bank of the Tenaru River, which snaked its way inland for two miles. On the west, the perimeter was defended by another line of marines, and northwest of the ridge two pockets were placed at strong points, one manned by men of the 1st Amphibious Tractor Battalion and the other by the 1st Pioneers (Construction Battalions). The fact that Vandegrift had to use specialists as infantrymen showed how thin the perimeter was in spite of the number of troops. He was not overly worried, however, because marines were trained first as infantrymen before they adopted specialties.

Vandegrift had four days to prepare, although no one was sure of the Japanese intentions. Admiral Ghormley's information indicated the Japanese might swoop down on Guadalcanal on the night of September 8 with cruisers and destroyers. The threat was real enough to have him call the destroyer transports *Fuller* and *Bellatrix* away from the beach before they were through unloading a slender string of supplies; he sent them eastward to avoid trouble.

On September 9, General Geiger reported that his pilots were nearly exhausted, and although he was driving them ("It's better to keep flying than get a Jap bayonet stuck up their ass."), the results of their flying were showing in mistakes and damaged aircraft. At least part of the reason for the heavy aircraft loss on the muddy field on

September 8 had been pilot exhaustion. The flight surgeon told Geiger that most of his pilots were unfit to fly, their nerves ragged from lack of sleep and their judgment impaired by exhaustion. Some of the pilots, who had been assiduous before, showed their combat fatigue in a growing unwillingness to fly. Major Robert Galer of Fighting 224 characterized his own squadron and two others as "almost worthless," except for Captains Marion Carl and John Dobbin, who seemed to be iron men. The pilots flew because they had to. They went up dazed, and they came back exhausted, and many of them opted out of fights if possible.

On September 9 the Seabees finished up a new airstrip, "the cow pasture," a mile and a quarter east of Henderson Field. From that point on the lighter fighters would take off and land on this strip, leaving the bigger one for the heavier bombers.

Initially, the improvement made little difference. On September 9 the Japanese sent over another large force of Betty bombers; the tempo had been stepped up with that call for help from Tasimboko, and at Rabaul the Japanese still were certain the Americans had made another major troop landing. The Japanese attack was directed mainly against the shipping in the sound. The marine fighters shot down five bombers and three Zeros. But the extent of the fatigue was shown again: Captain Marion Carl, the 12-plane "ace," did not return. The day ended with four more fighters gone, and three pilots wounded or missing. On September 10 the Bettys were back again in force, with 15 Zeros to guard them. The Americans claimed 5 Japanese planes, but by the end of that day only 12 F4Fs were operational. That day all the planes that had come off *Saratoga* were ordered to Guadalcanal.

Also on September 10, Ghormley's headquarters announced that a Japanese task force was coming to Guadalcanal, and could be expected to arrive by the 12th. No one was quite sure how large this force was; the reports spoke only of cruisers and destroyers. Admiral Yamamoto was being extremely careful to conceal from the Americans the whereabouts and number of his available carriers. His officers and the army officers tended to disparage the Americans, but Yamamoto had warned them against underestimating the enemy. The Americans thought there might be as many as 7 Japanese carriers operating in the area, and later on the 10th naval intelligence gave a new estimate. It was enough to frighten anyone: There were 7 carriers, 3 or 4 battleships, 8 or 9 heavy cruisers, 5 or 6 light cruisers, 20 or more destroyers, and seaplane tenders and transports capable of carrying 25,000 troops.

On the 11th the Bettys came again at the usual time with their Zero escort. This time the Cactus Air Force was sluggish, and before they could be intercepted, the Bettys had dropped a pattern of bombs in the service area on the east side of Henderson Field, causing 20 casualties and destroying one P-400. The commanding officer of the 67th Army Air Force Fighter Squadron was one of the injured who had to be evacuated.

The F4Fs came in trailing glory; they had shot down half a dozen bombers and fighters, but another U.S. pilot had been shot out of the sky, and swam for shore, and another F4F was gone. Now there were 11 F4Fs, but the Japanese at Rabaul had four times as many fighters, plus dozens of bombers and the seaplanes at New Georgia. That estimate was at four o'clock in the afternoon. At 4:30 the Cactus Air Force was augmented by 24 F4Fs from the *Saratoga's* "Fighting Five," the fighter squadron of Air Group Five, which was aboard the carrier.

Back at Nouméa, Admiral Ghormley again warned Admiral King that he would have to expect this sort of attrition for months to come and asked for a constant supply of aircraft capable of fighting in the conditions of the Pacific. The Army Air Force had suggested that the P-40 was an adequate airplane, but the pilots in the field quite disagreed. Besides, there weren't any P-40s or anything else available for Guadalcanal just at that time.

General Vandegrift had pleaded once more with Admiral Turner for reinforcement, but Turner had replied that the only possible force would be the 7th Marines at Samoa, who had no amphibious training. They would need at least a month to prepare.

To Vandegrift just then a month was a lifetime, Turner knew. He told Ghormley that day that in his opinion the situation of the Guadalcanal landings was perilous. Ghormley, in turn, sent a message to Admiral Nimitz that day: "Situation as I view it today extremely critical. . . ." What Ghormley knew, of course, was all secondhand information. He still had not visited Guadalcanal, although that very day Admiral Turner was going to see how bad it really was.

The Ghormley report was accurate enough. The food situation at Guadalcanal that day was critical. The Japanese air and sea strikes had grown increasingly effective against the American convoys coming from Nouméa. The air raids every day, and sometimes more than once a day, disrupted the unloading of the U.S. transports. The carrier task force had been reduced to two carriers, the *Wasp* and the *Hornet*, and Ghormley was worried about risking them. He sensed that the Japanese fleet was on the move, but he did not know precisely where it was going.

Just after midnight on September 12, Admiral Ghormley warned Admiral Leigh Noyes, commander of the carriers since Fletcher had gone, of an imminent attempt by the Japanese to occupy Henderson Field, using troops at hand and perhaps paratroopers and glider forces. The enemy, he said, had the field under constant observation. How true that was. For nights on end, the sleep of the marines had been disturbed by the droning of one Japanese fleet observation plane after another. "Washing Machine Charlie," they called the plane, or "Louie the Louse." One float plane sounded like another. "He" had been coming over since almost the first day of landing, but recently the visits had been more frequent and prolonged.

For the marines, September 12 began with an air alert at eight o'clock in the morning. It was a false alarm, and the F4Fs that had scrambled were back in half an hour having seen nothing. But at eleven o'clock came the usual Betty raid from Rabaul. The augmented force of F4Fs was in the air in a few minutes, and shot down seven planes, but again lost one plane, when one of the new navy pilots tried to make a dead stick landing, crashed, and was killed. The executive officer of the navy squadron, Lt. David C. Richardson, was wounded in the leg.

Shortly after the planes returned from the fracas, Admiral Turner and Admiral McCain arrived on the field in an R4D (the navy name for the Douglas Skymaster that the army called the C-47). When the admirals were closeted with General Vandegrift, Turner brought out a bottle of Scotch whiskey and poured three glasses. He handed one of them, with a situation report by Admiral Ghormley, to the general. For the first time, Vandegrift was informed of the extent of the Japanese plan. He knew something was afoot from daily messages and from the movement of Japanese troops to the island. But he did not know that Admiral Yamamoto was preparing to use the Combined Fleet to launch a major attack, and what Turner told him at this point, in the privacy of the command post, was that Ghormley had given up, thrown up his hands, and said there was nothing to be done.

The three commanders looked at one another. Their leader had quit. Seventeen thousand marines were stranded on that island with barely enough ammunition and food to last them a week, and if fighting developed, perhaps not that long. The Japanese fleet was in motion somewhere "out there," and it was apparent from the estimates that attack could come at any hour. If Guadalcanal was going to be saved, they were going to have to save it.

8

BLOODY RIDGE

THE three senior officers dined together that night in General Vandegrift's quarters. General Vandegrift showed them General Kawaguchi's dress white uniform complete with silk facings, which had been captured among the loot at Tasimboko. Admiral Turner brought out another bottle of whiskey, which was so precious on Guadalcanal just then that the only supply was in the hands of the flight surgeon, who doled it out after missions to the fliers.

As well as was possible under the circumstances the general and the admirals made plans. The 7th Marine Regiment simply had to be brought in to Guadalcanal to give the weary marines already in the line some rest. But this could not be done, disregarding training, for at least a few days. In the interim the marines would have to hold no matter what happened. As for the Cactus Air Force, McCain was doing everything possible to beg and borrow planes, and he would even steal them if he could find them.

As far as Turner was concerned, he proposed to go back to Espiritu Santo, board his flagship, and return to Guadalcanal with supplies in the transports, plus the 7th Marine Regiment. This move would be covered by all the warships and carriers that the fleet could produce.

Turner and McCain were asleep at Vandegrift's headquarters

when the Japanese bombardment began. That was the end of sleep. The Kawaguchi brigade began at daylight on September 12 to probe the marine defenses along the southern line. Kawaguchi, like General Vandegrift, had seen that the ridge south of Henderson Field was the most logical point of attack, since it would give the Japanese a sort of driveway with dense jungle on both sides; with luck, they might come down the ridge straight at the airfield and take control. One Japanese detachment broke through the line that day, surrounded a force of marines, and cut off communications. But the marines held in their pocket, and the Japanese did not launch the major attack expected.

On top of the ridge the Raiders had dug in. Some of them did not much like digging in the rock they found just below the surface, but an air raid that plastered the ridge with bombs from a number of Betty bombers killed several marines whose foxholes were inadequate, and the rest learned.

Just before noon the Bettys arrived as usual. This time the marine antiaircraft guns destroyed two bombers, and another was damaged and shot down later by a fighter. The marines and navy claimed 10 bombers and 3 Zeros that day, but the 42-plane bombing raid had done damage. One bomb hit the radio shack at the airport and cut off communications from Guadalcanal for four and a half hours.

Late on the afternoon of September 12, the dive bombers of Scouting Squadron Three went on their usual late patrol. This time they found the northern Solomons dotted with the gray shapes of Japanese warships. One pilot reported a cruiser and three destroyers forty miles off Rendova, another found a destroyer off Choiseul, and another found more destroyers off Santa Isabel. These ships were the cruiser *Tenryu* and her destroyers, coming in to open the combined assault that was to secure the airfield for the Japanese. The marines scattered the planes around the field as well as they could in order to protect them.

The Combined Fleet was behind these ships, waiting for word that General Kawaguchi had moved. As darkness fell, "Washing Machine Charlie" appeared, and just before 10 P.M. so did "Louie the Louse." The Guadalcanal night was lit up with ghoulish green flare light as the Japanese began their bombardment. But on this night neither the airfield nor the Lunga Point dumps were the prime target. General Kawaguchi had radioed to Rabaul a description of the marine dispositions, and the bombardment unit opened up on the ridge where Colonel Edson had dug in. After twenty minutes the ships shifted their fire to the airfield, and hit the marine scout bombing squadron camp, killing Lt. L. Baldinus, Lt. D. V. Rose, Lt. J. W. Weintraub, and wounding two others. More attrition.

When the bombardment ceased, the marines on the ridge knew what was coming.

A rocket flew up, red and trailing sparks, from the jungle below the ridge, and it was followed by the scraping of feet and metal on rock and Japanese shouting.

"Yankee you die."

"Drink marine blood."

"Banzai, Tenno Heika Banzai!"

The Japanese were coming.

At first the fury of their drive drove back the marines in the forward positions. The Japanese cut off the platoon on the right flank and then tried to encircle it. On the left they drove holes in the line held by the parachute troops. But the parachutists rallied and drove the enemy away. Marine artillery opened up from behind the Vandegrift command post, and the Japanese retreated.

When morning came, Colonel Edson surveyed his position and moved some forward positions back to better terrain. He could see that his marines were tired, but there were no replacements. Major Kenneth Bailey had a bullet through the top of his helmet, but his scalp was only grazed. Edson himself was dirty, bedraggled, and two Japanese bullets had torn through his blouse without hitting him.

But PFC Ray Herndon had been a member of a squad stationed on the south side of the ridgetop. When the Japanese made charge after charge against that position, this squad was hit hard. Finally only four men were on their feet. Then Herndon was hit in the belly. He thought surely he was going to die, and he took a .45 automatic from one of the others and told them to retreat. He would hold off the Japanese as long as possible. He did, but he was not seen alive again.

Lieutenant Colonel Lewis Johnson was wounded by a grenade during the night fighting, and next morning he was taken along with other wounded to a truck for evacuation to the field hospital. The road led down the ridge, and below, the Japanese were firing their mortars. A machine gunner somewhere on high ground also saw the truck and fired on it, wounding the driver. The truck stopped, and Johnson got out and tried to start it. It would not start. He put the truck in gear and used the power of the battery and starter to propel the truck jerkily for 300 yards, out of range of the Japanese gunner. Then he got the truck started and drove to the field hospital. Johnson let out the wounded and felt so much better that he went back for another load.

The wounded had to be moved, but the unwounded had to stay on. Edson knew that the night would bring an even more violent attack.

The morning of September 13 was quiet on the ground. In the air it was a different matter. Admirals McCain and Turner prepared to leave the field but were delayed when the coastwatchers reported enemy planes.

On the night of September 12 Admiral Yamamoto had expected General Kawaguchi to take the airfield as planned. By dawn on September 13, Yamamoto had no word from the army, but this was not unusual, because the two services never had learned to cooperate. Yamamoto ordered the 11th Air Fleet at Rabaul to send a scouting mission to Henderson Field to see if it was in Japanese hands as expected. Two observation planes guarded by 20 Zeros were assigned to the mission. If they saw that all was well, they were to land at Guadalcanal.

The Zeros arrived over Henderson Field early in the morning but to their surprise were met by a swarm of F4Fs. Just minutes before, 18 new F4Fs had been brought to Henderson Field from the carrier *Hornet*; for once there were plenty of planes available for the work at hand. The presence of the F4Fs gave the Japanese observation planes their answer. The American planes attacked, and only 17 of the Zeros went home, but once again the marines and navy had their losses: One U.S. pilot was shot down, two others were wounded, and two F4Fs were lost and one badly damaged.

Admirals Turner and McCain flew off just before the noon air raid. Ten minutes later the Bettys and Zeros appeared as if responding to a cue. The attrition of recent days had obviously caused the Japanese to bring in new, untried pilots. They were supposed to attack American artillery positions, but when the leader saw marine antiaircraft fire begin puffing up around his wings he dropped his bombs on the Japanese concentrations at Taivu Point. Others followed suit, and the damage to the Japanese was considerable. One Betty pilot did put his stick of bombs in precisely the right place, along the ridge line, but the marines were lucky and no one was hit. The American fighters shot down five Japanese bombers from that contingent. From the beginning, the marines and navy fliers had been told not to try to dogfight with the Zeros on a one-to-one basis, because the Japanese planes were so much faster and more maneuverable. As long as the Americans kept the two-plane unit, each protecting the tail of the other, they fared well. But on this day, perhaps intoxicated by their having received so many brand new F4F fighters, Capt. John Smith's fighter pilots made the fatal mistake of mixing at close hand with the enemy.

War correspondents Robert Miller of the United Press Associations and Richard Tregaskis of the International News Service had gone down to the Kukum Camps at Lunga Point that morning and there they got a worm's eye view of the aerial show.

The Japanese fighters had been instructed to strafe the Americans, and like the bombers, they had mistaken Taivu Point for Lunga Point and were strafing their own troops at the Tasimboko command post when the F4Fs jumped them. For the Zeros it was a quick pull on the stick and an increase in power and they were up, climbing fast and turning. The approved American technique called for the two pilots of an F4F two-plane section to stick together, turn, gain altitude and make another pass at the Zeros from above. Thus the superior diving ability of the F4F could be brought into play. But the combat deteriorated into dogfights, and the result was disastrous for all but the most experienced pilots. The cumulous clouds towered white and solid above Iron Bottom Sound and the island, and the correspondents and the marines in their foxholes had a great show as the F4Fs and Zeros circled and darted in and out of the clouds, trying to gain advantage and get on the tail of an enemy. The machine guns rattled incessantly. "As loud and magnificent as thunder," wrote correspondent Tregaskis.

"We saw one Wildcat (F4F) come diving down like a comet from the clouds," wrote Tregaskis, "with two Zeros on his tail. He was moving faster than they and as he pulled out of his dive and streaked across the water he left them behind. . . ." That pilot had escaped his enemies with the speed of his dive, which they could not match. Unfortunately, in a looping turn or a climb it was the other way around, and when the fight was over that day, Captain Smith and Lt. H. Phillips had each shot down a Zero, but they were old hands; they had been fighting at Guadalcanal for 23 days. Three other U.S. pilots, not so lucky or not so skillful, were shot down, and two more brought F4Fs back to Henderson Field so badly damaged that they were usable only for parts. Of the 18 brand new F4Fs ferried over from the *Hornet*, 4 were lost even before their Bureau of Aviation numbers could be recorded on the squadron rolls.

Henderson had more activity than usual that day. Late in the afternoon, a pair of Japanese float planes came in fast to examine the field again. They were at 500 feet, moving at top speed. They found an American dive bomber in the landing pattern above the field and shot it down before the shocked eyes of the whole Cactus Air Force. The bomber crashed, burned, and exploded, killing the pilot and gunner as the Japanese float planes disappeared over the end of the runway.

The marine antiaircraft gunners cursed themselves for being caught napping and vowed that it would not happen again. When a large formation of planes appeared ten minutes later they were ready, and they began firing furiously. As the planes came in despite the harassment, they saw the aircraft were navy SBDs and stopped shooting before they destroyed any planes. These also included aircraft of the unlucky carrier *Saratoga*, 12 dive bombers and 6 torpedo bombers.

The news of the Japanese ships in the waters north of Guadalcanal and the intimations from all sides of a major attack had left General Vandegrift more than worried. On September 13, he stopped by the Pagoda, which General Geiger was using as his headquarters as well as operations office. Vandegrift and Geiger had been in the Corps more than 30 years, and they were good friends. This day Vandegrift told Geiger that he did not know how long they could hold the perimeter against a concentrated Japanese attack, particularly if the Combined Fleet came down with an amphibious landing. It might well be that the perimeter would be overrun and the airfield would fall. If that seemed imminent he would get word to Geiger, and the general should have all his planes ready to fly out to Espiritu Santo where they would be safe. Geiger listened and nodded. He would arrange for that, he said. But as far as he was concerned personally, he would stay on and fight with Vandegrift even if it meant a fight to the end.

This sober thinking permeated the higher echelons of the marine headquarters that afternoon and evening. It was no laughing matter when the commander of the South Pacific force gave up the battle before it was fought, and the impairment of morale was obvious. The fact was that there was no real reason for the pessimism at that particular moment. Vandegrift did not know how greatly his force outnumbered the enemy, nor just how slender were the Japanese air forces at Rabaul. Admiral Tsukahara of the 11th Air Fleet was scraping the barrel and pleading with higher authority for more planes. He was also hampered because under the Japanese system, the navy was totally responsible for air defense in the South Pacific, and the army would not supply any aircraft. Admiral Ghormley at least had a unified command, with carrier planes, the Cactus Air Force, and McCain's land-based air force working for him. They could call on General MacArthur for some assistance, however reluctantly given. So the Japanese air forces were as badly off as the Americans. It was only in the matter of naval strength that the Japanese were fully superior. Their base at Rabaul and support base at Truk were close by, whereas the Americans had to be supplied from Pearl Harbor, half a world away. This, as much as the shortage of American fighting ships, was the truly serious problem of the moment at Guadalcanal. And true to his promise to help, Admiral Turner was on his way to bring the 7th Marines to reinforce Guadalcanal and supply the marines at the same time. Before he left Guadalcanal that day, he asked Ghormley for permission to move. Ghormley ducked the issue. "Definite approval cannot be given until present situation is known," he said, but copies of the messages went to Nimitz and King. Admiral King told Nimitz that Turner's request demanded action. Nimitz sent a sharp message to Ghormley: "Turner's [request] is approved."

Ghormley roused himself then to try to recover his lost prestige and issued orders to Turner to carry out the mission. He also warned Turner and Vandegrift that a major effort would be made on the night of September 13 by General Kawaguchi to capture the airfield.

That night of September 12 as darkness fell on the ridge above Henderson Field the Japanese began to move about, after an afternoon of silence. Colonel Edson's men were dog-tired, and their effective strength was 300 men in those foxholes on the ridge. Behind

them was General Vandegrift's command post, and behind that the
reserves, consisting of a battalion under Col. W. J. Whaling, and
behind them the artillery with its guns sighted in on the crest of the
ridge and the Japanese positions to the south of it. Beyond all the
soldiers lay Henderson Field, the prize the Japanese had vowed to
secure and the marines had promised to defend.

Japanese troop morale on Guadalcanal had been raised enormously by the bombardment of the night before and the continual
train of Japanese planes flying over Guadalcanal that day. That night
the reinforced Japanese set out to take the airfield at any cost.

As darkness fell, a red rocket shot up from the Japanese lines, and
men in the forward line began screaming.

"Marine you die. . . ."

The Japanese 90-mm mortars behind the ridge coughed, and the
mortar shells hummed in and exploded on the ridge line among the
marine foxholes. The Japanese on the edge of the ridge stood up,
and shouting "Banzai," ran forward with their bayonets, firing as
they came. The marines crouched in their foxholes and fired their
rifles on semiautomatic. The popping of Browning automatic rifles
was joined by the stitching sound of machine guns, the screaming,
the high "splat" of the .25 caliber Japanese rifles, and the staccato of
light Japanese machine guns. The Japanese probed the front of the
ridge and got nowhere; marines killed the enemy right up to and inside their foxholes. The Japanese moved to the right for the next assault, and on the west side of the ridge found an opening, squeezed
through and in the darkness outflanked one Raider company. Some
of the Japanese infiltrated as far back as General Vandegrift's command post before they were shot down.

Private First Class Jim Corzine saw four Japanese soldiers setting
up a Nambu machine gun on a hilltop, and he rushed at them,
bayoneted the gunner, and swung the gun around on the Japanese.
He fired, they fired, and he fell dead. But the Japanese were either
dead or wounded, and the gun was not put into action.

On the right flank of the marines the Japanese tried again to surround the forward element. Captain John Sweeney's Raider company was cut to pieces in this assault. His troops numbered only a
platoon at the end of the Japanese attack, not a company. Major
Torgerson's parachutists also took a heavy series of attacks, and in a

lull when the Tokyo Express came down again and shelled, the parachutists' position was hit.

"Louie the Louse" appeared over the marine lines and dropped one of his green flares. Another red flare went up, General Kawaguchi hurled more troops against the ridge, but still the marines held. As the infantry firing and the movement became intense, the marine artillery opened up and fired all night long, the "whompf" of the 105-mm howitzers the loudest sound in the jungle. The marine telephone lines to the ridge were cut by mortar fire. After that the marine howitzers fired at the Japanese by the light of the Japanese rockets, each of which went up over a new unit as it began to attack.

Off shore, the cruiser *Tenryu* appeared again with her train of destroyers, and they began a general bombardment of Henderson Field and the battle area.

Shortly before midnight the Japanese along the ridge line seemed to calm down. Then another red flare went up, and a howling line of skirmishers headed up the ridge against the left flank of the marines. The artillery behind the line began firing to its left. The Japanese loaded their mortars with smoke shells and laid down a screen.

"Gas attack!" the Japanese screamed, and charged forward, pushing back the marine left flank. Already the earlier attacks had pushed the right flank to the rear where it had reformed. Now the center company of marines was in danger of being cut off, so they were moved back to the last line on the ridge. Behind was the valley, and below that the pathway to the airfield. The Japanese were stopped by the heavy barrage from the 105-mm guns but some men managed to come through it, up the slope, and hurl grenades. They attacked intermittently, unit after unit, but each was sent reeling back. By 2:30 in the morning the edge of the Japanese offensive was blunted. The charges continued, but ever smaller and briefer. The marine machine guns rattled and the artillery boomed each time the Japanese moved. As dawn came, the last Japanese charge sent a handful of men to the crest of the hill, where the marines picked them off. But an officer and two men reached General Vandegrift's command post before they were shot down.

With morning came casualty reports, and General Vandegrift saw that the Parachute Battalion was down from the week before, down from 377 officers and men to 165 and the Raiders from 750 men to 526.

The shelling of the airfield and the marine positions had been a cover once more for a Japanese troop landing, and 1,700 troops of a 17th Army detachment had joined General Kawaguchi, but too late to be included in the last night's battle. He would need them; he had sent 2,000 men against the marine lines that night, and more than 600 had been killed and 500 wounded. As the sun rose in the sky, and the birds began to sing as if there had been no bloodletting the night before, the marines counted noses. That night 40 marines had been killed and 100 wounded on the ridge. A few others had been killed and wounded along the rest of the perimeter. The Japanese had staged lesser attacks on the bank of the Tenaru River against Colonel McKelvy's force, and another Japanese detachment, circling around in the jungle and thus arriving very late, had attacked on the other flank, where Colonel Biebush's 3rd Battalion of the 1st Marines dealt with them swiftly and mercilessly, aided by 75-mm pack howitzers.

As the morning sun rose along the ridge, General Geiger sent every available plane into the air to bomb and strafe. The three remaining operational army P-400s were admirably suited for this work, and they flashed in low over the ground, attacking—too low as it turned out, because two of the fighters were hit by accurate Japanese ground fire and were forced back to the field, their engines out, to make dead stick landings.

There was no quarter in this war. The Japanese bodies, five hundred at least, lay in grotesque positions around the ridge and on top of it. The insects moved in, and the heat began to bloat the corpses before noon. The Japanese made no attempt to brave the ridge in daylight, but under General Kawaguchi's orders, began to retreat to the headquarters established on the Matanikau River west of Lunga Point. They had to cut a trail through the jungle as they went, and many of the wounded did not survive the rigors of the journey.

On the ridge Colonel Edson's exhausted Raiders moved back while marines from the reserve advanced to handle the mopping up. Small pockets of Japanese had infiltrated the lines and been caught by daylight. They sniped and tried to move back as the marines came up that day. At one point, correspondent Tregaskis heard a strange foreign shout and then a burst of shooting. He walked up to the ridge and found two dead Japanese and a dead marine. Three Japanese had been flushed out and made a bayonet charge. The sounds Tregaskis had heard were the cries of "Banzai" by the Emperor's soldiers as they launched this suicide charge. One Japanese had caught the marine and spitted him and was then shot by other marines. The second Japanese had been tackled and then shot. A third had gotten away into the jungle.

The rest of the day was similar to that. The marines moved carefully, but the snipers still caused casualties, and had to be flushed out and killed. It took another 24 hours before the ridge returned to quiet.

The marines named the ridge then, in the fashion of American fighting men. "Bloody Ridge," they called it, and Bloody Ridge it would always be in the annals of the Marines.

9

THE SINKING OF
THE WASP

LONG after the Pacific war ended, the myth persisted in America that the Japanese submarine force had accomplished virtually nothing during the war. But the facts were quite the reverse: The Japanese submarines and particularly the big I-boats, which were superior to the American fleet-class submarines in many respects, were a real menace to the American fleet and particularly to the American carriers. By the time of the Battle of Guadalcanal, the *Saratoga* had been torpedoed twice, put out of action each time, and the *Yorktown* had been sunk by a submarine. The men of the U.S. Navy did not share the popular belief of the press, but at the beginning of the war the navy's antisubmarine tactics were ineffective. As of December 7, 1941, a chief petty officer was in charge of antisubmarine warfare in Washington. The sinking of the *Yorktown* and the two torpedoes that struck the *Saratoga* were largely the result of poor protective tactics, which were demonstrated by the carrier force's inability to sink any of the several submarines that shadowed the task force during the early days of the Guadalcanal campaign. One reason that Admiral Fletcher was so gun-shy could be traced to his fear that one of his carriers would be torpedoed, and this belief in the fragility of carriers was shared by Admiral Ghormley, who was also reluctant to expose the carrier force to danger.

On September 14, however, there was no recourse but to expose the carriers. In spite of Ghormley's reluctance, Admiral Turner had been given the green light by Admiral Nimitz to supply and reinforce the American beachhead on Guadalcanal. There was no way to protect the transports except by committing the American carriers and surface warships, since the Cactus Air Force was unable to build reserves in the war of attrition. At 6 o'clock on the morning of September 14, Admiral Turner sailed. The 7th Marine Regiment was aboard six transports, and they were escorted by all the cruisers and destroyers that Ghormley would let go. Far to the south was the task force that supported the *Wasp* and the *Hornet,* but it had to be prepared for action, because there were no other planes.

Admiral Turner knew that the Combined Fleet was circling somewhere north of Guadalcanal, and he charted a crooked course for himself, far to the east of the short approach to Guadalcanal, hoping to avoid detection by the enemy. If he were observed by the enemy he wanted to seem to be heading anywhere but to Guadalcanal. The ruse was effective, but perhaps by accident. The Combined Fleet had been at sea for a week, waiting for the past three days for General Kawaguchi to capture the airfields at Guadalcanal. The ships were running low on fuel, really low, and reluctantly Admiral Yamamoto called on them to retire temporarily from the danger zone to take on oil. The American search planes were operating competently for a change, and made many reports of sightings that were relayed to the naval commands. The *Hornet* sent a search group out on September 14, but the carriers were then 250 miles south of Guadalcanal, and the Japanese Combined Fleet was 200 miles north. Since the effective search range of American planes then was 250 miles, they did not come anywhere near the Japanese fleet.

On Guadalcanal on September 14, General Vandegrift shifted the 3rd Battalion of the 2nd Marine Regiment from Tulagi to the bigger island, since it was apparent that the action was going to concentrate on Guadalcanal. Early that morning four Zero float planes came over the island, perhaps encouraged by the easy success of the other two float planes the previous day, but these four were pounced on by F4Fs and shot down. The usual noon bombing raid arrived with the usual results. Early in the afternoon another raid came over the island, 25 Zeros escorting a handful of Betty bombers. The F4Fs shot down one Zero and one bomber. Just before dark, a dozen single-engine bombers struck Henderson Field again.

That day the U.S. destroyers *Hull* and *Sterett* appeared at Lunga Point, escorting two transports loaded with supplies for the beleaguered marines. They arrived in the morning and the transports began to unload. All was safe during the daylight hours as the planes from Henderson Field protected the ships in the harbor from Japanese warship incursions and enemy aircraft.

At dusk on September 14, however, the *Sterett* saw her first action against the Japanese. That bomber attack came in low over the island, and seaplane fighters strafed the ships. The *Sterett*'s five-inch guns brought down one of the planes. First there was an explosion next to the plane and then a spark and a trail of smoke.

"It was a beautiful sight," wrote Lt. Thomas McWhorter, an officer aboard the *Sterett*. "Soon after that our target imitated his unfortunate comrades and added his wreckage to the Savo Sound. . . . The *Sterett* had drawn her first blood! The next day we painted our first Jap flag on the bridge."

That night, as darkness closed, the two destroyers moved across the channel to anchor in Tulagi Harbor. Three hours later down came the Tokyo Express, one cruiser and four destroyers, to speed along the Guadalcanal side, bombard Henderson Field, and then speed back. They did not pay the slightest bit of attention to the American ships in Tulagi Harbor.

The next day the events were much the same: a heightening of air activity, but no naval activity near Guadalcanal, and the Japanese troops moving back to the area around Taivu Point.

As a matter of course, intelligence officers looked over the pieces of Japanese aircraft wreckage that fell on the island. At this time they discovered that almost all the planes shot down were just off the assembly lines of Japanese aircraft factories. That said something about attrition and also about the Japanese ability to resupply their air forces in a hurry. Observing and questioning the F4F pilots, intelligence also learned that the skill of the Japanese fliers was on the decrease. Major Smith and Capt. Marion Carl, who had walked in to Henderson Field after a five-day sojourn that included rescue by friendly islanders after he had landed in the water, could remember those first encounters with the cream of the Japanese naval air fleets.

But the rate of attrition had been so great, that the new group of fighter and bomber pilots seemed to be as fresh from the assembly lines as their planes.

Around Bloody Ridge, the marines spent three days mopping up after the big battle. The snipers were the worst problem, for having been trapped behind the American lines, they had no real recourse by their standards but to fight to the death and make every shot count as long as they lived. So the marines had to keep scouting and clearing out the trees, and they suffered a certain number of casualties and much more inconvenience.

South of Guadalcanal the *Hornet* and the *Wasp* were cruising. The *Wasp* was surrounded by four cruisers and six destroyers. A few miles away was the *Hornet*, accompanied by the battleship *North Carolina*, three cruisers, and seven destroyers. On the morning of September 15 the combat air patrol shot down a Kawanishi four-engined flying boat. But since the big plane was far beyond visual range of the force, and had been detected by radar, no one worried much about having been reported to the Japanese, and also the searches indicated the Combined Fleet was far away.

On September 15, General Kawaguchi sent a reluctant message to Rabaul and the Combined Fleet. He had met stiff enemy opposition, he said, and had to abandon the drive on the airfield.

Aboard Combined Fleet flagship *Yamato* the news was greeted first with disbelief and then with disappointment.

"We stamped our feet in bitter anger," said one officer. Admiral Yamamoto was no better pleased. The army had completely underestimated the enemy and suffered the bitter results of that error. It would take at least a full division of troops to reinforce Guadalcanal and take the airfield. Until the army could supply the troops, there was no point in pursuing the action. Yamamoto turned the Combined Fleet back and headed for Truk.

Flight operations continued all day. At two o'clock in the afternoon the *Wasp* made ready to launch a new search and combat air patrol. She turned into the wind and slowed down from the 16 knots cruising speed. She launched 18 dive bombers and 8 fighters. Admiral Noyes did not know that even as the carrier launched her planes she was being watched by one of Japan's most celebrated submarine captains. He was Commander Takaichi Kinashi, in the *I-19*, who had made his reputation in the first days of the war operating off Malaya.

When Commander Kinashi spotted the task force through his periscope, he worked around until he had the *Wasp* group ahead of him, silhouetted against the *Hornet* group. That way, if he fired torpedoes and they missed the *Wasp* group, they would go on through and give him a second chance.

Kinashi moved in as close as he could to the *Wasp*, and fired a full spread, six torpedoes, from the forward tubes. Three of the torpedoes headed directly for the *Wasp*'s course.

Captain Forrest P. Sherman, the commander of the *Wasp*, swung into the turn demanded just then by their base course, and as he did so, lookouts warned that torpedoes were approaching the starboard beam of the ship. Sherman tried to escape by turning right again, but three torpedoes struck. The explosions were enormous. The flight deck bucked up, and planes jumped into the air to crash back onto the deck. Planes suspended in the hangar deck fell. Fire broke out in the ammunition and fuel supplies; the water mains forward burst, and the fire could not be fought with water. Captain Sherman turned the *Wasp* so that the flames and smoke blew aft away from the undamaged parts of the carrier. The ship listed, but the engineers corrected the list, and kept her going.

All this activity had not really communicated the danger to the *Hornet* task group, so unprofessional was the American antisubmarine approach. From six miles away no one could fail to see the smoke and flame rising from the deck of the *Wasp*, but the men aboard the *Hornet* wondered if perhaps she had not suffered an operational accident. Just then, with no more warning from the protective destroyers than the *Wasp* had, the *Hornet* came under attack from the remaining three torpedoes of the *I-19*. As Commander Kinashi had hoped, the three that missed the *Wasp* ran straight on. When the torpedoes neared the *Hornet* group, the lookout aboard the destroyer *Mustin* sighted one wake and spread the alarm by voice radio and by hoisting the torpedo warning flag. But the battleship *North Carolina* had no time to maneuver, and one torpedo struck forward on the port side of the ship. It hit 20 feet below the waterline and killed five men instantly. A hole 32 feet long and 18 feet high was torn in the battleship's side, and it seemed she must sink. Certainly, one of the old battleships of the Pearl Harbor vintage would have. But the new fast battleships were constructed with many watertight compartments, and although four of *North Caro-*

lina's compartments were flooded, the captain also flooded the nearby forward magazines for safety. The ship could still make 25 knots, and in a few minutes the damage control party adjusted ballast so that the list was gone.

Commander Kinashi's fifth torpedo raced across the *Hornet* formation, and so did the sixth. The destroyer *O'Brien* was steaming off the *North Carolina's* quarter. One of the *O'Brien's* lookouts saw the fifth torpedo to port and yelled. The bridge responded and swung to the right, so the "fish" passed just astern of the ship. But at that very second the gunnery officer spotted the sixth torpedo. It was too late to move out of the way. The sixth torpedo struck the *O'Brien* in the bow and ripped it open. It was not a mortal wound, but the *O'Brien* was badly hurt.

So Commander Kinashi had accomplished one of the rare feats of the war: he had expended six torpedoes and left one carrier burning, one battleship crippled, and one destroyer crippled (her back was broken and she sank on the way home to the United States). Commander Kinashi was not discovered.

The American destroyers rushed to and fro seeking a second submarine but they found no clues. Much later U.S. naval historian Samuel Eliot Morison concluded in his history of U.S. naval operations that the *North Carolina* and *O'Brien* had been hit by torpedoes from *I-15*, which was also assigned in that same southern area; but Admiral Morison misunderstood the Japanese use of submarines. Almost never were two submarines in a position to cross paths; the Japanese kept them carefully apart. Morison did suggest that it was barely possible for *I-19* to have attacked both carrier groups, and in his defense it must be said that it seemed so nearly impossible that Kinashi could have made such a sweep with one spread that any other explanation seemed more reasonable.

The carrier force, moreover, was thoroughly occupied in the task of trying to save the *Wasp*. The fires of hell burned below her decks and the forecastle was red hot. No one in the wardroom at the time of explosion could have survived; it was smashed and gutted. Much of "officers' country" was located directly below the torpedo hits, and men in their bunks had no chance. But up forward men were alive, although cut off from the main part of the ship by fire, smoke, and white-hot metal. On the water, a film of burning gasoline encircled the bow, and many were afraid to leap into the sea, the only possible way of saving themselves. Those who raised the courage made the jump and some swam successfully beneath the fires. Some men also burned.

In fighting the fires the major trouble was the lack of water pressure, and in the absence of it, the fires gained headway. At three o'clock the carrier was suddenly shaken by an enormous explosion of gas that had built up below deck. The bridge and the island structure was smashed. The fighter director office, the radar, and the air commander's cubbyhole were all wiped out. On the bridge, Admiral Noyes was thrown flat on the signal deck, his clothes afire, and several officers and men on the port side of the bridge were blown overboard.

The admiral and Captain Sherman survived. The captain made his way aft to the Battle II station to control the rescue effort. As he reached this point, another explosion blew the No. 2 elevator out of its housing and high into the air to crash down onto the flight deck.

The carrier burned fiercely. The hangar deck was turned into a fire pit. The ready bombs, machine gun bullets, and torpedoes began to explode. After twenty more minutes of distressing effort, Captain Sherman decided that there was no hope and that the ship must be abandoned. He gave the order.

The retreat was remarkably orderly, considering the raging fires and the constant danger of explosion. The injured men were found and taken off, and chiefs searched the wreckage for survivors before leaving the ship. Mattresses, lumber, life preservers, anything that would float was hurled from the deck to help the men who struggled in the water. The evacuation took an hour; it was nearly four o'clock in the afternoon before Captain Sherman left the ship.

Belatedly the destroyers were throwing depth charges at "submarines." (Commander Kinashi had marveled for a moment at his handiwork and then slipped silently away beneath their noses.) The depth charges did more harm to the survivors in the water than anything else, but after the carrier was evacuated, and all the rescued were picked up by ships of the task force, the statistics showed that of the 2,250 men aboard, about 200 were killed and 375 wounded. All but one of the planes that had just flown off as the torpedo struck were able to land on the *Hornet*. Considering the extent of the tragedy, Admiral Noyes, Captain Sherman, and the men of the *Wasp* had rallied heroically.

If there was a lesson to be learned from the enormous damage done so easily by one submarine in the presence of 13 destroyers, there was also something to be learned about American torpedoes, a lesson that went unremarked that day. The *Wasp* continued to burn fiercely, and Rear Admiral Norman Scott in the *San Francisco*, who had taken command when Admiral Noyes was in the water, ordered the destroyer *Lansdowne* to torpedo and sink the carrier. The *Lansdowne* fired five torpedoes at the *Wasp*, and all five were hits. But only three exploded. They did the job, and the *Wasp* sank that afternoon, 250 miles northwest of Espiritu Santo. When Admiral Ghormley received the report of the affair, he suggested that Noyes was at fault for remaining in the same area for a long period of time (the area was 300 miles east-west and 140 miles north-south), and that this "hanging around" had been the cause of the sinking. But when the report reached Admiral King, who had all year been experiencing the devastation of the German U-boats off the American coast, King knew better than Ghormley that the fault lay in the entire American technique of dealing with submarines. Admiral Noyes could not be faulted for the errors of the past, nor could anyone else. An investigation made by Rear Admiral John Shafroth said as much. Admiral Nimitz agreed that no one could be blamed for the loss of the *Wasp*. But in all this investigation, sight was lost of a matter equally important: Why did two U.S. torpedoes strike but not explode? This was one of the mysteries of the early days of the war, one that would not be solved in 1942 or the next year. At the moment many other problems seemed far more pressing, especially the fact that as of September 15, 1942, the United States had only one operational carrier in the South Pacific, while as far as Admiral Nimitz knew, the Japanese had eight carriers available. The United States had one battleship available, the *Washington*, while the Japanese had nine battleships, including the *Musashi* and *Yamato*, the most powerful ever built; and the Japanese force of cruisers and destroyers far outnumbered the American. These statistics were enough to give anyone pause.

10

THE JUDGMENT
OF ADMIRALS

ADMIRAL Yamamoto's Combined Fleet was fueling on the day the *Wasp* was destroyed. Commander Kinashi wasted no time in surfacing well outside the American task force; he sent the word of his victory and of the course and speed of the 20 remaining warships and the *Hornet*. But the Combined Fleet carriers were too far away, and for some reason the Japanese did not choose to take the aggressive stance of earlier times. Japanese postwar writers have suggested that the defeat at Midway had made Yamamoto more cautious, and that was certainly true of the naval staff in Tokyo, which did not urge immediate action.

Admiral Turner was seriously worried on September 16, after learning of the sinking of the *Wasp*, but no one ever accused him of being faint of heart. He was also spurred by a new sense of urgency. That day Vandegrift's Cactus Air Force was down to 5,000 gallons of aviation gas, not enough supply for a week of limited operation. It was imperative that Henderson Field be resupplied. In the absence of any definitive information about the enemy Combined Fleet, Turner decided that any risk must be taken, and he pushed on toward Guadalcanal with the reinforcements and the supplies. He was lucky; the Japanese submarines were not working the waters north-east of Guadalcanal at the moment, and the Japanese air force at Rabaul was kept heavily occupied by B-17 raids which, although they did little damage, did manage to keep the planes busy. While Yama-moto was finishing up with the fueling process in the north, Turner came into Lunga Roads at dawn on September 18. The ships brought the 4,000 fresh troops of the 7th Marine Regiment, plus food, tanks, jeeps, field guns, and ammunition. That day, while the transports unloaded, the destroyers *Monssen* and *MacDonough* moved up and down along the shore of Guadalcanal, bombarding all known enemy positions. The damage was not very great except to Japanese morale. For days the Japanese on the island had talked of the coming victory, but the Kawaguchi force had failed to take the airfield, and the Japanese airplanes had skipped two days of bomb-ings, and now the American ships seemed to have control of the sea. The Japanese ashore on Guadalcanal suffered an enormous reverse in morale, which was not helped by the fact that in bringing the troops in night after night during the first two weeks of September, the Jap-anese transports had not brought enough supplies for them and the existing garrison, and food was running short in the Japanese camps.

On the American side the reverse was true. The marines were get-ting three meals a day. Morale had not been higher since the third day of the landing, when the marines had watched the transports deserting them. The reinforcements were like "a shot in the arm," and so were the scores of drums of precious aviation gas. The unit that had suffered more casualties than any of the other marine units on Guadalcanal was the paratroop battalion, which had been hard hit in the desperate fight for Tulagi and then had helped the Raiders hold on Bloody Ridge. The paratroopers were loaded aboard the transports, bound for Nouméa and a rest.

All day long the transports unloaded and loaded, and then at eight o'clock that night they pulled out, for Turner knew well that the nights still belonged to the Japanese Navy.

How right he was. His ships left Lunga Roads at eight o'clock that night, and just after midnight four Japanese destroyers showed up to bombard the island and particularly the airfield once again. This gave a little lift to the Japanese morale, but it would also take rice and some basic supplies and more troops to meet the growing Ameri-can force. But even knowing the state of the American carrier force and of the damage to one American battleship, the Imperial High Command did not make a move in this vital period in September. Even with the 4,000 new troops and a few tanks brought in to replace those destroyed in the battle of Bloody Ridge, the marines were in short supply and short of supplies. It seemed probable they would remain that way until something could be done about the air situation besides simply replacing the fighters destroyed by attrition.

Actually, the Japanese were moving into action. Admiral Yamamoto called more conferences. Admiral Tanaka, who had supervised the piecemeal reinforcement of Guadalcanal, spoke up in disgust and insisted that the army must land at least a division if they wanted to recapture the island and not simply sacrifice Japanese lives. His message got through, and Admiral Yamamoto became a believer. He told the Imperial General Staff that the army must stop thinking in terms of Guadalcanal as a momentary roadblock to the invasion of Papua and the capture of all New Guinea. If the Japanese did not destroy the American presence at Guadalcanal, Yamamoto told Tokyo, the entire war effort would soon be in jeopardy. The army must divert at least a division from its New Guinea operations and might have to employ more troops. But it was essential that the struggle for Guadalcanal be won, or the Papua adventure would most certainly end in failure.

As if to underscore the importance of victory, Admiral Yamamoto reorganized the striking force of the Combined Fleet. What Admiral Ghormley was worried about was certainly true: The Japanese had an eight-to-one carrier advantage over the Americans; but until this time Yamamoto had not taken the American threat seriously enough to bring most of them down. In late September, he ordered Rear Admiral Kakuji Kakuta to come south from Japan to Truk. Kakuta was the commander of the 2nd Air Fleet, and his carriers numbered the 27,500-ton *Hiyo* and *Junyo* and the 13,000-ton *Zuiho*. By Japanese standards these were light carriers, although two of them were as large as the American fleet carriers. These would be added to the 40,000-ton *Zuikaku* and *Shokaku* and give Japan a five-carrier fighting force to add to the battleships and cruisers in the South Pacific. The Americans could not match this strength.

Had Yamamoto made these decisions in August, the battle for Guadalcanal might have ended in Japanese victory by the first of October. But because of the intricacies of the Japanese system of divided commands, the response to the U.S. initiative was extremely slow. The Achilles' heel of the Japanese military-naval system was this failure to achieve unified command on a theater basis. One of the real strengths of the American system was its opposite approach: Admiral Nimitz was in command of the South Pacific operations, and Army, Army Air Force, Marines, and Navy were all directly responsible to him; he was responsible to Admiral King, who in turn had to answer to the Joint Chiefs of Staff, which included the senior officers of all services. To be sure, at Guadalcanal and for the rest of the war in the Pacific, Nimitz struggled with MacArthur for control of operations, but once the control was established by the Joint Chiefs, the Americans operated in general cooperation. As for the Japanese, the cooperation was only at the lowest levels, and became truly operative only when the Japanese forces found themselves in desperate circumstances. Guadalcanal was their most serious challenge to date, but desperation had not yet set in, and so army and navy remained aloof from one another, and neither Admiral Yamamoto nor General Hyukatake knew more than vaguely what each other was doing about Guadalcanal.

Late in September, Yamamoto was preparing for a new operation when word came from Imperial General Headquarters in Tokyo that the Guadalcanal situation was indeed serious, just as Yamamoto had been saying. Headquarters concluded that it called for temporary abandonment of new moves in Papua and full attention to the Solomons, also just as Yamamoto had also been saying. The Imperial Army 2nd Division was ordered from Java to Rabaul to prepare to assault Guadalcanal in an amphibious landing as early as it could be achieved.

Meanwhile, the Japanese did not stop the trickle of reinforcements to Guadalcanal. Virtually every night, the destroyers came down The Slot escorting barges or destroyer transports. Five hundred men landed one night, six hundred the next. By the last week in September the losses of Bloody Ridge had been more than made up by the Japanese forces, and their headquarters area west of the Matanikau sector had received new guns and ammunition. The food supply was still not keeping up with the size of the force, and that was the major problem.

In the air, the last two weeks of September (except for the last two days) were quiet. The rainy season was at its height, and heavy cloud cover interdicted Japanese attacks against Henderson Field. The marine and navy dive bombers took off daily for missions against the Japanese ships coming down The Slot, but they also were hampered so badly by weather that in this period they were ineffective.

On September 21 Admiral McCain was relieved of command of the South Pacific Air Forces by Admiral Fitch, and started back to Washington. McCain was a victim of Admiral King's prejudices and was saved from being sent "out to pasture" only by Nimitz's and Turner's vigorous defense. Even so, King could not forget that the disaster of Savo Island was caused largely by air search failure, and no matter the reason, McCain was the man responsible. For the next two years he would "fly a desk" as chief of the Bureau of Aeronautics in Washington. Although it was a personal tragedy, it was fortunate for the aviators in the field to have in Washington a friend of the fighting men, a man who was more concerned with getting aircraft to the scenes of operations than in shuffling papers.

After McCain was relieved and had started homeward, Admiral Nimitz flew to Palmyra on September 24 to meet McCain and question him about the air situation in the South Pacific. Actually, Nimitz wanted much more information than that; the Commander in Chief of the Pacific Ocean Areas and the Pacific Fleet was on his way to Nouméa to find out what was wrong with the Guadalcanal operation that was making it so costly and so ineffectual.

An indication of the desperation with which Nimitz considered the air problems in Guadalcanal was his inquiry to McCain regarding possible use of the New Zealand Air Force to be integrated into the American force there. Nimitz did not have planes for the New Zealand pilots; McCain told him the services were so different in discipline and outlook that it would never work.

McCain told Nimitz the number one problem in the South Pacific was aircraft, not pilots. Actually, at that moment, the Cactus Air Force needed pilots, but no one outside, not even McCain, understood the severity of the combat fatigue suffered by virtually every man after these six weeks. But McCain did know that planes, parts, and aviation gas had to be on hand and constantly siphoned in to Guadalcanal if the island was to be held.

In his own leathery way, the wizened McCain got across to Nimitz the need to replace Fletcher, and not just on a few weeks temporary duty. "Two or three of these fights are enough for any one man. A rest will do him good," said the air admiral.

One of the big problems in the South Pacific had been the relative ineffectiveness of the B-17 bombers that were so successful in Europe. The Japanese Navy had real contempt for the B-17s. "They never hit anything," said one Japanese officer when his ship was under B-17 attack, and while that was not strictly true, the big plane's bombing results were minimal at this stage of the Pacific War. General Millard Harmon, commander of the South Pacific Army Air Force, was trying to work out a new method to better the B-17s' bombing. The Navy would have liked to see the B-17s abandoned for other planes, but Harmon said that the Army Air Force had too much invested in the B-17 and simply had to make it work in the Pacific as well as the Atlantic. His current thinking was to bring them down low to bomb. At low altitudes their size as a target could pose a danger, but that hazard could be reduced by adopting "weaving" tactics, much like ships' zigzagging, until almost on target. McCain had developed a considerable respect for the B-17 but not for the way they were employed. He had seen pictures taken at Rekata Bay, where the big planes had caught five seaplanes on the water near their tender. The B-17s came in low and strafed; they destroyed the five seaplanes, and one of them attacked the tender, clearing its decks. The bomber was in turn riddled by low-level Japanese antiaircraft fire, but one of the great virtues of the B-17, like the F4F, was its tough hide. With 20 or 30 holes as big as saucers, that one B-17 flew back to its base.

Admiral McCain headed for San Diego. When he got there he talked to Fletcher as Nimitz had asked him to and when he reached Washington he reported back to Nimitz that Fletcher had best have a long rest. Afterwards McCain could report that Fletcher had virtually said so himself. McCain also said he had talked to Admiral King on the telephone and asked for 50 high-altitude fighters to be sent to Guadalcanal right away. That was when King began shouting (a habit for which he was famous in Main Navy, the rickety "temporary" building put up in World War I for an expanding Navy, which was still headquarters in 1942).

Nimitz headed south toward Nouméa, knowing that in McCain he had an ally going to Washington who would try to get every plane possible for the Pacific. The Fletcher matter had been handled

easily. Admiral William Halsey had shown up back at Pearl Harbor
a few days before, hale and hearty after three months in the hospital,
itching to get into action, and Nimitz knew very well that with Halsey in charge of the carrier force in the South Pacific there would be
no need to wonder if his carrier commander was willing to fight. He
had not asked McCain about Ghormley; that would have been most
unseemly, since Ghormley was the area commander. But as Nimitz
went south the question of Ghormley was paramount in his mind.

Admiral Nimitz flew down to Canton Island, and then to
Nouméa, where he arrived on September 28. He wasted no time, but
called a meeting for 4:15 that same afternoon aboard the U.S.S. *Ar-
gonne*, Ghormley's flagship. On hand were Admiral Turner, General
H. H. Arnold, chief of the U.S. Army Air Corps, General Millard
Harmon, and General Sutherland, MacArthur's chief of staff.

Part of Nimitz's reason for coming down was to wring from Mac-
Arthur a greater degree of cooperation than the South Pacific Command was getting from the jealous general. But above that, Nimitz
had to get to the bottom of the command and morale problem. The
meeting lasted four hours, with Nimitz asking hard questions all the
time. He quickly discovered that although Ghormley was the commander of the Guadalcanal force, after two months he had still not
visited the island. Nimitz's displeasure was obvious. He told Ghormley to go to Guadalcanal immediately and see for himself what was
happening there. It was not a request. It was a sharp order.

No detail was too small for Nimitz. He and Ghormley discussed
coastwatchers and torpedo nets, salvage tugs and labor problems—
whether to use native labor, Seabees, or army labor battalions for
construction of roads and trails on Guadalcanal. Ghormley said the
Americans had at least prevented the Japanese from landing troops
in daylight by barge.

Nimitz probed Ghormley's ideas for the future, and Ghormley
made the mistake of saying "can't." If the Japanese wanted to make
a maximum effort to retake the Solomons, he could not stop them,
Ghormley said.

Nimitz said nothing.

Why, the Japanese might even attack Hawaii, Ghormley said.
They were strong enough. The Rabaul area was still alive with troops
—maybe 60,000 of them.

Nimitz said nothing.

Ghormley indicated the Japanese might move 75,000 men against Guadalcanal by small boats.

"But their movement by small boats, you say, has not been successful," Nimitz observed.

Ghormley was silent.

Nimitz asked about plans.

Ghormley replied that until they had Guadalcanal in hand there was no use making plans.

Nimitz said nothing. He remembered that the demand for plans had come from Admiral King in August, and that King was embarrassed because he had been asked by the Joint Chiefs of Staff for future plans for the Solomons. If they were not forthcoming, then the Joint Chiefs might well turn to General MacArthur for the next move. MacArthur had plans and had given assurances that he could carry them out.

The Nimitz-Ghormley meeting broke up, but it was apparent that Nimitz was not pleased.

During the next two days Nimitz fulfilled his obligations as Pacific Fleet commander. He spoke to Admiral Fitch who had just taken over as land-based air commander and was learning the ropes. He awarded medals. He inspected the troops at Nouméa and Espiritu Santo. And on September 30, Admiral Nimitz went to Guadalcanal to see for himself what was happening. He almost didn't make it. The young army B-17 pilot who was assigned to take the Nimitz party to Guadalcanal got lost in heavy weather and had no navigator nor any maps aboard. Nimitz's aide, a string saver, had brought along a *National Geographic* map of the South Pacific, and Captain Ralph Ofstie, Nimitz's air officer, used it as a navigational aid to bring the B-17 into Henderson Field.

Nimitz visited with General Vandegrift, who told him his troubles, but never gave any sign of quitting. He awarded medals and managed to get up to the marine lines and see for himself what his men were up against.

On October 2 he was back in Nouméa for one more meeting with Admiral Ghormley. At that meeting Nimitz urged Ghormley to take a more aggressive stance. He gave him specific instructions, and then he left Nouméa for Pearl Harbor. He had some heavy thinking to do.

11

CAPE ESPERANCE

BACK at Pearl Harbor, Admiral Nimitz sent messages to Admiral Ghormley insisting that Ghormley "put the fleet at risk," which meant that Ghormley was to stop pussyfooting and fight. The *Washington* was the only battleship in the South Pacific then, and Ghormley had sent it out of harm's way. Nimitz said that Task Force 16 must be brought up close to Cape Esperance to protect the transports from Japanese attack. Nimitz also wanted the carrier task force, even though it was reduced to one carrier, to be brought up where it could fight.

Even when Nimitz had been on Guadalcanal, the respite of the closing days of September had begun to end. On the island, the marines encountered Japanese patrols that were obviously probing for information about the American dispositions. On September 30 the Betty bombers were back. The Japanese in Tokyo had begun to pour aircraft into the pipeline for the navy forces at Rabaul despite army opposition to any cutback, even temporary, in their supply of aircraft, which never seemed to get into action.

Still, every night, the Japanese destroyer transports and barges landed supplies and men. The SBDs bombed them, and the P-400s strafed trucks and troops moving along the new roads the Japanese had built. It was apparent to the pilots that Japanese ground activity had increased in the previous week.

On October 2 the coastwatchers were caught unaware, and before anyone knew it, 9 bombers and 36 Zeros swept in from the west. The gong rang at Henderson Field and the American fighter pilots scrambled, but the Japanese fighters caught them from above as they were gaining altitude and shot down six of them, while the Americans shot down 4 Zeros. At the end of the day General Geiger had only 26 operational fighters. The Japanese at that point had nearly 100 Zeros at Rabaul.

The Japanese demonstrated their fighter strength on October 3, when the usual noon bombing raid was escorted by 27 Zeros. But the quality of the pilots was also showing. On this day, the Americans had warning, and they climbed high long before they saw the Japanese, then swooped down on them in the approved diving passes. They shot down nine Zeros—a visiting pilot, Colonel Joseph Bauer, shot down four of them; and then two more Zeros made the mistake of zooming low across Henderson Field to strafe. Both were shot down by the antiaircraft gunners. At the end of this day the picture looked better; two American planes were lost but no pilots.

Back at Rabaul, the enormous loss of 10 percent of the fighter force caused consternation. Admiral Yamamoto from Truk relieved Admiral Tsukahara as commander of the 11th Air Fleet and installed Vice Admiral Jinichi Kusaka in that post. At Truk there was at long last a growing feeling of urgency about Guadalcanal. The nightly resupply from Shortland Island was increased, and Admiral Tanaka carried out the mission day after day, although his grumbling about piecemeal reinforcement was heard clearly at Truk.

On the ground at Guadalcanal action was confined to patrols on both sides, but the size and activity increased. In the air and on the sea, however, it was a different struggle. On the afternoon of October 3, the SBD air searchers found three destroyers speeding toward Guadalcanal, something they had not seen for many weeks. Then, another group sighted an enemy seaplane tender north of the island, escorted by six destroyers.

Back at Henderson Field the bombers were put in the air, and they attacked the seaplane tender *Nisshin* at dusk, but the Japanese antiaircraft gunners were good; they put up such heavy fire that the bombers missed their target. By midnight the Japanese force was at

Cape Esperance and beginning to unload its supplies of tanks, 150-mm howitzers, guns, men, and food. The Cactus Air Force launched another attack just before midnight, but since the night was dark and they didn't make contact with the enemy until late, their bombs missed.

During the last week of September, General Vandegrift planned a move to envelop the Japanese west of the Matanikau River. On September 23, Lt. Col. "Chesty" Puller took his 1st Battalion of the fresh 7th Marines on an expedition that was to move six miles southwest of Henderson Field. The Vandegrift staff was operating on the principle that the Japanese had been badly mauled ten days earlier and would be in no condition to mount a strong defense. But they failed to count on the effectiveness of the nightly resupply program and the high standard of combat readiness of the Japanese reinforcements, all of whom were veterans of previous military action.

Colonel Puller's battalion was supposed to cross the Matanikau River, but failed, and on the night of September 26 reached the mouth of the river. The 1st Raider Battalion had gone upstream that day to cross and join Puller. The 2nd Battalion of the 5th Marines was already at the mouth of the Matanikau as reserve. The Raiders made a long march, but the Japanese were waiting for them atop a hill near the bridge where the Americans intended to cross, and they ambushed the force. Lieutenant Colonel S. B. Griffith, the new commander of the 1st Raiders (Red Mike Edson had been promoted to command the 5th Marines), was wounded in the fierce struggle for that hill, and Major Kenneth Bailey was killed, as were a number of marines. The Raiders retreated to the mouth of the Matanikau. Three companies of the Puller battalion crossed the river the next day by landing boat, landed between two Japanese positions, and were promptly ambushed by the enemy, who got between them and the beach. Surrounded, they suffered many casualties and called for help by spelling out the word with clothing on a grassy meadow. A plane from Henderson Field spotted the HELP sign and reported by radio to General Vandegrift's headquarters. Colonel Puller then took passage on the seaplane tender *Monssen* and found them not far from the beach. By hand semaphore the ship signalled that the marines should move down the coast, while the *Monssen* covered their retreat with its guns.

Under constant fire from Japanese machine guns, mortars, and field pieces, seamen from the *Monssen* brought the marines off the beach in landing boats. Finally the marines had to call Henderson Field for air support to aid the retreat, and by the end of September 28 they were back where they had started, having suffered 60 killed and more than 100 men wounded. At least they had learned that the Japanese had been strongly reinforced.

As for General Hyukatake, he still underestimated the Americans; he believed there might be as many as 7,500 U.S. troops on Guadalcanal, when there were more nearly 20,000. But in order to make fast work of the Americans, the army had decided to use real force and sent in another 15,000-man division, bringing the Japanese force on the island up to about 25,000 men. From the Japanese point of view, the operations of late September and early October were simply holding actions, while they brought in troops from China, Java, and the Philippines to assist in the South Pacific operations. The army had never lost sight of its intention to move in strength against New Guinea, and most of one division would be retained at Rabaul to be used for that purpose as soon as the troublesome gnats were removed from Guadalcanal. Meanwhile, the troops were moving in from the Shortlands, and the major offensive was a few days away.

While Admiral Nimitz had been in Nouméa, he had authorized Ghormley to use any troops he could get to help at Guadalcanal, and from General MacArthur came word that he would send immediately the 164th Regiment of the Americal Division, a National Guard unit. The additional 3,000 troops would help. So that plan was in the works. Admiral Ghormley made arrangements to send them down by transports, protected by the best force he could muster. There was an increased confidence now, too, because in recent weeks the Japanese had been given a thorough working-over on the sea anywhere within 250 miles of Guadalcanal that they happened to appear during the daylight hours. The force of bombers in the MacArthur command had grown much larger, and the bombing had become effective enough that the Japanese could no longer sneer at the B-17s.

On October 4 Admiral Yamamoto was ready to move. That day he issued his operational orders for the invasion and naval and air attack that would drive the Americans off Guadalcanal. General Hyukatake would go to Guadalcanal personally to take over from General Kawaguchi, who had failed to do the job. The general would be accompanied by 22,500 troops of the 2nd Army Division, all of them veterans of Asian action. The first target would be Henderson Field, and after that was taken, the American troops would be fought, defeated, and captured until General Vandegrift surrendered. The Japanese had planned it all. Vandegrift's surrender would come on October 15.

First the air attacks by the 11th Air Fleet would be increased even above the high level of the past week. The battleships *Kongo* and *Haruna* would come to Guadalcanal to bombard the American beachhead, and Admiral Kondo's 2nd Fleet would operate north of Guadalcanal with three carriers, while Admiral Nagumo's 3rd Fleet would operate east of the islands with the *Shokaku* and *Zuikaku*. The cruiser and destroyer resources of the Combined Fleet would be available to take whatever action seemed called for. Lieutenant General Maruyama and General Hyukatake were landed with the troops by the Tokyo Express. The increased Japanese activity was a signal to General Vandegrift that a major offensive was coming, and he deployed six marine battalions to secure control of the Matanikau River. But the Americans and the Japanese had the same idea simultaneously, and on October 8 Vandegrift's marines ran into elements of the Japanese 4th Infantry Regiment and flushed them out, marching up the Matanikau to the crossing point called Nippon Bridge. On October 9 the American troops crossed and marched back down the opposite side of the river. Colonel Puller's battalion trapped a thousand of the troops of the 4th Infantry Regiment in two ravines, and when marine artillery began firing on the Japanese, they tried to escape up the sides of the ravines and ran into marine machine gun fire. In the battle that day 700 Japanese soldiers died. The marines returned to their lines with casualties of about 200 killed and wounded. The Matanikau area seemed secure.

On October 8 the Japanese seaplane tender *Nisshin* made another trip to Guadalcanal and successfully landed heavy guns, tanks, and supplies for the 2nd Division. On October 10, Admiral Kakuta's task force steamed out of Truk with the three carriers to support the Guadalcanal recapture, and that night the last of the 2nd Division was landed at Guadalcanal, bringing almost to a par the numbers of American and Japanese troops on the island, although neither side knew it.

One reason that Admiral Yamamoto had delayed the combined

operation was to secure a new air base at Buin in southern Bougainville. As Yamamoto knew, one major reason for the high Japanese losses in the air battles of the last two months had been the inordinate distance the Japanese planes had to fly to reach the Americans. If a plane was damaged, its chances of making the 500-mile return journey to Rabaul were not good. But with the new fighter bases halfway between Rabaul and Guadalcanal, a much more effective air cover and attack would be possible. From Buin, constant air cover of Japanese operations could be managed on a daily basis. The fighter strip was finished on October 8, and the 11th Air Fleet sent down 30 planes, a combination of Zeros and "Hamps," the carrier version of the Zero.

From October 5, then, the increase in activity at Guadalcanal had been enormous, with the Japanese sending hundreds of planes to Guadalcanal, the marines fighting them off, the Japanese landing forces by night, and the marines trying not very successfully to interdict the landings.

On October 9 Admiral Turner sailed from Nouméa with the 3,000 troops of the Americal Division in his flagship *McCawley* with the transport *Zeitlin* and eight escorts. Their destination was Lunga Roads, and their schedule called for them to pass north of San Cristobal Island, through Lengo Channel, to arrive at the Roads on the morning of October 13.

To protect them, Admiral Turner called on three task forces: the *Hornet*'s force 180 miles southwest of Guadalcanal, the *Washington* and her lesser ships, 50 miles east of Malaita, and Admiral Norman Scott's cruiser force near Rennell Island. Scott, in particular, was to keep his eye on Cape Esperance, and if any enemy ships showed up, he was to attack them.

Scott was travelling in the cruiser *San Francisco* and had with him the heavy cruiser *Salt Lake City* and the light cruisers, *Helena* and *Boise*, and the destroyers *Buchanan, Duncan, Laffey, Farenholt*, and *McCalla*.

The attacks mounted by General Geiger's Cactus Air Force on October 9 and 10 were more than vexing to Admiral Mikawa, and he asked Admiral Kusaka to do something drastic with the 11th Air Fleet to stop the Americans. On October 10 that demand was repeated after 42 American planes attacked the Japanese ships returning from the nightly Tokyo Express run. Not much damage was suffered by the Japanese ships, a few near misses and a few casualties, but Mikawa's exasperation was nearly complete. Since the 11th Air Fleet had failed him, he sent down a task force under the command of Admiral Aritomo Goto to take care of Henderson Field, and, he hoped, to provide sufficient cover so that the night convoy would not be disturbed. The heavy cruisers *Aoba, Kinugasa,* and *Furutaka* and the destroyers *Hatsuyuki* and *Fubuki* were to do the job. This was the night scheduled for delivery to Guadalcanal of the last and largest part of the 2nd Division.

For once, the American air intelligence system was working better than the Japanese. Admiral Mikawa was totally unaware of the American cruiser force lurking off Cape Esperance. Admiral Scott knew of the presence, destination, course, and speed of the two Japanese forces, the reinforcements and the covering warships. By six o'clock that evening, Scott knew that the enemy was less than a hundred miles from Savo Island, and he sped 29 knots to catch them.

The Americans were ready for action this time. As they sped toward Guadalcanal the ships came to action battle stations and made ready for the call "General Quarters" that would signal the fight. The Americans came around the western coast of Guadalcanal, and Scott launched two of his four float planes. The other two were lost due to operational mishap, but the two that did get into the air headed out to find the enemy.

At 10:30 that night Scott's ships were fourteen miles off Cape Esperance, moving toward Savo to intercept the Japanese.

Admiral Goto had warning. When one of the *Salt Lake City's* float planes was launched, somehow the flares she was carrying caught fire, and the plane burned on top of the water. The flames were visible 50 miles away, where Admiral Goto's cruisers and destroyers were moving down, but when a lookout called attention to the flame, the Admiral and his staff decided it must be a signal from the Japanese troops on the beach. He replied with signal blinkers, but did not really suspect a problem even when there was no answer. The Japanese were still suffering from an enormous sense of superiority, which seemed quite justified, for so far on the sea, except for Midway, which was an aerial fight, they had proved themselves far superior to the Americans.

Just before 11 o'clock that night, the *Salt Lake City's* observation plane reported three ships six miles from Savo Island. That was about the end of the usefulness of the float planes. One had engine trouble and had to land, and the other found nothing. Admiral Scott kept cruising between Savo Island and Cape Esperance, waiting. In waiting, the American force became thoroughly confused. The *Helena*'s radar found a target at 11:08, but the *San Francisco*'s radar did not pick it up. Scott continued to maneuver, unaware of the closeness of the enemy. At 11:32 the column turned about, and ten minutes later the captain of the *Helena* announced that he had a target six miles away, heading northwest. Then the *Boise* delivered a strange report speaking of "bogies," which usually meant aircraft, although her captain was speaking of unidentified ships. The destroyers followed Admiral Scott's maneuvers and came up alongside, except for the *Duncan*, whose captain got the impression that the other destroyers had seen the enemy, as he had, and were attacking. The *Duncan* staged a lone attack at 30 knots, straight at the radar contacts.

So the *Duncan* was going one way and the rest of the task force another at 11:45. The American communications got fouled up so that no one seemed to know what anyone else was doing, but at 11:46 the *Helena* opened fire on the radar contacts. None of the Americans knew it, but unwittingly they had "crossed the T" of the Japanese force.

"Crossing the T" is a naval term as old as warfare, and it refers to the use of a ship's guns. When a warship is running south, as the Japanese ships were, its guns trained straight ahead, only the forward guns can be brought to bear on the target. The ideal position for firing is at right angles to the target.

On the night of October 11, Admiral Goto's ships were moving in a column, and suddenly, Admiral Scott's ships crossed the T.

Ideally, the U.S. ships would have stayed in line, which meant every American vessel could bring all its guns to bear on the various Japanese ships, while if the Japanese vessels in the rear fired forward, they might hit one of their own ships. The American position was ideal.

Actually, Admiral Scott achieved it without even knowing it at the time, or until the battle was reconstructed much later. And in fact the crossing of the T lasted only a brief time since the various ships began to maneuver independently, a development that would have made Lord Nelson spin in his coffin in St. Paul's Church in London.

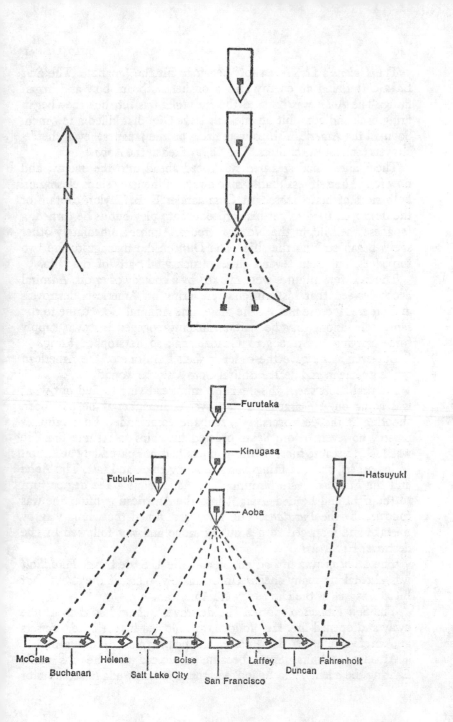

N

Furutaka

Kinugasa

Fubuki

Aoba

Hatsuyuki

McCalla
Buchanan
Helena
Salt Lake City
Boise
San Francisco
Laffey
Duncan
Fahrenholt

The *Helena's* first few shots began to hit the Japanese. The *Salt Lake City* found an enemy cruiser on her starboard bow and began firing. The *Aoba* was hit and the *Furutaka* was hit, but they began firing back and got a hit on the *Salt Lake City* that killed a few men. Soon all the American ships were firing on the Japanese; even the destroyers took on the cruisers. The *Laffey* fired at the *Aoba*.

The *Duncan* had steamed full speed ahead into the enemy, and now found herself less than a mile away, with enemy ships closing on both sides of her. Lieutenant Commander E. B. Taylor, captain of the destroyer, tried to get his torpedoes into play but as he turned, a Japanese shell hit in the No. 1 fireroom. Almost immediately other shells began striking the ship. The *Duncan* did manage to fire two torpedoes, but then several shells struck vital parts of the ship.

The next few minutes were marked by a comedy of errors. Admiral Scott decided that his cruisers were firing on American destroyers and ordered a cease fire. At the same time Admiral Goto came to the same conclusion, that he had mistakenly engaged his own supply force carrying the troops to Guadalcanal, so he stopped firing.

But even as he gave the order, a shell from one of the American cruisers came in and dealt Admiral Goto a mortal wound.

Admiral Scott spent the next few minutes trying to find out what was going on. He asked his destroyer commander if he had been shooting at the destroyers. No, said the commander. Four minutes passed, however, before Scott ordered his ships to resume fire. He was lucky, because most of the gunners had not payed any attention to his orders, and the firing was still going thick and fast. The *Aoba* and the *Furutaka* were burning. The *Aoba* made a 180 degree turn to the right and headed straight into the American gunfire. She was followed by the *Furutaka*. The *Kinugasa* turned the wrong way by mistake and managed to get out of range and was followed by the destroyer *Hatsuyuki*.

The *Duncan* was in bad shape and the U.S. destroyer *Farenholt* was also taking many shells. Unfortunately, most of the shells that hit her, as well as the *Duncan*, were American.

The *San Francisco* spotted the destroyer *Fubuki* less than a mile away and opened fire. Her action was followed by the other cruisers and in five minutes the *Fubuki* stopped, exploded, and sank.

At 11:55 Admiral Scott became convinced that he was really fighting the enemy, and he looked around, then swung his column of

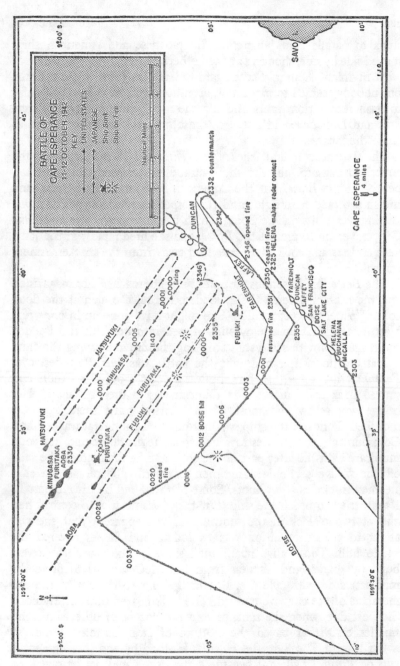

BATTLE OF
CAPE ESPERANCE
11-12 OCTOBER 1942

KEY
UNITED STATES
JAPANESE
Ship Sunk
Ship on Fire

Nautical Miles
0 1 2 3 4 5

HATSUYUKI

KINUGASA 0005
0010

FURUTAKA 1140
0000

0000 firing
2346
0001
0000

2355

FUBUKI

2346 HELENA makes radar contact
2325
2346 opened fire
2350 ceased fire
2351 resumed fire

LAFFEY

FARENHOLT
DUNCAN
LAFFEY
SAN FRANCISCO
BOISE
SALT LAKE CITY
HELENA
BUCHANAN
McCALLA

2355

0001

0003

0006

0012 BOISE hit

0016

0020 ceased fire

0028

0033

AOBA

0030 FURUTAKA

KINUGASA
FURUTAKA
AOBA 2330
HATSUYUKI

DUNCAN
2332 countermarch
2342

FANSHENLT

2303

CAPE ESPERANCE
4 miles

SAVO I.

9°00' S.
05'
45'
10'
05'
9°00' S.

159°30' E.
159°30' E.

ships to parallel the Japanese. The Japanese and American ships moved side by side, shooting at each other.

At midnight Admiral Scott again ordered his ships to cease firing, but nobody seemed to pay much attention until he ordered all ships to flash recognition lights and assume a column formation. *Farenholt* and *Duncan* could not, but the others did, and they began to chase the Japanese.

The Japanese fought back. The *Kinugasa* began firing at the American flagship, but the shells straddled her wake. She sent torpedoes at the *Boise,* but the American lookout spotted them, and the ship turned hard right, and the torpedoes sped away. The *Aoba* got in several hits on the *Boise,* which began to burn. The *Salt Lake City* moved up to protect the *Boise,* and she fired rapidly at the Japanese cruisers and took their attention away from the stricken American ship.

The *Boise* was in serious trouble. Fires approached her magazines, and the captain ordered them flooded, but all the men at the flood control panel had been killed. She might have gone up in one great blast, except that an enemy shell ripped into her hull and flooded the magazines with sea water, stopping the fire and saving the ship.

Half an hour after midnight the battle was over. The destroyer *Farenholt* had a bad list, but she was able to move at 20 knots and started back to Nouméa. The *Duncan* was in dreadful shape. Her bridge was askew and most of the control units there were demolished. Forward, the ship was burning and the metal was red-hot. Communications were destroyed so that the captain could not communicate with the after part of the ship, and he finally took the men off the bridge section. Many men were still aboard, as the ship steamed in circles at 15 knots. Some of them, led by Lt. Herbert R. Kabat, tried to beach the ship, but there was no way to control her, and at two o'clock in the morning, it was apparent that she was about to go. Ammunition was exploding and flames covered the whole hull. Those alive abandoned ship. In the water they were beset by sharks, and rescuers from the *McCalla* had to drive the man-eaters off with rifle fire. But in the end 80 percent of the 250 members of the crew were saved. The hulk floated until nearly noon the next day, when she sank to join the dozens of other ships and smaller craft that paved the bottom of Iron Bottom Sound.

Off toward The Slot, the *Hatsuyuki* stood by and took the survivors off *Furutaka* when it became certain she could not be saved. As dawn came up, the *Aoba* retired. She had been hit more than 30 times, but she still sped along at highest speed, because the captain feared an American air attack as dawn arrived. She left behind the *Fubuki*, which sank, but the destroyers *Shirayuki* and *Murakumo* returned to rescue survivors and picked up 400 men from the *Furutaka* and the *Fubuki*.

As this battle was waged, Admiral T. Joshima, commander of the Japanese reinforcement force, landed his men and 150-mm guns and stores near Kokumbona on Guadalcanal and then turned around. There were still many Japanese in the water, and the Americans tried to rescue them. Some refused, but about 110 Japanese sailors were pulled from the water to become prisoners of war.

When the night battle ended, the American ships requested Ghormley to send air cover at dawn. The Japanese ships headed back to Shortland Island. At 5:15 the next morning 16 bombers and an escort of F4Fs and some P-39s that had just flown in to help the Cactus Air Force strength took off from Henderson Field looking for any Japanese ships that might have been crippled or left behind. As they neared Savo Island they saw a series of oil slicks on the sea, with small boats moving around. They saw one destroyer, dead in the water, burning, and drifting slowly with the current. She was the *Duncan*, and circling around her, with boats out, was the *McCalla*, picking up survivors. The American planes recognized the American ships and did not attack.

North of the Russell Islands, the bombers and fighters came upon the *Shirayuki* and *Murakumo*, which had stayed behind the cruisers to rescue the survivors of *Furutaka* and *Fubuki*. The American bombers peeled off to attack. The first section missed; the second group scored so near a miss on the *Murakumo* that the pilots could see it losing oil, which spun out in a long trail behind as the ship speeded up to escape. At eight o'clock that morning another group of planes found the two destroyers and attacked again. The F4Fs came in strafing the two ships, which attracted the attention of the antiaircraft gunners, while the dive bombers attacked and scored three more near misses on the *Murakumo*. The six new torpedo bombers then attacked, three at the bow of each destroyer in an inverted "V" pattern to give a good chance of a hit no matter which way the destroyer captain turned his vessel. The attack against the *Shirayuki* failed, but that against the *Murakumo* succeeded, and at least one torpedo scored a direct hit. The ship was obviously hit in the boilers, because she came to an abrupt stop and stood, blowing an enormous cloud of steam into the air and smoking from the fires that had been set. She began to list, and by early afternoon she sank.

As the *Murakumo* was sinking, the *Shirayuki* sped on northward to escape and was joined by the *Natsugumo*. The American planes went back to Henderson and were refuelled and rearmed, and in midafternoon set out again to find the enemy destroyers. They discovered them just before 5 o'clock in the afternoon. Ten dive bombers attacked the ships. The *Natsugumo* was hit by a bomb amidships, and the bomb must have found either a magazine or a boiler, because the ship blew up and rolled over. The *Shirayuki* escaped.

Since this battle was the first since Midway in which the Americans had not been roundly defeated, it was hailed in the United States as an enormous victory. The Japanese had lost their oldest cruiser (*Furutaka*) and one of their oldest destroyers (*Fubuki*). The cruiser *Aoba* had to go to Japan for repair. The United States had lost a modern destroyer, the *Duncan*, and the cruiser *Boise* was sent to Philadelphia Navy Yard for repair. The *Salt Lake City*, also damaged, was repaired at Pearl Harbor.

Tactically, then, the Battle of Cape Esperance was an American victory. The Japanese were furious with Admiral Goto for failing to note the signs of the presence of an American task force, but there was nothing they could do to him, since his soul had already gone to the Yasukuni shrine. Admiral Mikawa put the blame on Captain K. Kijima, the successor to command after Goto was mortally wounded, and relieved him, perhaps because he claimed to have sunk two heavy American cruisers and a destroyer when he had not.

Admiral Scott was the luckiest man in the Navy just then, because the victory concealed the bumbling of his tactics. His claim to have sunk four destroyers and two cruisers was accepted for a short time.

But strategically, the Battle of Cape Esperance was at least a standoff for the Japanese. The Americans had not stopped the landing of the major part of the 2nd Japanese Army Division and its heavy equipment. Nor had the Japanese cruiser force stopped the American reinforcement of Guadalcanal. On October 13, at sunrise, Admiral Turner's transports arrived in Lunga Roads bearing that regiment of infantry from the Americal Division. The marines were getting more of the help they so desperately needed.

12

X-DAY

THE reason that Admiral Mikawa was so angry with the dead Admiral Goto and all of Goto's immediate subordinates for the failure at Cape Esperance was far more than a matter of pique, bad temper, or ego. It was a serious setback to Admiral Yamamoto's Plan X. On October 9 Yamamoto had sent staff officers from the flagship *Yamato* to Rabaul to give the orders to the 11th Air Fleet, the 8th Fleet, and to the army, and to answer any questions. Plan X had provided for the combined operations to retake Guadalcanal. On October 12 the army would begin shelling the airfield and so would naval vessels coming in offshore. On October 13 the shelling would be increased dramatically by both army and navy. On the 14th six high-speed transports would arrive at Guadalcanal, anchor, and begin unloading supplies and the last men of the army reinforcement group. On October 15 at 11 o'clock the transports would finish unloading and move back up Sea Lark Channel to the Shortlands. At noon the Japanese army would begin the operation that would overrun the airfield and force the Americans to surrender. During all this operation the 11th Air Fleet and all other aviation organizations would make a maximum effort to strike Henderson Field and keep the American aircraft from operating.

So, Admiral Goto's carelessness had put a monkey wrench in the plan, although in spite of the disgrace of the Cape Esperance "defeat," the Japanese Navy had not really suffered much in that engagement, and for the next few days the Japanese reaped an unexpected harvest from it. The damage to two American cruisers and one destroyer meant that that force had to move back to base, leaving Cape Esperance unguarded. The Japanese Navy then was free to continue the buildup for the major battle it was planning. The 2nd and 3rd Japanese Fleets had left Truk on October 11 to move north and east of the Solomons. The 11th Air Fleet at Rabaul was ordered to make a maximum effort to destroy the U.S. air umbrella that covered The Slot in the daytime, and this meant knocking out the planes of Henderson Field.

On October 12, because of the Cape Esperance defeat, Admiral Yamamoto officially postponed X-Day, but the operation of the fleet air arm and the supply organization continued the same. Admiral Kusaka took his assignment seriously. By this time, the Japanese were well aware of the effectiveness of the Allied coastwatching network. They had tried unsuccessfully to root it out on the ground, but the Australians had built up goodwill with the islanders, who would usually protect or warn them against Japanese land searches. But Kusaka had another means of avoiding raising the alarm. On October 13 he sent the planes on a wide route at high altitude, and when the 27 Betty bombers and 18 Zero fighters came in at noon at 30,000 feet above Henderson Field, General Geiger had only a few minutes to put up 42 F4Fs, but they were still climbing to reach the bomber level when the bombs began to fall. The bombing was very accurate, putting 13 craters in the runway and destroying much of the Marston mat that was so hard to keep in place. (Only this metal matting made the runway usable on wet days by the dive bombers and torpedo bombers.) The bombs also burned a 5,000-gallon fuel dump. As the bombers sped away, one F4F shot down the leader, but was riddled in return, and the pilot, Lt. William Freeman, had to ditch the battered plane. Another pilot shot down a Zero.

The marines were refuelling the fighters, working over the Marston matting, and moving drums of aviation fuel out of the disaster area, when the second raid of the day arrived, 18 twin-engined bombers and 18 Zeros. Captain Joe Foss and the members of Marine Fighter Squadron 121 had just arrived at Henderson Field four days earlier, but they had learned much in those last 96 hours. Operations managed to get a dozen F4Fs in the air, and Foss led them out, shot down one Zero and was nearly shot down by three others, before he landed at such speed that an ambulance chased him down the fighter strip. The dozen fighters scarcely hindered the Japanese bombers. This raid did more damage and destroyed several aircraft. The pilots agreed that it was the most aggressive and damaging series of raids during all the days they had been at Henderson.

Just after dark, a single twin-engined bomber flew across the island, and the antiaircraft guns pounded, and the marines' searchlights stabbed the sky to find it, but the plane completed its mission and flew away. No one knew what the mission was.

An hour later the newly unloaded Japanese 150-mm howitzer mortars began to shell Henderson Field and its environs. The destroyers *Sterett*, *Gwin*, and *Nicholas* were dispatched from the area where Admiral Turner was unloading troops and supplies, to the area west of the Matanikau, and they bombarded what they thought was the firing zone. Soon the howitzers were silent.

While these events occurred, in the darkness off Guadalcanal two Japanese battleships were coming down The Slot. Their target was Henderson Field, and they were instructed to bombard it thoroughly to destroy the American fighters and bombers there.

Vice Admiral Takeo Kurita was in direct charge of the operation. He had nearly 1,000 shells for the 14-inch guns of the *Kongo* and the *Haruna*. As the ships neared the island, Kurita sent aloft one of his float observation planes. Just before midnight of October 13, the marines heard the familiar "Washing Machine Charlie" as the plane flew over the airfield and Iron Bottom Sound, looking to see that no surprises were lying in wait. At one o'clock on October 14, the eight big guns of *Kongo* and the eight big guns of *Haruna* began to fire in a continual roar. The float plane dropped a flare that lighted up the airfield, and observers in the plane and in the mountains gave coordinates to correct the battleships' fire. No part of the airfield was to be untouched this night, Admiral Kurita vowed. The shells started fires in the fuel dumps, and blasted one plane after another in the revetments, which were not well hidden. Marines crouched in the slit trenches and tried to duck down even lower. In the next hour and a half the battleships threw 918 shells at Henderson Field. With this bombardment raging, there was no chance that an aircraft could safely take off and get into the air. Along the shore, marine and navy searchlights tried to find the Japanese ships, but the ships were a mile offshore, and the lights and the gunfire from Guadalcanal were totally ineffective.

Four PT boats had recently been brought to Tulagi to assist in the defense against the Tokyo Express, and these went out to fight. They scurried about the fringes of the battleships' destroyer screen, firing machine guns and torpedoes, and although they did not score any hits, the Japanese destroyers were forced to fire back. The PTs also caused Admiral Kurita some concern. But it was only when he had exhausted his allocated ammunition that Kurita finally ended the bombardment at 2:30 on the morning of October 14 and retired to the north.

When dawn came, and the marines began to count the cost of the bombardment, they found that only 42 planes remained intact of a total of 90 on the field the previous day. Most of the aviation gas had been destroyed, and 41 men had been killed and a hundred wounded. That morning the 150-mm howitzers kept the men at the airfield off balance, and then at noon, once again without warning, Japanese bombers arrived and attacked the airfield again. At the end of this raid, General Geiger announced that the bomber airstrip with the Marston matting was out of service until further notice. All planes would have to use the "cow pasture" that had been used only for the fighters.

The fires at Henderson Field burned all the next day, and the Japanese troops on the island gained an enormous boost in morale. They had messages from Yamamoto and 17th Army Headquarters to expect more reinforcements and a strong attack on the Americans that next night. The Americans had the same sort of dispatches. Admiral Ghormley estimated that six Japanese transports supported by cruisers and destroyers would land thousands of troops on Guadalcanal that night. The Combined Fleet's carriers had been reported 250 miles north of Malaita. Unfortunately, the American carrier force was north of New Caledonia and could not arrive in the area before October 15, and the cruiser force was at Espiritu Santo, and could not arrive until the 16th.

As Admiral Yamamoto had expected, the combination of air raids and bombardment had destroyed the ability of the Cactus Air Force to control the waters around the island. Before the Battle of Cape Esperance, the Japanese had been unable to bring ships down The

Slot in the daylight hours, but on October 14 they had no such fear. Six transports, escorted by destroyers and covered in the air by large flights of Zeros, moved down The Slot unopposed. Of the 39 dive bombers that had been on the field on October 13, 4 dive bombers, 3 P-400s, and 4 P-39s were all that were left. All the torpedo bombers had been destroyed.

At 9:30 on the morning of October 14, the alarm rang, and the fighter planes scrambled. Admiral Kurita's air intelligence had failed in one respect: the little fighter strip had gone unnoticed by the observers, and so of the 42 F4Fs on the ground on the night of October 13, 29 remained operational. The alarm the next morning came from the coastwatchers, but when the fighters got into the air they found nothing, and they came down almost immediately to save precious fuel. Again the search for every quart of aviation gas on the island was pursued and what could be found was poured into the fighter tanks. They were still on the ground when the usual noon raid arrived: 26 Betty bombers attacked the main airstrip, tearing more holes. But again, they did not seem to see the "cow pasture" 100 yards away, and the fighters went unnoticed. The leader of this first raid announced to Rabaul that American air strength on Guadalcanal had been completely destroyed, and so when the next raid of 18 bombers came in an hour later, they were careless. The F4Fs were alerted and waiting in the sky above them. They claimed nine bombers and three Zero fighters. The bombers that escaped did not drop their loads successfully; the raid was a failure.

The search planes in the waters north of Guadalcanal found the transports heading fast down The Slot, and they also spotted Admiral Mikawa's 8th Fleet, the cruisers *Kinugasa* and *Chokai* with two destroyers. Without a force of bombers, there was nothing the Americans could do about it. Undoubtedly, the afternoon of October 14 was the low point of the defense of Guadalcanal. Colonel Toby Munn, General Geiger's aide, drove around the airfield to the bomber and army pilots' quarters and warned them that the situation was desperate. The Japanese were sending troop reinforcements and warships to pound the airfield again. If they sent enough troops and did enough damage to the airfield, the marines might not be able to hold. They had gasoline enough for only one more mission for all the planes; they were to load up the SBDs and the P-400s with bombs and attack the Japanese ships. That would probably be the last mission. Then the aviators would have to join the ground troops in defense of the perimeter.

The bombers and the army planes were patched up that day by mechanics who worked under shelling from the Japanese 150-mm howitzers on the other side of the island. The mechanics "cannibalized" one plane after another and drained the gas out of two wrecked B-17s. From other wrecked planes and from the slender store of remaining drums they got enough fuel. At 2:45 four bombers and the seven army planes took off. They bombed the transport group and did some damage to the destroyer *Samidare* but scarcely enough even to slow her down. They were driven off by the umbrella of Zeros.

By four o'clock in the afternoon, the "cannibal" mechanics had managed to put together nine more bombers. Accompanied by the army planes and fighters, they attacked the transports, but were again driven away by the large force of Zeros, and one of the army planes was shot down. They came back in the dark, and one more army plane crashed on landing. That was the end of air operations for the day.

As darkness covered Guadalcanal, General Vandegrift faced the stark future. The Japanese would land six transports full of troops and supplies, and as matters stood there was no way he could do anything to stop them. He sent a message whose very bleakness told the story: "Urgently necessary that this force receive maximum support of air and surface units."

At Espiritu Santo, Admiral Fitch received that message and looked over the previous files to add up the difficulties of the Cactus Air Force. He had on hand eight bombers from the *Enterprise* air group and nine spare bombers but no pilots to fly them. He solved the problem by ordering fighter pilots of Marine Fighting 212 to ferry the bombers to Guadalcanal, come back by transport plane, and be prepared to move their fighter planes, too, to Guadalcanal at a moment's notice.

Aviation gasoline was on its way to Guadalcanal by barges that had been shipped from Espiritu Santo on October 10, each towed by a tug and accompanied by two cargo ships and two destroyers. But in view of the Japanese control of the sea around Guadalcanal, at 1:30 on the morning of October 14, the commander of the force had told Ghormley the danger was too great to continue the journey. Instead, he suggested sending the barges on with the destroyers *Vireo* and *Meredith* and the old destroyer seaplane tender *McFarland* loaded with drums of aviation gas. Fitch accepted that, and also arranged for an airlift to ferry drums of fuel by transport plane from Espiritu Santo starting the next day. So as the night wore on, the wheels were beginning to move.

But on Guadalcanal the blackness brought nothing but misery. The Japanese, scenting victory, were stirring. Their attack plan called October 15 X-Day, and that was the day the American forces were to be assaulted with enormous force from air, sea, and land.

That night of October 14 the howitzers boomed out their deadly messages, and patrols moved along the marine perimeter seeking weak spots.

Midnight came but not quiet. Then, at 2 o'clock on the morning of October 15, the cruisers *Chokai* and *Kinugasa* arrived on station, a few hundred yards off Guadalcanal, and began firing their eight-inch guns at the airfield. They fired 750 shells at the field, and under that cover, the Japanese transports began unloading their 4,000 troops and more big guns, tanks, and ammunition.

Dawn came, and with it the sight of the Japanese calmly unloading their transports, while the Americans could do nothing to stop them, and an umbrella of Zero fighters circled overhead. They did not bother to strafe Henderson Field, because Admiral Kurita was sure that he had finally destroyed American air power on Guadalcanal. He was very nearly right.

Before the dawn, General Geiger counted airplanes. He had three dive bombers that could still fly. Two of them were filled with gasoline drained from wrecked planes, and one started to taxi up to the head of the "cow pasture." No one noticed the crater in the taxi strip, and the dive bomber rolled into it, smashed undercarriage and wing, and was still. The other plane got to the end of the runway, turned, and pilot Lt. Robert Patterson pulled back the throttle and began moving with increasing speed along the ground. But then a wheel caught in an 8-inch shellhole made by one of the guns of those cruisers, and the plane slewed around into a ground loop, which wrecked it beyond repair.

Lieutenant Patterson begged to take up the last remaining SBD and did manage to take off with a bombload. Although his hydraulic system was leaking, he made an attack, hit one of the transports, and returned safely to the field. The Zeros apparently were so surprised that they paid no attention. But that one SBD on the morning of October 15 represented the striking power of the Cactus Air Force.

That morning General Geiger was beleaguered but not in despair. This tough, stocky marine officer with the heavy crow's feet that marked many hours of looking into the sun from the air was first a marine, then an officer, and then a pilot. He was prepared to fight as long as there was anything with which to fight. His chief of staff, Colonel Louis Woods, had been sent off to Espiritu Santo, where he had been promoted to brigadier general and given a command of his own, but on this desperate day someone on the staff recalled that Louis Woods had cached some gasoline around the island. "By God," said General Geiger, "find some."

So the staff officer went off to find gasoline drums, and Geiger made him take another officer along, so that if one were killed, someone would know the secret of the caches. They found 200 drums of gasoline on the edge of the marine perimeter and another 100 on the beach south of Kukum, where they had been unloaded in an enormous hurry in those first days when the transports sat off the beach. They found other caches, and by noon General Geiger had a two day supply of aviation gasoline, and life was not quite so desperate as it had been. For General Geiger had been an extremely worried man for the past ten days; much later, General Woods returned to Guadalcanal on a visit and found that Geiger was still carrying around a letter he had written about the gasoline caches, unopened.

For the moment, the gasoline problem was solved, but what would General Geiger's pilots fly? That morning the mechanics managed to paste together five F4Fs, which strafed the transports with some effect. One pilot shot down a Japanese float plane. Several bombers were patched up well enough to fly, but one at a time, and they went on dangerous single missions that did not prove effective. General Geiger's second aide, Major Jack Cram, had brought two torpedoes back to Guadalcanal on his last supply mission in the general's personal PBY, but Cram discovered that all of the torpedo planes were wrecked, and that most of the men of the torpedo squadron had gone off to join the marines on the perimeter, convinced that the Cactus Air Force was finished.

The Japanese could raid Henderson Field at will, and General Geiger had neither the planes nor the gasoline to send fighters up every time bombers came over. The situation was so critical that the order was issued that there would be no scramble unless at least 15 bombers came over. Major Cram had the idea that maybe he could drop the two torpedoes from the PBY with a homemade bomb release, and so near desperation was General Geiger, that he agreed to the scheme. Cram took the PBY out to attack, accompanied by several dive bombers, whose attack diverted attention from the slow amphibian. Miraculously, he managed to put one of the torpedoes into the side of a transport, and although attacked by several Zeros, he also managed to bring the bullet-battered PBY back to Henderson Field and land without crashing.

Admiral Fitch did everything he could that day to help Geiger. He sent a flight of 11 B-17s from Espiritu Santo, and they bombed one transport successfully. The dive bombers set fire to another, which meant that three of the six Japanese transports were in trouble.

By two o'clock on the afternoon of October 15, the *Kyushu Maru*, *Sasako Maru*, and *Azumason Maru* were all afire. Admiral Tanaka took stock. He had unloaded all the troops from all the transports and most of the supplies from the three undamaged transports. The American attacks were becoming more frequent and troublesome, so he decided to move out with his undamaged transports and destroyers and leave the three burning ships until night, when he would bring the destroyers back and complete the unloading. So he moved out, and that was the first indication that the Japanese plan to overwhelm Guadalcanal on X-Day had failed.

As the day drew to a close, the Americans again counted planes. They had lost 3 dive bombers, 1 F4F, and 2 P-39s. They had shot down 7 Zeros, the ponderous PBY had torpedoed a ship, and the dive bombers had set another afire. During the afternoon, in spite of Japanese air raids, 3 twin-engined Douglas transports each brought in 12 drums of gasoline. It was not much. A fighter plane used a third of one of those plane loads on a mission. But it was something, and there was something more. Six of those dive bombers from Espiritu Santo appeared, ferried by the fighter pilots. So the Cactus Air Force was still in operation as night fell. General Geiger had 10 SBDs, put in operational condition by heroic mechanics, 4 P-39s, 3 P-400s, and a handful of fighters. The major problem of the moment was still fuel.

The tug *Vireo*, the destroyer *Meredith*, and one of the big gasoline barges were still moving slowly toward Guadalcanal on October 15, although the transports with other supplies had turned back.

These vessels were spotted by a Japanese search plane that morning, and just before noon two bombers attacked. The convoy was just 75 miles from its destination. The captain of the *Meredith* decided to continue, but a few minutes later he was informed that two Japanese warships were close by. He wanted to reverse course then, but the *Vireo* was damaged and could not keep up; he ordered the crew to board the destroyer and prepared to sink the tug. As he was making ready to fire the torpedo, a flight of 27 planes from the Japanese carrier *Zuikaku* attacked and in five minutes sank the *Meredith* with bombs and torpedoes. The *Vireo* and the barge were abandoned, although a few men from the *Meredith* managed to get aboard. Tug and barge drifted down towards Sealark Channel, deserted. The men of the *Meredith* who had survived the attack took to life rafts, and some in the water clung to the rafts. As in the case of all the ships and planes forced down at sea in the Guadalcanal area, the men faced an immediate and serious danger of shark attack, for over hundreds of years the Melanesians had disposed of their dead by setting them afloat at sea, and generations of sharks had acquired a taste for human flesh. As with the survivors of the Battle of Savo Island and the Battle of Cape Esperance the survivors of the *Meredith* were attacked, and in the end of the 275 men of the *Meredith* only 88 survived.

That night of October 15, the cruisers *Myoko* and *Maya* visited Guadalcanal and poured 1,500 eight-inch shells into Henderson Field.

That night morale reached a new low among the Americans on Guadalcanal. Vandegrift reported the bad news to Ghormley. The Japanese had brought in big guns, bigger than anything Vandegrift had. With these guns the Japanese could shell any point on the island, including the airfield. The enemy had control of the sea and was now able to move around day or night and shell at will. If this continued, said Vandegrift, he could not hold out forever. General Geiger had told him that there was no use trying to repair planes if they could not get more gas and no use trying to fly them if the airfield was going to be shelled so heavily. The only effective air strikes as of the afternoon of the 15th could be launched from Espiritu Santo.

That same day Admiral Fitch reported that he was sending away from Espiritu Santo all merchant ships except one oiler. He could no longer guarantee their safety with the Japanese Combined Fleet on the move.

Admiral Nimitz had some idea of how tough it was in those days, and on October 15 he sent Ghormley a message saying that he had sent Admiral Kinkaid south with the *Enterprise* and several capital ships to help. "I realize that this is a difficult phase of our campaign and I have complete faith that we will come out on top."

Nimitz also sent King an urgent message calling for the Joint Chiefs to make available major assistance. But even as he sent it, he knew it would never arrive in time. If the battle was to be won, at least the first phase of it must be won with the forces at hand in the South Pacific. And if he could not change troops, he could change commanders. At the early October meetings Nimitz had not been happy with what he saw of Ghormley's handiwork, and he had the feeling that Ghormley's heart was not in the battle, that he had given up before he began, and each setback only confirmed in Ghormley's mind the "impossibility" of the Guadalcanal invasion. On October 15, Admiral Ghormley sent Nimitz a situation report with a copy to Admiral King, in which he showed his despair. The situation was critical, he said, aviation gas on Guadalcanal was low, enemy surface forces were attacking at night with heavy bombardment, the shore-based aircraft contingent had been reduced to a critically low number, enemy striking forces of an unknown composition were forming south of Truk, and enemy ground forces were infiltrating into Guadalcanal. With the forces available Ghormley could not stop the Japanese if they made a determined effort to break through, he told Nimitz.

If ever there was an admission of defeat, Ghormley had made it. Nimitz had all the same facts from the intercepts of the desperate messages from Fitch and Vandegrift, but Nimitz expected them all somehow to hold on until help arrived. Admiral Ghormley had shaken his confidence. As the Japanese prepared for their all out assault to take the island back from the Americans on the night of October 15, Admiral Nimitz decided to relieve Admiral Ghormley.

13

HALSEY ENTERS

ON the night of October 15, after Nimitz had consulted with his staff and made the painful decision to relieve Admiral Ghormley, he sent Ghormley a message to that effect.

"After carefully weighing all factors have decided that talents and previous experience of Halsey can best be applied to the situation by having him take over duties of COMSOPAC (Commander, South Pacific) as soon as practicable. I greatly appreciate your loyal and devoted efforts towards this accomplishment of a most difficult task. . . ."

Admiral Halsey was then en route to Nouméa by plane, expecting to take over the task forces at sea. Admiral Murray with the *Hornet* task group was on his way to a point northeast of Espiritu Santo to join up with Admiral Kinkaid in the *Enterprise*. Halsey was to take over command of the whole force, and to do so he had brought his old chief of staff, Captain Miles Browning, and his intelligence officer, Marine Colonel Julian Brown. The PBY bringing them down arrived at Nouméa at two o'clock on the afternoon of October 17, and a whaleboat came alongside the plane. Admiral Halsey and his staff stepped in, and an officer immediately handed Halsey a sealed envelope marked MOST SECRET and URGENT. He tore it open there in

the boat and inside found another envelope marked SECRET. Inside
were the orders giving him command of the whole South Pacific.

"Jesus Christ and General Jackson!" Halsey exclaimed. "This is
the hottest potato they ever handed me."

He was under no illusion about the task ahead. Nor was he critical
of Admiral Ghormley's performance. Technically Ghormley was
doing everything that had to be done, that could be done. But as Admiral Nimitz knew better than anyone else after that October visit,
technical performance was not the highest qualification of a successful battle commander. Ghormley had no confidence in the operation, and consequently no confidence in himself or in the ability of
his subordinate commanders to accomplish the difficult task set
them by Admiral King. Halsey had the quality of self-confidence. He
had always had it, since the days at the Naval Academy when he was
the most popular man in his class. There was something about Halsey that inspired confidence, and if he said it could be done, then
men would do it.

Halsey took command of the South Pacific on October 18. The
military situation was no better than it had been three days earlier.
On October 16 the destroyer-seaplane tender *McFarland* arrived at
Guadalcanal carrying 12 torpedoes for the moribund torpedo
bombers, but also crates of 37-mm ammunition for General Vandegrift's guns, and above all, 40,000 gallons of aviation fuel for Henderson Field.

Lieutenant Commander John C. Alderman had not slept well on
the voyage over, sitting on that explosive keg, and he was no more
comfortable at Guadalcanal either. The ship anchored off the beach
at Lunga Point and began discharging gasoline from the ship's tanks
into barge tanks. They were still pumping gas at five o'clock when
someone said he saw a submarine periscope. Captain Alderman decided to move out of the area for the night, and headed away, with
the barge still alongside. Fifty minutes later nine Japanese dive
bombers attacked the *McFarland*, giving Alderman and the crew a
terrible fight. The gunners shot down one dive bomber and damaged
a second, but the planes blew up the gasoline barge and put a bomb
into the ship—luckily at the fantail, where the depth charge racks
were located. The bomb blew up several depth charges, blew off the
rudder, damaged the engines, and threw a cargo of hospital patients
into a panic. These were ambulatory patients, men who were suffer-

ing from what was once called "shell shock" or "battle fatigue," and they scared easily. They very nearly disrupted the crew's efforts to save the ship, but Alderman and his men somehow brought them under control and managed to coax the damaged vessel across the channel into Tulagi harbor pulled at the end by a tow, and saving that precious aviation gasoline in the tender. Several times each day the marines at Henderson Field welcomed the R4D transport planes that shuttled as quickly as possible between Guadalcanal and Espiritu Santo, bringing precious drums of aviation gas. The submarine *Amberjack* was loaded with 9,000 gallons of gasoline and ten tons of aerial bombs and made the voyage. Necessity was obviously the mother of invention; if some of the high command seemed to have given up, the same could not be said of the troops.

On October 16 and 17 the Japanese on Guadalcanal were very quiet. General Hayaguchi's reinforcements had continued to arrive night after night in groups of about 1,000. Although the general was troubled by the beaching of those transports that never could be completely unloaded, and although the bombardment of the Kokumbona area destroyed enough supplies to give him concern, he was busy with his planning. Since the timing for the full-scale attack had been thrown off, X-Day had been allowed to pass and was supplanted by Y-Day. General Hyukatake could not ask for more seasoned troops than he had in General Maruyama's 2nd or Sendai Division from northern Honshu. This division had fought in China, and was famous in Japan and infamous in the rest of the world for its "Rape of Nanking."

General Geiger and Admiral Fitch combined forces with Admiral Murray to try to squelch the Japanese land buildup. On October 16 Geiger sent his ten operable dive bombers against targets on the island. He also sent the seven army planes, which were more useful for striking ground targets than for any other purpose. The Cactus Air Force flew seven ground attack missions that day, with a loss of one SBD. The *Hornet's* planes spent most of the day over the island, striking at troop concentrations and supply dumps. Late in the afternoon, as the *McFarland* had unloaded 20,000 gallons of her gasoline and was being attacked, the dozen fighters of Marine Fighter Squadron 212 flew into Guadalcanal to reinforce Henderson Field. Squadron Commander Joe Bauer saw the Japanese dive bombers attacking the destroyer, went after them, and shot down four of them in a few moments, before landing at Henderson.

On the night of October 16 Pearl Harbor's radio intelligence team intercepted messages indicating that planes from the Japanese carriers *Hiyo* and *Junyo* had been flown in to Buka and would attack Guadalcanal on the morning of October 17. So early that day the F4Fs of Henderson Field were in the air, and at 7:30 the Japanese came over, 18 dive bombers and 18 Zeros. The Americans shot down 6 bombers and 4 Zeros, while losing 1 fighter.

That night of October 17, Admiral Yamamoto sent the Tokyo Express down The Slot once again. Three cruisers and eight destroyers anchored off Tassafaronga, and another five destroyers anchored off Cape Esperance. Several of them shelled the American positions, including the fighter strip, which they seemed finally to have discovered as a separate entity. The shelling kept the American planes from taking to the air while several of the Japanese destroyers landed more thousands of troops.

Admiral Yamamoto had grown more than a little impatient with the army, when General Hyukatake indicated that he was not quite sure when the big land offensive would take place. The Combined Fleet had sailed, and the men expected to fight, but instead, after October 11, they were milling around north of the Solomons waiting for word from the army. Finally Yamamoto had called off X-Day and was now awaiting General Hyukatake's indication of the date on which he would be prepared to take Henderson Field. Hyukatake was so pleased with the navy performance on the night of October 17 that he made the decision: Y-Day would be October 20.

On October 17, the marines were given a hand by the navy when the destroyers *Aaron Ward* and *McCalla* moved in west of Kokumbona in one of the Japanese sectors of the island and did to the enemy what the Japanese destroyers, cruisers, and battleships had been doing to the marines. The two destroyers fired 2,000 rounds of five-inch ammunition at Japanese supply dumps and destroyed large quantities of enemy ammunition and food. General Hyukatake had not yet assessed the damage done by the raid begun by destroyers *Aaron Ward* and *McCalla* and augmented by the Cactus Air Force and *Hornet* planes. The big loss was in transport: trucks and armored vehicles and their fuel supplies had been blown skyhigh, so many of them that Major General Tadashi Sumiyoshi, commander of the 17th Army Artillery, was very much concerned.

That same day, October 17, Admiral Nimitz showed how much he was trying to help: He was at last ordering the diversion of some Pacific Fleet submarines to the Guadalcanal area. He also had suggestions. The Japanese Combined Fleet was dependent on a small number of fleet tankers, and if Admiral Fitch and General MacArthur could send planes after those tankers it might relieve the pressure. Nimitz was getting a new task group of ships built around the new battleship *Indiana*, and he sent that straight from the Atlantic through the Panama Canal to the South Pacific. The 25th Army Infantry Division on Oahu was ordered to move south. From the army, Nimitz got fighter planes and B-17 bombers to augment Fitch's slender forces. They were coming as fast as they could.

In this hour of crisis, even General MacArthur seemed to rouse himself from his policy of minimal cooperation. He had resisted employment of the Brisbane-based submarines for tactical purposes at Guadalcanal, but now he would send them.

All that Halsey had to do was hold out until the help arrived.

Halsey did not need much of Admiral Ghormley's time and no more of his advice. He had brought some staff, and he brought in more of his own men, not to denigrate Ghormley's, but because his own staff knew his ways, and they had not been contaminated by defeatism.

The flagship was the old destroyer tender *Argonne*, but Halsey moved into the former Japanese consulate and set up his headquarters. On October 18 the word began to move through the fleet and to Guadalcanal: Halsey had come! The morale on the island, never apparently as low as that back at headquarters, received a sudden boost. Halsey was one commander that every marine and sailor could respect, for he was aggressive and outspoken in his intent to win the war.

"Kill Japs, Kill Japs, Kill More Japs" was his slogan, and within a matter of hours it had been painted and hung up all over the command, from the walls of Nouméa to the fleet landing at Tulagi.

So the morale of the Americans, most of whom did not know the critical situation, went up. But the morale of those who did know the problems and the deadly nature of the threat posed by Admiral

Yamamoto was another matter, one that would not respond to a gesture.

Halsey took command on October 18. That day he had an inkling of the possible future. Admiral Kusaka sent 15 more Bettys and 9 Zeros to Guadalcanal on the noon raid. The augmented Cactus Air Force, with enough gasoline for a change, shot down 3 bombers and 4 fighters, with the loss of 1 F4F. But the Japanese army was now causing trouble at Henderson, firing with the 150-mm howitzers and other artillery on both runways, so that even the fighter strip was not usable most of that day. General Geiger ordered the engineers to begin construction of another airfield east, out of the range (he thought) of the Japanese guns west of the Matanikau River.

The next day, Guadalcanal was still quiet, but it was the ominous quiet of preparation. On the ground, General Sumiyoshi's attack force was cutting its way through the jungle from the supply area at Kokumbona toward the positions from which it would launch the attack on Henderson Field on the night of October 20. Having lost some of his heavy equipment on the 17th, General Sumiyoshi was finding the Guadalcanal jungle the hardest terrain his men had ever encountered, but they pressed on, day and night.

On October 19, Admiral Halsey called his commanders to Nouméa for a fateful meeting. Much as he wanted to fight, there was no way he could win if the commanders were as depressed about the prospects as Admiral Ghormley had been. Halsey did not say so, but he had no intention of quitting the battle. But he must find out the strengths of his command and be prepared to change if necessary, ruthlessly and without warning.

One by one the commanders came in to Nouméa on October 20. General Vandegrift came from Guadalcanal. Generals Alexander Patch and "Miff" Harmon from the Army came up too. Admiral Kelly Turner came from Espiritu Santo.

Admiral Halsey asked one question:

"Are we going to evacuate or hold?"

Then he looked around the cabin of the *Argonne*, where the commanders sat at the conference table.

"Hold," said General Vandegrift, "if we get the help."

"Hold," said General Harmon.

"Hold," said General Patch.

"Hold," said Admiral Turner. "You'll get the help."

So the meeting was brief and positive. Admiral Halsey sent them all back to their commands with promises that he would do everything possible, and that immediately he would do *something*, and he did. Ghormley had begun the building of an airfield at Ndeni in the Santa Cruz islands. The construction was stopped, and the troops were sent to Guadalcanal to reinforce General Vandegrift's slender perimeter. Next, said Admiral Halsey, he would build a new airfield on Guadalcanal to take the pressure off Henderson Field. And, said Halsey, the carrier forces were now going to come out of mothballs and get into action.

Halsey had come, Halsey had acted, and the skies over the South Pacific seemed somehow immeasurably clearer for it.

14

Y-DAY

ON the night of October 18, the Japanese force heading for Henderson Field had made miserable progress, and at 8:30 on the morning of October 19, General Masao Maruyama had to send a shamefaced message to Admiral Yamamoto, postponing Y-Day, the decisive battle for Guadalcanal's Henderson Field. Sumiyoshi was ready to attack along the line of the Matanikau River; in fact he made a feint on October 19 there to test the marines' line. But Colonel McKelvy's troops had held firm, and the Japanese had lost a tank and several men before they retired to pelt the marines with mortar and artillery fire. Sumiyoshi was not the stumbling block; the trouble lay with the two-pronged drive that was aimed at the envelopment of Henderson Field. Major General Kawaguchi was to lead the eastern prong and Major General Yumio Nasu the western prong. But on the night of October 19 it was apparent that they would never be in position by morning to strike, and it would take them at least two more days to hack their way through the jungle. Even so, they were forced to leave much of their heavy equipment and their heavy guns behind, because the steep mountain trails simply would not accommodate such weight. So General Maruyama set October 22 as Y-Day.

Admiral Yamamoto had kept his end of the bargain. The new

airfield he had ordered for Buin was completed, and 30 new Zero fighters were moved down there, cutting in half their flying time to Guadalcanal. His ships were ready, except Admiral Kakuta's flagship, the carrier *Hiyo*, which suddenly developed a deficiency in her engines. She had been designed as a tanker, and converted on the ways to a carrier, but her power plant had never been adjusted for the extra weight. Admiral Kakuta decided he might have to transfer his flag to the carrier *Junyo* and send *Hiyo* back to Truk to see what could be done with her. That would reduce the Japanese carrier force from five to four against the American two.

The 11th Air Fleet also did its part. On October 20, a force of 30 Zeros swept down from Buin, and into the skies above Henderson Field. The Japanese army artillery was also doing its part; shells kept falling on the Henderson Field main airstrip so that it was unusable. The fighter strip had still not been located by the artillery, and any shells that fell there were accidental. So the F4Fs got into the air and fought the Zeros, and when the usual Rabaul bomber raiders came over at noon, 16 Bettys and another 18 Zeros, they fought them too.

During two and a half months of air fighting on Guadalcanal, there had been one development that worked for the Americans. Over this long period, operating against such geographical odds, the Japanese had sacrificed many pilots, and most of the highly trained navy fighter pilots were gone. That meant the new crop of Zeros was manned by young men without experience, and every day the F4F pilots gained in experience and in confidence. Joe Bauer, who was as confident as any man, told his pilots to get in and dogfight with the Zeros. Two months earlier that advice probably would have cost Foss and his wingmates their lives, but in October they were able to dive, turn, and maneuver with the Japanese and win much of the time. There had been no change in the aircraft of either side.

On October 20 the Japanese lost three bombers and four fighters, while the Americans lost three planes and at least temporarily two pilots.

At Espiritu Santo, Admiral Fitch was sending up as much gas as he could by any means possible. He commandeered two minelayers, the *Southard* and the *Hovey*, had them loaded with 175 drums each, and sent them to Guadalcanal. As the barges came in, they were unloaded and then sent back hastily to Espiritu Santo for another load. The barge towed by the tug *Vireo* on the day the *Meredith* was sunk was discovered floating in the channel, and brought to shore. It held 2,000 drums of aviation gas, about a ten-day supply for the Cactus Air Force.

Again on October 21 Admiral Kusaka's 11th Air Fleet did its job. From Rabaul came the usual noon raid, only 7 Bettys this time, escorted by 20 fighters. The Americans shot down 6 fighters and the antiaircraft guns downed a bomber. Two American planes were lost. In view of the activity along the Matanikau River, the P-400s were sent on ground strafing missions that day and they claimed to have destroyed two antiaircraft batteries.

On that night of October 21, General Sumiyoshi's troops were probing again along the river. They sent several light tanks across the river, but they were pushed back by American 37-mm and 75-mm guns.

That day the Joint Chiefs of Staff in Washington showed some new appreciation of the importance of the Guadalcanal battle. In spite of the demands of General Eisenhower and others in the European theater, Admiral King managed to get some new assignments. There would be two groups of heavy army bombers, which meant 70 planes, and two groups of army fighters, which meant 150 planes, one group of medium bombers, or 52 planes, and five squadrons of patrol bombers, or 60 planes, plus about 1,000 navy planes. But the trouble was that they would not begin arriving until the following month, and the problem was immediate.

On October 22, the new Y-Day as proclaimed by General Hyukatake, the Japanese kept up the pressure, but the flying weather made it impossible for any aircraft to operate effectively that day.

Once more General Maruyama's force was not ready for the "decisive attack" on October 22, and Admiral Yamamoto had another false start. Admiral Kakuta did transfer his flag, and the *Hiyo* went limping back to Truk to see what could be done to make her fleetworthy.

On October 23 Admiral Kurita again dispatched 16 twin-engined bombers with 28 Zeros to strike Henderson Field. On this day the F4F pilots outdid themselves. They put up 3 eight-plane flights of F4Fs and 4 P-39s, and they went after the Zeros in dogfights, no matter the violation of navy fighter doctrine. The planes suffered—one F4F was virtually destroyed in the air although the pilot got back safely, and seven others were damaged. But the pilots all came back that day, and they claimed 20 Zeros—a figure that as usual with pilots was more effusive than accurate. But the marines on the line in Guadalcanal could attest to the smoke plumes that followed Zero after Zero down to the ground and the explosions that sent clouds of flame and smoke above the island when the planes hit. One Japanese pilot parachuted from his burning plane and floated down behind the Japanese lines.

Once again, Admiral Kurita's 11th Air Fleet had made the "maximum effort" called for in the battle orders from Admiral Yamamoto. Once again the surface fleet had word at the last moment to hold up, for the ground troops were not ready. The new date set for the all-out attack was October 24.

Admiral Yamamoto's search planes had been keeping good track of U.S. Admiral A. W. Lee's Task Force 64, built around the battleship *Washington* and the cruiser *Atlanta*. That day "Ching" Lee was about to move out to meet Admiral Scott and his cruiser force. They would patrol south of Guadalcanal, but be prepared to move up and engage any enemy force trying to run through The Slot. Admiral Yamamoto was concerned, because the Americans were doing just what he did, and they had managed to conceal from him the whereabouts of their carrier force. It had been a long time since his planes had sighted a carrier, and he did not at this point know how many he might be facing. In fact, on October 23, the American carriers were 1000 miles southwest of the Japanese fleet, just below the New Hebrides. Admiral Murray still commanded the *Hornet*, and Admiral Kinkaid the *Enterprise*, but with Admiral Halsey in command of the South Pacific forces, he in effect was the commander of the carriers, and he issued specific orders to the two groups: they were to run along the New Hebrides, around the Santa Cruz Islands, and then head southwest to cover Guadalcanal.

On October 23 Admiral Halsey also had several American submarines at his disposal, unlike during the previous months, and he put them out on patrol in the waters north, east, and west of Guadalcanal to watch for the Japanese fleet.

On the morning of October 24, the Japanese troops who had been assigned the pincers operation against Henderson Field were still struggling to reach their jumping off place for the major attack. General Sumiyoshi's troops attacked again, believing that the major assault had begun. The marines called for artillery and air support, and the field guns began to work over an area on a ridge, and army planes came in to bomb and strafe. General Sumiyoshi was stalled again.

General Maruyama's 2nd Division of the 17th Army had marched for ten days, but they had made only a little more than ten miles progress by that morning. The terrain had been unbelievable, up one steep ridge, down into a gulch, over the stream that flowed there, back up another ridge and down again, all the while cutting through the dense mass of trees, bushes, thorns, and creepers that were slippery and wet. The Japanese soldiers' canvas and rubber shoes slipped on the rotten jungle floor, and hauling the heavy equipment across gullies and three major streams had been exhausting work. Late on the morning of October 24, they arrived finally before Bloody Ridge, and were ready to launch the attack.

Colonel Chesty Puller had disposed 1st Battalion of the 7th Marines along a wide U-shaped line on the south side of Henderson Field with Bloody Ridge well enclosed in the perimeter. The marines were dug in along the edge of the jungle and the west bank of the Tenaru River. The Army's 164th Infantry Regiment was posted at the end of the river line, with one battalion in reserve.

During the past week while they had been waiting, the marines had hacked out fields of fire across the tall grass that led out south from the jungle. They had strung barbed wire and put an outpost patrol of about 50 marines on the top of the grassy hill 3,000 yards ahead of the line. The outpost and the marine pickets were connected to the main line by lengths of string that could be pulled to announce the coming of the enemy. Along the barbed wire, the marines had hung bits of metal that would clink and clank if the Japanese tried to sneak through.

At midmorning on October 24, the outpost saw signs of Japanese activity. General Nasu's left flanking troops had arrived at the jumpoff point, and they were milling about, waiting for General Kawaguchi's right flank attack force to come up.

General Nasu waited all day for the Kawaguchi troops, but they did not come. Finally, General Nasu decided he could wait no longer; it was inconceivable that Y-Day could be postponed again. His scouts and patrols reported that the thinnest part of the American line was located at the point where the jungle met the grassy field. General Nasu selected that point for a frontal attack. Without

Kawaguchi the pronged drive was out of the question. He attacked at 9:30 at night, in a driving rainstorm. The marines on the hill out front gave the warning, and fought to hold, then those who could fell back, because the hill and the entire position were overrun by Japanese troops rushing into the marine line. The point of the attack was the corner (the marines called it Coffin Corner) where the lines emerged into the grass from the jungle. The Japanese charged with bayonets, grenades, and samurai swords, and the marines aimed their machine guns and rifles and mowed them down as they came. In the darkness the tinkling of metal could be heard as some Japanese came through the wire and attacked the marines in their foxholes and entrenched positions. But the marines were ready for hand-to-hand combat. The Japanese stormed up shouting and screaming; the marines were silent except for their weapons. But one Japanese company-sized unit managed to get through the lines and behind the marines to the edge of Henderson Field. The colonel who led them sent back a message that Henderson Field, at long last, was in Japanese hands, and General Maruyama passed it to General Hyukatake, and he sent the message along to Admiral Yamamoto, whose fleet was waiting, itching to move.

The Japanese push threatened the slender American line, and Colonel Puller began bringing up small units of the reserve battalion of the 164th Infantry to plug holes as they developed. The Japanese attacked and were driven off, fell back, reformed, and attacked again. Altogether that night they attacked six times, and each time, except for the colonel and his men who had gotten through the perimeter, they were driven back. At sometime during the night, General Nasu saw that his attack was failing, and he led his men out personally and fell with them in the battle. Finally the Japanese retreated. The next day, the marines counted 1,000 bodies along the line of attack.

The next morning, General Kawaguchi's brigade began to arrive at the assembly point. The Y-Day plan was already a failure as he could see, and there was no question about running a two-pronged attack. He prepared to send his men in a frontal attack against the line south of Henderson Field.

On October 24th the Cactus Air Force had been unable to operate with any effectiveness. The rain had pelted down all day, so the planes had flown only a handful of individual missions in fire support of the marines. That night, once again the Japanese sent barges with supplies and more men to press the attack. At Coffin Corner the Japanese renewed the assault, but during the day Colonel Puller had brought in more troops from the 164th Infantry, and the line held, while more Japanese were killed in wave after wave. A part of the Sumiyoshi force split off that night to try to outflank Colonel McKelvy's troops, but they ran into the 2nd Battalion of the 7th Marines, who had been pulled back to a defensive position east of the Matanikau to guard the McKelvy flank. The Japanese managed to take one important ridge and place several machine guns on the high ground. The marines enlisted the fighting support of the cooks and headquarters personnel early on October 26, and that crew of fewer than 20 men braved the hill with hand grenades and recaptured it.

The misinformation about the capture of the airfield had caused Admiral Yamamoto to put the fleet in motion. His battle plan called for the 8th Fleet to move immediately down to a point 150 miles northwest of Guadalcanal and the 2nd Fleet to move to a point equidistant from the island on the northeast. Meanwhile Rear Admiral Tamotsu Takama's Destroyer Squadron Four would advance to Guadalcanal to support General Maruyama's troops with gunfire where necessary.

Although the brief message had been sent claiming the capture of Henderson Field on the afternoon of October 24, Admiral Nagumo was not at all sure. He had suffered nothing but disappointment since the debacle at Midway, and now, in his cabin aboard the *Shokaku*, he wondered if the army really had managed to take the airfield. Nothing more had been heard since that one message.

That day one of the admiral's radiomen who read English had copied down a United Press radiogram. The United Press was still serving many clients in the Pacific, war or no war, including newspapers in Australia, and those periodicals received the service by radio every day. In the U.P. report of October 24, the operator had noted a story from Hawaii indicating that the United States Navy was preparing for a major sea battle in the South Pacific. It could have been pure propaganda, of course, but the operator took it down and delivered it to the Nagumo staff. The admiral also had kept track of all the sightings of U.S. warships in the past two weeks, and they added up to a powerful fleet of at least two carriers, probably three battleships, perhaps eight cruisers, anywhere from fifteen to twenty destroyers, plus seaplane tenders and other unidentified ships. But in the past week, the search planes had completely lost track of the American carriers, and Nagumo, having learned at Midway that it was never wise to make any assumptions as to the whereabouts of the enemy, was a worried man. He became more concerned when the radio operators reported large numbers of coded messages in the air. That meant that the American forces were up to some action. (What Nagumo's staff was getting was the spate of messages sent out by Admiral Halsey in the reorganization of the South Pacific Forces for the battle that was obviously coming up.)

One of Nagumo's staff officers suggested that he send a message to Combined Fleet raising some of these worries. Nagumo did send such a message to Admiral Ugaki, Yamamoto's chief of staff. Nagumo pointed out that they were moving ahead blindly in the assurance that Henderson Field had been captured. But had it really? And where were the American carriers? Nagumo suggested that they stop moving south until they had some definite word about the enemy.

When Admiral Yamamoto received that message from his chief of staff, he was in no mood to listen. He still held Nagumo personally responsible for the Midway defeat, and he was not about to listen to counsels of timidity. He told Ugaki to send Nagumo a message ordering him to proceed quickly to find the enemy. That settled the matter.

On that night of October 24, the Japanese carriers and their attending ships fueled, and they were almost ready to move when a staff officer rushed a message to the admiral, reporting the destruction of an American carrier scout plane. Nagumo was up from his bunk in a flash.

"Stop refueling," he ordered. "Turn the carrier and head due north."

So at dawn, the Japanese carrier force began steaming directly away from the enemy. He slowed only to send out scout planes in all directions to make sure that he was not surprised again at the Solomons as he had been at Midway. They found nothing, and the American planes that came out searching later also found nothing where the Nagumo force had been a few hours earlier.

Nagumo headed north for 12 hours until he was certain that he

Japanese soldiers killed in the Battle of Tenaru, August 21, 1942.

Copy of a photo found on a Japanese captured on Guadalcanal.

Raiders' Ridge (looking north), Guadalcanal Island. This photo was taken from the second Raiders' position, held throughout the battle. Some Japanese got behind the position and attacked, and for a time the Raiders were cut off. But the Japanese were forced to retreat and contact was reestablished September 13, 14, 1942.

Japanese POWs. A very low percentage of Japanese troops surrender. Most preferred to die for the Emperor.

Small Marine tanks on Guadalcanal.

A captured Japanese tank.

Running a gauntlet of anti-aircraft fire, four Japanese bombers com
in low at Guadalcanal to attack U.S. transports at extreme left.

Amphibian tractors come ashore at Guadalcanal.

Sinking of the carrier *Wasp*, torpedoed on September 15, 1942 while covering the movement of supplies and reinforcements to Guadalcanal.

Major General
Vandegrift, left, con-
venes a staff meeting
on a transport.

General Vandegrift in his tent on Guadalcanal.

A Japanese Betty bomber.

American troops waiting out a Japanese air raid.

Major Gregory "Pappy" Boyington and his pilots at Henderson Field.

The planes of the Cactus Air Force were often all that stood between the Americans and defeat.

was beyond attack. Then he stopped, completed the fueling, and turned south once more.

That morning, as the sun rose, Henderson Field was still shut down. The Japanese artillery was firing on the runway every ten minutes, and the fighter strip, which was not covered with Marston matting, had been turned into a mud flat by the two days of rain. The strip could be used, but not very many planes would be able to take off. The decision was made to fly off six dive bombers. They left at dawn on the regular morning search around the waters of the island. Not fifteen mintues after takeoff one of the planes sighted Admiral Takama's destroyers in The Slot. They were rushing down on Guadalcanal at 20 knots.

Back at Rabaul that early morning, Admiral Kurita acted on the basis of the information from the army that Henderson Field was occupied by Japanese troops. He sent down a reconnaissance plane with an escort of eight Zeros to inspect the field. Below, the observers could see the main strip, badly holed by shells and bombs. They saw many wrecked aircraft around the perimeter and some that looked whole. But no planes rose in the air. The big twin-engined bomber came down low, and made a long slow sweep along the length of the central runway and then came along the fighter runway, right down "on the deck."

As the Japanese plane came winging over, every gun on Henderson Field was firing at it, and at the end of the runway, the plane pulled up as if to gain altitude, then suddenly dropped one wing and dove straight into the ground to explode with what to the marines was a most satisfying roar. The Zeros circled above, keeping the American planes down, or so they thought. What was actually keeping the American fighters grounded was the state of the runway. It would take several hours of baking sun to dry out the mud.

Two hours later, the fighter pilots decided the field was dry enough to support takeoffs. Five F4Fs took off, led by Captain Joe Foss, and by sticking close together, turning into the Japanese, and firing every time the Zeros came at them, they managed to gain 6,000 feet of altitude and then had room to engage the enemy. They shot down several of the Zeros.

The speeding Japanese destroyers stopped off at Lunga Point to destroy the tug *Seminole* and a small patrol boat that had been enlisted to carry gasoline. Two old four-stack destroyers carrying supplies were very nearly caught at Lunga Point, but managed to escape under the cover of an air attack against Admiral Takama's ships by a handful of fighters from Henderson Field. The planes buzzed around the Japanese ships like gnats, and disconcerted them so that they lost track of the old American supply destroyers, which managed to get away. The Japanese ships were also harried by the marine shore guns, and one five-inch gun put three shells into one destroyer, causing the Japanese to move away from the shore.

In Admiral Kusaka's mind, Guadalcanal's airfield was held by the Japanese, and as noon came no one had informed him to the contrary, so he continued to send in Zeros to land at the field. Not being able to land, they circled around and engaged the Americans as they took off and landed. The rate of attrition on both sides was high that day.

At noon, a group of five dive bombers took off from the half-dried field to attack the Japanese ships in The Slot. They found the three destroyers, and then Admiral Takama's flagship, the light cruiser *Yura* and five more destroyers. They attacked. Lieutenant Commander John Eldridge, Jr., made one of the first runs, and bombed the *Yura* squarely with his 1,000-pound bomb. The ship was hit hard in the after engine room, and she slowed to a crawl. Another bomber dropped on the destroyer *Akizuki* and damaged that ship. The Japanese turned to escape, but more American planes appeared, and they attacked again. They scored near misses and added to the damage. That afternoon the captain of the *Yura* was trying to beach her near Santa Isabel Island, which was in Japanese hands, but he was caught by a group of planes from Henderson Field, and then by six B-17s. The near misses and the bomb hits were too much for her; she began to burn from end to end, the crew abandoned ship, and she was sunk by two Japanese destroyers.

The *Akizuki*, which had been dodging planes and bombs all afternoon with relative success after that first hit, managed to crawl back to Shortland Island, and the rest of the destroyer squadron sped back up The Slot as well.

At the end of the day General Geiger reported on the activity to Admiral Fitch. The report was one paragraph long and only hinted at what had been happening:

"Enemy fighter planes over area at irregular intervals since seven o'clock. 17 destroyed. 16 heavy bombers here at 2:30. Five bombers shot down. 9 bombers Aichi class (dive bombers) attacked 3 P.M. Only minor damage by bombs. Two Grumman pilots jumped. Both rescued."

That terse report summarized the busiest day the Cactus Air Force had ever had. Antiaircraft gunners scarcely left their guns all day long. The mechanics no sooner got a plane airborne than another was coming in, probably shot up, for rearming, regassing, and even repair. Japanese planes swooped down during this work to strafe, and the mechanics ducked under wings or into slit trenches. As for those two Grumman pilots who bailed out, each had a story. Here is one of them:

Lieutenant J. E. Conger was flying over the water off Guadalcanal when he was attacked by a Zero. Conger was out of ammunition, but he still had to escape. In maneuvering, he found himself suddenly below on his enemy's tail at close range, and he started to climb sharply. His propeller chewed off a hunk of the Zero's tail, and then flew into a thousand pieces. The two fighters began to spin down out of control, and both pilots took to their parachutes. A landing boat picked up the marine lieutenant, and then headed over to the point in the water where the Japanese pilot had landed. When the boat arrived, the pilot tried to kick it away. Someone snagged the pilot with a boat hook, but he pulled out a pistol and tried to shoot his rescuer. The pistol didn't fire. The pilot tried to shoot himself. The pistol still didn't fire. A sailor grabbed the pistol, and another grabbed the pilot, and the marines had another prisoner of war.

Y-Day had ended. It had been a complete failure for the Japanese; they had not captured the airfield, nor had they cleared the skies of American planes, nor had they exerted any force against the American fleet.

Rather, they had lost at least 3,000 men in the attacks against the American perimeter, while the American casualties were about 500 killed and wounded. During the air combat that day, the cost had been high. General Geiger had 35 fighters that morning; at night he had 12 left, plus 11 dive bombers and 6 army planes. The Japanese in the last few days had lost more than 100 planes, and the 11th Air Fleet force was so reduced it could not launch another major attack against Guadalcanal. The Japanese surface fleet had lost a cruiser and once again learned the lesson that as long as the Americans controlled Henderson Field they could not move in the waters around Guadalcanal during daylight. So the decisive attack planned by Admiral Yamamoto and General Hyukatake had come to nothing, and the war was just about to enter a new phase.

15

SANTA CRUZ

AT two o'clock on the morning of October 26, two PBYs of Admiral Fitch's land-based air force searched for the Japanese carriers as they headed south again in response to Admiral Yamamoto's orders. These big flying boats were an experiment of sorts, part of a new PBY night striking force that had been devised in the desperation of plane shortages. They carried bombs and torpedoes, slung under their long wings.

It was a hot night aboard the Japanese ships, and the sailors were restless. Admiral Nagumo was sitting in his cabin, surrounded by staff officers and worrying because he was once again heading toward the enemy and still did not know where they were. The memory of Midway rested heavily on his mind. From time to time, an officer slipped into the room to report that enemy radio traffic was still heavy but indeterminate in direction.

The sky was clear that night and the moon bright as two of the PBYs headed north. Suddenly, one of the pilots saw ships gleaming on the silvery surface of the sea, and as his eyes focused, he saw two big carriers. He put the PBY into a dive and headed for the nearest carrier, and when he approached at low altitude, he pulled the release lanyard and four bombs fell close enough alongside the carrier *Zuikaku* to send geysers of water at her bridge.

Aboard the flagship *Shokaku*, the air raid alarm blasted every man from his rest. One of Admiral Nagumo's staff officers rushed to the flag bridge just in time to see the waterspouts. He did not see the torpedo launched by the second PBY, which missed the *Zuikaku* because the hastily contrived firing apparatus was defective.

But from a defensive point of view, the results of the impromptu air raid were all that an American could wish. Admiral Nagumo seemed to be riveted to his chair in his cabin. The staff officer returned to announce with relief that the *Zuikaku* had escaped damage.

"Let's turn around," said Admiral Nagumo, and his staff agreed enthusiastically. In a few moments the signal blinkers of the flagship began to work.

"All ships turn 180 degrees starboard. Speed 24 knots. Course 360°."

The Japanese 3rd Fleet, the main carrier striking force of the Combined Fleet, was heading due north, directly away from the enemy. It consisted of the carriers *Shokaku* and *Zuikaku*, the light carrier *Zuiho*, and a screen of warships. South of them was a force of battleships, cruisers, and destroyers that were to protect the carriers from attack by offering an imposing target.

Admiral Nagumo, who had not seen the attacking planes, had assumed that they were from a carrier and that at any moment he might feel the weight of an enemy air strike. But the minutes passed and then the hours, and nothing happened. On hearing that the carriers were moving north, Admiral Kondo, commander of the 2nd Fleet, also turned around and headed north. Kondo's ships and Mikawa's were then a little less than 200 miles from the American carriers and a hundred miles from each other. Kondo's force consisted of two battleships, five cruisers, destroyers, and the carrier *Junyo*, commanded by Rear Admiral Kakuji Kakuta.

Admiral Kinkaid's carrier force was concentrated, unlike the Japanese force. The *Enterprise*, Kinkaid's flagship, was accompanied by four cruisers and six destroyers. The *Hornet* was screened by more ships, but altogether the two Japanese fleets heavily outnumbered the American. In a surface battle they would have an enormous advantage; in an air battle they would have an advantage, too, because the Japanese carriers mounted 212 planes and the Americans only 172. In addition, the pilots of the *Shokaku* and the *Zuikaku* were the cream of the Japanese naval air force, and their experience went back to the Pearl Harbor raid.

As the American carrier force steamed north that night, they were looking for the Japanese without success. All day long on October 25 they had searched. At noon a PBY from Espiritu Santo reported directly to the fleet the sighting of two carriers and attendant ships heading southeast. At that time the American ships were 360 miles away. They headed toward the position indicated, but by then Nagumo had turned around, and gone north for the first time.

At 2:30 in the afternoon, Kinkaid had sent 12 bombers searching for the Japanese. But the search planes' radius of 200 miles was not enough, and they found nothing. An hour later, Kinkaid sent off an attack in the hope that these planes would find the Japanese carriers if the others had not. A dozen dive bombers, 6 torpedo planes, and 11 fighters took off from the *Enterprise*. But at the end of their radius they found nothing, and when they returned, darkness had fallen, and the Americans witnessed an example of the tragedy of their training tactics: seven aircraft and one pilot were lost as the planes tried desperately to make unfamiliar night landings. The *Enterprise*'s Air Group 10 was the first of the new crop of navy pilots to get through training in the U.S. and be assigned to the Pacific.

The American fleet was west of the Santa Cruz Islands, north of the New Hebrides, and southeast of the Solomons. Admiral Kinkaid headed north at 20 knots, and so during the night after Nagumo turned north for the second time, the Japanese kept the distance between the fleets.

The PBYs kept contact with the Japanese carriers. At one o'clock in the morning one PBY reported "enemy" and gave coordinates. But which enemy? Kinkaid wanted the carriers. He waited that night as they moved north. At 3 o'clock one of the PBYs reported on the enemy and mentioned the carriers, and the report went back to Espiritu Santo. But there, once again, American communications failed, and the report was delayed in reaching Admiral Kinkaid until five o'clock. All night long a striking force of bombers and fighters from the *Hornet*'s experienced air group was waiting for the word to attack; it did not come.

Back at Nouméa, Admiral Halsey was at his desk, reading the dispatches, and he saw the report of the PBY. He sent out a single message to all ships.

"Attack—Repeat—Attack."

There could be no question in Admiral Kinkaid's mind as to what was wanted this day. Although the sun would not rise for another half hour, at 5:12 Admiral Kinkaid launched an air search of 16 dive bombers carrying the usual 500-pound bombs. He had lost an invaluable two hours' advantage through the communications confusion.

An hour earlier the Japanese battleship group had moved. The credit must go to Admiral Hiroaki Abe, commander of the battleships that had been interposed between the carrier striking force and the probable position of the Americans. At 4:15 Abe launched seven float planes to search for the enemy. The report seemed to galvanize Admiral Nagumo into action. He ordered 13 scout planes launched from the *Shokaku* and *Zuikaku*, and once again turned the Japanese fleet southward to seek battle. The operations officers of the two carriers were told to be ready to launch a strike on a moment's notice, and the pilots got their gear. Admiral Nagumo donned his uniform, complete with white gloves, and left his cabin to go to the bridge.

By 5:30 in the morning, as the sun shed a growing light on the South Pacific, the planes of the opposing fleets were fanned out, searching for each other.

The American dive bombers were searching in pairs. About 85 miles out from the *Enterprise* two of her planes spotted a Japanese bomber heading toward their carrier. The planes were piloted by Lt. V. W. Welch and Lt. (jg) Bruce McGraw. No one had instructed them to break off a search pattern to attack an enemy plane, even so close to the ships, so they didn't and flew on. The Japanese plane took their reverse course and soon found the *Enterprise*. Meanwhile, one of the float planes from Abe's battleships had found the *Hornet*, and the carrier nature of two of the American search planes had been noted. Aboard the *Shokaku* and *Zuikaku*, 67 planes were ready to go. Just before seven o'clock the *Shokaku* scout plane that had passed the two American scouts reported:

"Large enemy force at KH 17 [Japanese grid coordinates]. Force consists of one *Saratoga*-class carrier and 15 other ships heading northwest."

Admiral Nagumo felt relieved and justified when he plotted the American position and found it was only 210 miles away and northeast of him. If he had continued to run south on the 25th instead of turning around twice, he told his staff, they most certainly would have been trapped by the enemy. If the reasoning was specious, it nevertheless restored his confidence, and he was swift to act. Within 12 minutes the air strike was leaving the Japanese carrier decks. Admiral Nagumo could still remember how indecision had kept his carrier decks crowded with planes at Midway and helped to cause the disaster. On this day the 67 fighters and bombers were all off the deck within fifteen minutes of the launch of the first plane.

After passing the Japanese scout bomber, pilots Welch and McGraw had continued on their assigned task, and at 6:17 they saw Admiral Abe's battleships and cruisers below. It would have been easy for them to assume that *this* was the Japanese force, but they did not take Admiral Yamamoto's bait and flew on. They reported back at 6:30 that they had seen the battleships, moved to the end of their sector, and did not find anything else. On their way back to the carrier they passed over the Abe force again and this time drew antiaircraft fire, but it did not stop them. On the way home they passed the Japanese scout bomber again, and again they ignored it. This time it would have made no difference; the damage was done when the bomber had sighted the *Enterprise*.

At 6:50, as the Japanese scout bomber was reporting to Admiral Nagumo on the discovery of the *Enterprise*, two American scout bombers discovered the Japanese carriers to the west of the Americans. They attacked but were attacked in turn by the Japanese fighters of the combat air patrol, and escaped by ducking into clouds. Two other American scouts, who had found nothing in their search, heard the American broadcast to the *Enterprise* and came over to join the attack on the Japanese carriers. Lieutenant Stockton Strong and Ens. Charles Irvine came through the clouds, undetected, and before the combat air patrol could intercept them, they had bombed the *Zuiho*. One bomb went through the flight deck and blew a fifty-foot hole upward that made it impossible for the *Zuiho* to recover aircraft. The captain reported this sad state of affairs to Admiral Nagumo and was instructed to launch all his planes (which he could do) and then withdraw to Truk for repairs. The *Zuikaku* and the *Shokaku* would recover the *Zuiho*'s aircraft. As the American scout planes disappeared, Admiral Nagumo was already ordering up the second air strike.

The American planes claimed to have destroyed seven Zeros in this and other attacks, and the SBDs were extremely fortunate that day, because every one of them made it back to the *Enterprise.*

Following the 6:50 report by two pilots about the position of the Japanese carriers, it was a full half hour before the two American carriers were able to launch planes. The *Hornet* launched 6 torpedo planes, 15 dive bombers, and 8 fighters. Another half hour later (8 A.M.), the *Enterprise* launched 3 torpedo planes, 8 dive bombers, and another 8 fighters. The *Hornet* launched a second air strike at 8:15, this time 9 dive bombers, 9 torpedo bombers, and 7 fighters. So the Americans had 73 planes in the air, but the Japanese soon had many more: a second strike from the three Nagumo carriers and a separate air strike from Admiral Kakuta's *Junyo,* even though that carrier was 330 miles away from the American fleet. To the Americans at that period of the war, 330 miles was an impossible distance—the U.S. planes could not make a 660 mile round trip—so here the Japanese had a great advantage that persisted throughout much of the Pacific war.

Kakuta was not worried by the distance. In the first place he was heading toward the enemy with his carrier, which would decrease the distance of the return flight. And if the planes got in trouble, he assumed they could land on the *Shokaku* and *Zuikaku,* not being party to the information that those carriers were already committed to take on the *Zuiho*'s aircraft.

The two enemy air attack groups passed one another in the air. The Americans did not turn aside from their appointed task, and the Japanese fighters had the advantage of sun and altitude. The Japanese force first saw the *Hornet*'s dive bombers, but by the time the Japanese leader realized that these were enemy planes they had gone by. Five minutes later the integrated Japanese force encountered the 19 planes of the *Enterprise.* So new to combat were the *Enterprise* pilots that they were completely unprepared for a fight in the air before they reached their targets. Several of the TBF pilots had not turned on their radio transmitters. Several of the fighter pilots had not charged their guns, which meant they could not fire them. The torpedo bombers were flying at 6,000 feet and climbing slowly. At 7,000 feet the F4Fs were idling along to keep pace with the slower TBF bombers, and no one seemed to be keeping the sort of lookout that would protect them. The Japanese fighter contingent from the *Zuiho* was closest, and those nine Zeros came down out of the sun to attack. In the first pass they shot down two torpedo bombers and damaged two others so badly they never got back to their carrier. The F4Fs committed the fatal error of trying to dogfight with the Zeros. Perhaps the marines on Guadalcanal could get away with it after much experience and having whittled away the layers of experienced Japanese pilots. But these *Enterprise* pilots were as new to the game as any of those young Japanese at Rabaul, and three F4Fs went down, one after the other. A fourth was damaged and had to turn back. Of the *Enterprise* strike force, only three dive bombers and five torpedo bombers were left, protected by one division of four fighters. Half of the *Enterprise*'s attack strength had been wiped out before they cast eyes on an enemy ship.

As the American planes droned on toward the enemy, the Japanese planes, being faster and having been launched first, were nearing their objective. At 8:45 came the first report of the Japanese air presence from the outbound planes, but so many planes were heading out in such small groups that the radar operators found it hard to differentiate one group of blips from another. Only just before nine o'clock did the radarmen definitely single out the Japanese attack force, and then the enemy was only 45 miles out. At almost that moment the American combat air patrol above the ships saw the first Japanese dive bombers at 17,000 feet. The Americans were 5,000 feet higher and ten miles away as the Japanese headed in for the *Hornet*.

At 9:10 the Japanese mission leader, Lieutenant Seki, sent the word back to Admiral Nagumo:

"Enemy carrier sighted. . . . All planes attacking."

The Japanese dive bombers then peeled off and began their high-level runs, while the torpedo bombers moved down to low level and began their attack.

The planes of the American combat air patrol charged in to stop the Japanese, but they were too late. The dive bombers were already screaming downward in attack by the time they caught up, and although they chased them and shot down a number of bombers, the Japanese had already released their bombs.

The *Hornet* was ready for the attack. Her antiaircraft guns and those of her support ships were firing rapidly, and they too brought down some Japanese planes. But at 9:12 the first Japanese bombs fell, near misses that battered the hull and broke equipment inside. Lieutenant Seki's bomber was hit and dove into the ship, glanced off the stack, and started a fire on the signal bridge, which forced the sailors off. The plane was carrying one 500-pound bomb and several 100-pound bombs, and it smashed through the flight deck and blew up. The 500-pound bomb did not, but lay on the hangar deck as a fire raged about it for two hours.

As the dive bombers kept the eyes of the sailors of the *Hornet* scanning the sky, the torpedo bombers came in astern. Two torpedoes exploded in the engineering area, and the *Hornet*'s engines slowed, then stopped. She erupted in clouds of steam and smoke and went dead in the water. Three more bombs struck and went down to the fourth deck, destroying compartments and machinery. A torpedo plane that had dropped its torpedo came in, was hit by antiaircraft fire, and the pilot steered his plane into the ship to explode near the number one elevator shaft and start another bad fire.

The gunners of the carrier were having a field day. They counted a dozen planes they had sent into the sea, but their carrier was dead. The other ships formed a circular screen around the *Hornet* and some of the destroyers came alongside to train their hoses on the fires, even though the carrier had a list of 8 degrees to starboard and rolled heavily, endangering the destroyers' superstructures.

As the *Hornet* group fought the fires, the *Enterprise* was coming under Japanese attack. In the beginning, at nine o'clock, it seemed that she might escape, because she went into a rainsquall and the Japanese planes could not see her. The dive bombers that had already started their attacks completely lost track of the carrier. But soon enough she came out of the squall. And just then a torpedo wake appeared near the *Enterprise*. The torpedo ran wild but threatened two accompanying destroyers that had slowed to pick up air crewmen from a U.S. dive bomber that had crashed alongside the carrier. One of the *Enterprise* fighter planes saw the torpedo circling the destroyers and attacked it, although the trigger-happy gunners of the whole flotilla fired at him. But he was not successful; the torpedo turned madly and then blew up against the side of the destroyer *Porter*, which was so seriously damaged that she had to be abandoned later. (This torpedo was fired by the Japanese submarine *I-21*, which had penetrated the destroyer screen and was never touched.)

The second group of Japanese planes hit the *Enterprise*, and there were no fighters there to stop them. But the *South Dakota* and the cruiser *San Juan* had five-inch antiaircraft guns among them, plus scores of 40-mm guns. Plane after plane came into attack and was shot down, to fall in the sea trailing smoke and explode or sink like a rock. The *South Dakota* gunners enthusiastically claimed 26 planes, although there were only 20 in the attacking group—but that meant that several guns were after the same plane at the same time. The score was high enough, as the observers could see from the smoke plumes and crashing planes.

The Japanese pilots, however, did not falter. They came in on the heels of their dying comrades and tried to find the openings. One dive bomber put a bomb through the *Enterprise*'s flight deck forward. It smashed down through the forecastle deck and out through the ship's plating, blowing one plane over the side, but the bomb did not explode. Another bomb hit near the forward elevator, smashed down three decks below and exploded, killing 43 men, injuring 75, and putting the elevator out of working order. The attack was over in ten minutes, and the shattered remnants of the Japanese dive bomber force headed back toward their carriers. Most of them did not make it, but a few did.

The torpedo planes of this second attack group came from the *Shokaku*; they were led by Lt. Comdr. Shigehara Murata. He had helped plan the Pearl Harbor torpedo attack, had worked months earlier to adjust the torpedoes to run in that shallow bay water, and then had led the torpedo planes from the Japanese carriers on December 7.

He led ten other torpedo bombers in the attack against the *Enterprise*, only to be attacked from above by four F4Fs that swooped down on them from 10,000 feet. One after another the torpedo bombers were hit, caught fire, and slid off into the sea. One of them crashed into the destroyer *Smith* and blew up, sending the whole forecastle into flame. But the ship was saved and continued to fight the battle.

The fighters, the antiaircraft gunners, and Captain Hardison of the *Enterprise* together put up a remarkable battle against the determined Japanese. Of the whole squadron of dive bombers, only five got close enough to drop their torpedoes effectively and Captain Hardison managed to evade those. All but two of the Japanese torpedo bombers were shot down, and Lieutenant Commander Murata was not one of the lucky ones to return.

After that torpedo attack, the *Enterprise* had forty-five minutes of respite from attack but that did not mean rest for the crew. Planes from the combat air patrol and aborted missions were coming in circling and asking to land. In addition to the *Enterprise*'s own, she would have to handle the planes of the *Hornet*, too. Some of these aircraft were low on gas, and some were in trouble. The "airedales" (plane handlers) and the others on the flight deck scurried about with the damage control parties, trying to get the flight deck into shape to handle landings.

Up above, the sky was clouding over and the cover obscured the arrival of the *Junyo*'s attack group. Admiral Kakuta had sent out 18 dive bombers and 12 Zeros. The leader of the attack, Lieutenant Masao Yamaguchi, could not at first locate the carrier beneath the murk, but he did find the battleship *South Dakota* and radioed back to his carrier for permission to attack.

"No," said Admiral Kakuta. He must find one of the carriers and strike it.

At 11:21 the first half of the *Junyo* group did find the *Enterprise* in a break in the clouds, and headed in to attack. Flight operations had just begun to land the *Enterprise* and *Hornet* aircraft when the dive bombers appeared. They were severely hampered by the cloud structure, which prevented them from coming down from 8,000 or 10,000 feet in a steep dive, to bomb and level off. Instead, they had to approach in shallow dives if they wanted to keep the carrier in sight. Coming down in these long shallow dives, the Japanese planes were ideal targets for the antiaircraft gunners of the American ships. The *Enterprise* gunners claimed to have shot down eight of the attackers. One bomber scored a near miss that flooded several compartments and jammed the forward elevator to the flight deck so that it could not be lowered.

The second half of the *Junyo* group showed up a few minutes later, and one dive bomber put a bomb into the *South Dakota*'s forward turret. It wounded the captain and fifty crewmen and knocked out the steering on the bridge. The battleship turned, out of control, and aimed at the *Enterprise*, moving at 28 knots. But the carrier captain saw what was happening and moved out of the way, and soon the *South Dakota* had managed to transfer the steering to the emergency compartment aft. Another Japanese bomber put an armor-piercing bomb into the cruiser *San Juan*. The bomb went all the way through the cruiser, out her bottom plates, and exploded under the keel. She was shaken from stem to stern, and her steering was knocked out. The *San Juan* then twisted and turned through the formation, with the other ships speeding and turning to avoid her. All this excitement lasted just a few minutes, and at 11:45 the Japanese attack was over. The *Enterprise* could begin landing her planes and those of the *Hornet*.

But the number of planes that would have to land was uncertain, since the American attack force was still far away from home base.

They had found the Japanese carriers just about 9:30 that morning, as the *Shokaku* was taking aboard several of its search planes. One of the search planes came in fast, obviously badly damaged, and ditched near the stern of *Shokaku*. The destroyer *Amatsukaze* raced in to rescue the crew, and as it was making the rescue the American dive bombers broke out of the clouds above the carriers.

The Japanese antiaircraft gunners opened fire, and from above the Japanese combat air patrol jumped them. The fighters went after the torpedo planes, and the antiaircraft guns concentrated on the dive bombers. The American fighters were engaging the Japanese combat air patrol as the melee increased in tempo. Two F4Fs were shot down early, even before the bombers reached the carriers, but the American fighters did their work well, and most of the bombers got through to attack. Two of them were shot down attacking *Shokaku*, but 11 dive bombers made their attacks, in the steep swooping dives that were so effective. They were doubly so this day; at least three 1,000-pound bombs struck the carrier forward and amidships. The flight deck bulged up, and flames shot upward from the hangar deck. Admiral Nagumo ordered the flagship turned about and headed at 30 knots northward, away from the trouble. The *Zuikaku* stayed behind to take aboard the returning planes of all three carriers in the 3rd Fleet.

Once the American dive bombers had made their attack, the *Zuikaku* could concentrate on plane recovery. No more attacks came in against her, because the *Hornet*'s torpedo planes had failed to find the carriers, and so had returned to attack Admiral Abe's battleship and cruiser force. They did not score any hits. The *Hornet*'s second attack wave also missed the carriers, and the planes went back to drop their bombs on the cruiser *Chikuma*. Several near misses caused severe damage on the bridge and many casualties, including the wounding of the captain, but *Chikuma* was able to steam back for Truk.

What was left of the *Enterprise* attack force also struck at the Abe force, but did no damage. Then, the American planes were gone, and the sea around the Japanese fleet was quiet. Soon the Japanese strike planes began to come back to the carrier, many of them seriously damaged. The first order of business was to get those planes aboard.

But even as the *Zuikaku* took on the planes, her captain was planning a new attack. Interception of American talk between ships had told the Japanese something they had not known—that there were two carriers in the area, not just one. One carrier looks much like another from the air, and although both American carriers had been attacked—by different Japanese units—no attacking pilot had seen *two* carriers.

Back aboard the *Hornet* the crew was fighting the fires and had them under control by ten o'clock that morning. Down below, the engineers managed to connect three working boilers up to the undamaged engine room, and the cruiser *Northampton* came alongside to tow. Just then a single straggler from the Japanese dive bomber force appeared and attacked, stopping all salvage activity as it was fought off and its bomb fell into the sea.

By 11:30 the salvage had begun again, and the *Hornet* was being towed by the *Northampton*. Then came a jerk, and the towline parted. It was 1:30 in the afternoon before a heavier cable was rigged and the tow begun again.

All this while the *Enterprise* was busy with the battle. The enemy air attack had ended just after 12:30, but that was not all the task force had to worry about. Apparently *I-21* was still firing torpedoes, because the cruiser *Portland* reported narrowly escaping four wakes. A little later the *San Juan* sighted a periscope and turned sharply to starboard to avoid torpedoes. Then the sea quieted down and the *Enterprise* began recovering planes.

The Japanese, however, were not through with the carriers yet. At 1:15 the *Junyo* launched its second attack group, which consisted of her entire torpedo squadron of 9 planes with an escort of 5 Zeros, plus the 6 remaining dive bombers and 9 more Zeros. The flight leader, Lieutenant Yoshiaki Irikiin was instructed to attack a damaged carrier. At three o'clock in the afternoon he sighted a damaged carrier and the torpedo planes attacked.

Twenty minutes later the dive bombers came in, but did not inflict any damage nor were any planes lost.

No air cover appeared above the *Hornet*. Admiral Kinkaid had begun retiring at high speed at about two o'clock fearing a new Japanese air attack while one of his elevators was not operating, and the decks were jammed with fighters and bombers.

Had Admiral Halsey personally been conducting this operation, perhaps the story would have been different, but Admiral Kinkaid refused to provide the air cover, although he continued to mount flight operations all afternoon, partly to protect his own carrier, and partly to send the *Hornet*'s dive bombers off to Espiritu Santo to relieve the crowding on the decks of the *Enterprise*. Even so the congestion was not too severe because the Americans had lost nearly 70 planes that day.

The men of the *Hornet* were furious with Kinkaid for abandoning them, but Kinkaid had the last operational American carrier in the Pacific, and if it were lost, the Japanese could have a field day.

Admiral Nagumo did not realize this fact, and withdrew in the *Shokaku*, leaving the *Zuikaku* to pick up the pieces for the Japanese. Their plane losses were even more severe, 100 planes in the various attacks. But back at Truk, Admiral Yamamoto saw what was happening as he read the dispatches, just as Admiral Halsey saw as he read his.

That afternoon Admiral Murray had to decide what to do with the *Hornet*. As he moved away, Admiral Kinkaid had put the whole responsibility in Murray's hands when he also told Halsey, "Am retiring southward."

Halsey could tell the extent of the disaster: *Hornet* dead in the water under tow, more plane attacks, the *Porter* torpedoed, the *Enterprise* damaged. It added up to defeat, and Halsey was not surprised later that afternoon when Admiral Murray reported two more air attacks, one by twin-engined bombers that must have come from Rabaul, and more bomb hits on the *Hornet*.

Just before four o'clock the carrier was attacked again by six bombers and took another bomb on the flight deck. Without air cover, without power, Admiral Murray saw no way that he could save the ship from a constant series of air attacks that could do nothing but cause more casualties. He ordered the ship abandoned.

At five o'clock that afternoon his judgment was justified when six fighters and four bombers from *Junyo* dropped another bomb on the ship. But by dark all living men of the carrier crew were off and aboard other vessels. She had lost 111 dead and 108 men had been wounded.

Admiral Kinkaid gave the order for the destruction of the carrier. The destroyer *Mustin* stood a mile away and fired eight torpedoes at her one after the other. Again, the American high command was to have evidence of the American torpedo performance. Two of the torpedoes ran wild and did not hit the carrier at all. Three simply did not hit, and no one knew why. Three did strike the carrier and explode, but she did not sink. At 7:20 that night the destroyer *Anderson* fired eight more torpedoes. Six hit, but two were duds. Still the *Hornet* did not sink, and finally, fearing a Japanese night attack, the destroyers and other ships of the U.S. task force abandoned her, leaving an American vessel to the mercies of the enemy for the first time.

Admiral Kakuta in the *Junyo* had been responsible for the latter air damage and finally for the American decision to abandon the ship rather than try to save her. His aggressiveness was not shared by others in the Japanese fleet, however. Admiral Kondo was ordered to make a night attack, but he was not enthusiastic. He dispatched Admiral Abe's two battleships and five destroyers only after direct orders came down from Admiral Yamamoto at Truk to "chase and mop up the fleeing enemy." Harsh words for an American to read, but they were truthful; Admiral Kinkaid was fleeing as rapidly as possible to get out of Japanese range. He was successful; soon the American ships were 300 miles from the Japanese fleet, and Kondo could never catch them. In the absence of Admiral Nagumo, Kondo was also upset when a "black cat" night bomber from Espiritu Santo very nearly torpedoed the *Zuikaku*, and another did torpedo the destroyer *Teruzuki*.

That night the destroyers *Makigumo* and *Akigumo* did find the *Hornet*, and chased away the *Mustin* and the *Anderson*, whose captains expected the Japanese heavy ships must be close behind. It took the Japanese only four of their "long lance" torpedoes to finish off the burning carrier.

Admiral Nagumo had returned to the battle area on the morning of October 27 in the destroyer *Arashi*. He transferred his flag to the *Zuikaku* and tried to find the Americans. But his searches found nothing, and at evening he called off the operation and returned to Truk.

The Japanese immediately took up their usual policy of overstating their achievements. It was a great victory, said Radio Tokyo; once more the victorious Japanese Navy had shown its superiority over the Americans by sinking one carrier and damaging another and several other ships. Nothing was said about the damages to *Shokaku* that would keep her tied up for months or those to the carrier *Zuiho.* Yet it really was a Japanese victory, and a worse American defeat: the battleship *South Dakota* collided with the destroyer *Mahan* on the way to Nouméa.

The battle had been an American loss, but not one that made it impossible for the Americans to hold on to Guadalcanal. Since the Japanese had not followed up, the carrier *Enterprise* had escaped, and the Americans had gained some time to reinforce their naval contingent and their air force.

Admiral Yamamoto understood what had happened, and he was furious with his commanders for letting the Americans escape with so little damage. He was particularly angry with Admiral Nagumo for leaving the scene of the battle aboard the *Shokaku* instead of staying to direct operations and destroy the *Enterprise.* A few days after Nagumo's return to Truk, he was summarily transferred to become commander of the Sasebo Naval Station in Japan.

The long awaited action, and the action itself, had exhausted the ships of the Combined Fleet. Yet the indecisive nature of the battle of Santa Cruz had made it impossible for Admiral Yamamoto to give his fleet a rest. There were to be more battles, more attrition, in the days to come.

16

BUILDUP

ADMIRAL Halsey recognized the defeat at Santa Cruz, but it did not lessen his determination to hold Guadalcanal and win this campaign. To do so, he had to make the best use of the forces at hand, and bring in more troops, planes, and ships, knowing all the while that Admiral Yamamoto and the Imperial Japanese Army would be doing the same thing.

On October 27, at Rabaul, 19th Army Headquarters had a do-or-die radio message from Imperial Headquarters in Tokyo: the troops on Guadalcanal had to be reinforced, and the attack absolutely must succeed.

At Rabaul the Imperial General Staff promised Tokyo what it wanted, but General Hyukatake and his officers had grave doubts as to their ability to win the victory demanded in the name of the emperor. The trouble was that it had become apparent (all too late) that the American marines were on Guadalcanal in much greater force than Tokyo ever believed possible, and that those marines had proved to be first class, well-trained fighting men of a sort the Japanese Army had not hitherto encountered.

A landing at Koli Point was ordered, but the chief of staff of the 38th Division objected. It would be suicidal, he said. Koli Point was far too close to Henderson Field. Landing would be difficult and resupply virtually impossible.

The only way it could possibly work was if the navy took the responsibility for escort and unloading of the troops and if maximum air cover could be achieved. Chief of Staff Ohmae of the Soruku Number Two Aviation Group objected to this as suicidal, but in an historic meeting (because they were so rare) officers of the Imperial General Staff, Yamamoto's Combined Fleet, and the 17th Army met at Rabaul and thrashed out the details of a new operation. The fate of the 38th Division was sealed at that series of meetings.

On October 27, Admiral Halsey ordered Admiral Scott to form a new task group centered around the cruiser *Atlanta*. He would have four destroyers plus his cruiser. On October 28, Scott would steam into Lunga Roads via Sealark Channel and pick up liaison officers from Vandegrift's staff. Then the task group would move around Guadalcanal to bombard Japanese positions as indicated by Vandegrift's officers. That work would take them all day, and at night they were to retreat out of The Slot to stay out of trouble during the Japanese hours of activity, then return the next morning to bombard the Japanese again.

Halsey's next step was to ask General MacArthur for a maximum bombing effort, day and night, against Japanese shipping around Bougainville, for it was from this area and the Shortlands that the resupply and reinforcement of Japanese troop units originated.

On Guadalcanal, the marines had a respite from Japanese air attack, because the 11th Air Fleet had been heavily depleted during its support of the land-sea Y-Day attacks aimed at giving the Japanese control of Henderson Field. Nor could the Combined Fleet continue air attacks with carrier planes, even if Admiral Yamamoto had been agreeable to such a tactic. Admiral Nagumo's striking force had emerged with fewer than 90 operational aircraft after the Battle of Santa Cruz, and the fleet had lost nearly all its experienced squadron commanders in the battle. The *Enterprise* had landed 14 fighters, 20 dive bombers, and 7 torpedo planes from *Hornet*'s air group. When she steamed into Nouméa, her own air group consisted of 40 fighters, 31 dive bombers, and 9 torpedo bombers.

On the ground, the Japanese 2nd Division continued to attack the marine perimeter, but without the ferocity of October 25. One attack on the night of October 26 did break through the marine lines, but a marine counterattack sent the Japanese back, and the marines restored the barbed wire perimeter. After six days of continuous fighting all the marine positions were still as they had been.

Reports from intelligence officers indicated that the failure of the Y-Day operation had dealt a serious blow to Japanese morale, but General Vandegrift was not persuaded by this information to lessen his vigilance. He believed the Japanese had powerful reserve forces that they had not committed and could stage an attack as strong as that of October 25. So he ordered continual ground and air patrols.

On October 27 the Cactus Air Force dive bombers and P-400s attacked an eight-gun Japanese antiaircraft battery at Kokumbona and destroyed an ammunition dump, which went up with a satisfying explosion. The guns were quiet, which indicated that they had been put out of action. The planes also attacked known field gun positions that day and silenced them. Henderson Field no longer suffered that nagging fire from the 150-mm howitzers.

The next day the fliers again attacked Japanese land positions. One fighter was shot down by antiaircraft fire, but the pilot made a parachute landing into the water.

Japanese submarines continued to be a threat to the American naval forces, and the U.S. Navy still had not perfected antisubmarine patrol. On October 27 the battleship *Washington* was nearly torpedoed. A Japanese submarine attacked her, fired several torpedoes, and missed. Two hours later the Japanese vessel attacked again and fired more torpedoes, but again they all missed, although one exploded four hundred yards off the port of the *Washington*.

Back at Pearl Harbor, Admiral Nimitz was making every possible effort to strengthen Halsey's hand. In the last days of October he established a new task force built around the carrier *Saratoga*, now repaired. Rear Admiral DeWitt C. Ramsey was given command of the carrier, two cruisers, and eight destroyers. The force would join Halsey.

Admiral Halsey also established another task group in the South Pacific, Task Group 64.4. (Those decimal numbers indicated that the group was the fourth task group of Task Force 64, which was Halsey's force of surface combat vessels.) This group was led by Rear Admiral Daniel Callaghan in the cruiser *San Francisco*. It included the cruiser *Helena*, and the destroyers *Laffey*, *Buchanan*, and *McCalla*. Immediately, Callaghan was assigned to escorting supply ships into Guadalcanal, as Admiral Halsey kept his promise to give General Vandegrift and General Geiger the help they needed to hold the island. Callaghan would join other ships, take over this augmented group, which would be called Task Force 65, and they would deliver 6,000 troops of the 8th Marine Regiment to strengthen General Vandegrift's force. They would also bring tanks and heavy artillery.

Admiral Turner was hastening his efforts to supply Vandegrift. The transport *Fuller* was loaded with two batteries of 155-mm guns as well as ammunition and stores. The *Alchiba* was loaded with stores and sent to Guadalcanal, to arrive around November 3, when the 8th Marines would land. Then General Vandegrift proposed to launch an offensive operation against the Japanese. It would be the first real offensive the marines had tried since the landing in August. Since that time, because of Turner's difficulties with supply and the pressure on Henderson Field, the marines had been constantly on the defense.

The 8th Marines would soon be followed by an aviation engineering battalion, an army infantry regiment, and the 2nd Marine Raider Battalion to replace the 1st Marine Raiders who were recuperating after their heavy casualties and difficult days on Bloody Ridge.

As the month of October drew to an end, the marines continued to spar with the Japanese. On October 29, west of the Matanikau River, members of a patrol captured two enemy 75-mm guns, which they spiked. The Japanese seemed very quiet, and although Admiral Scott reported enthusiastically about his bombardment mission against boats and buildings, the Cactus Air Force found it hard to see targets on the ground. The scout planes did find a pair of Japanese destroyers off Tassafaronga on October 29 and bombed, but without making any hits. Those destroyers then headed west of the Russell Islands. A second raid made an attempt on them, again without success, and this time one dive bomber was lost to antiaircraft fire. The fighters went hunting for Japanese aircraft and found a seaplane base at Rekata Bay, which they attacked, destroying three planes, but eight or nine others escaped. The fighters strafed the area and set fire to a fuel dump.

Admirals Halsey and Turner had been distressed that on Y-Day the Japanese were able to stop traffic on the main airstrip at Henderson Field and to threaten the little fighter strip. Halsey decided that a new airfield was needed so that never again could the enemy put the bombers out of action. Admiral Turner selected a spot at Aola Bay, fifty miles east of Lunga Point, for the second airfield. On the map it looked good, but the terrain was actually totally unsuited for a field, as Generals Geiger and Vandegrift saw as soon as they heard of the decision. But at the end of October Admiral Turner was already moving to build his airfield. Since Aola Point was well behind the Japanese lines, it would mean another amphibious operation to set up the base. Turner selected the 2nd Marine Raider Battalion, which had just arrived in the area for the task. The Raiders would make the assault, an army infantry regiment would then take over, and the Seabees would build the base. It all looked so simple that Lt. Col. Evans Carlson, commander of the 2nd Raider Battalion, decided he needed to employ only two of his companies.

They boarded the old four-stack destroyers *McKean* and *Manley* on October 30 and headed for Aola Point.

The Raiders landed without opposition—they were too far east of the Japanese lines. Shortly after they landed, it began to rain, and having established the camp, the Raiders huddled on the beach and waited for the landing craft to come back and relieve them with the army garrison.

On November 1, General Vandegrift's offensive began. The 5th Marines crossed the Matanikau River and attacked to the west supported by B-17 bombers. The Cactus Air Force sent its dive bombers and P-400s against Japanese troop concentrations, and the marines moved forward about two miles that day in very rough terrain that the Japanese contested.

That night Vandegrift's reports from the Pearl Harbor radio intelligence organization indicated that the Japanese were going to begin landing troops that night with five destroyers.

On November 2 the American attack west of the Matanikau River progressed, but slowly. The Japanese fought hard, and one Japanese stronghold west of Point Cruz stopped the marines. They had to mass to take the position, which included a 170-mm gun, six 37-mm guns, and many machine guns. It took most of the day, but they did it, and then began moving forward once more.

The planes of the Cactus Air Force maintained fighter patrols, and the bombers and army P-39s carried out troop support missions. Two fighters were lost that day in operational accidents, and three dive bombers went out to attack an enemy task force of a cruiser and a number of destroyers, and did not come back. That was ominous. Also another dive bomber reported seeing a destroyer near Kokumbona at 9:30 that night. That plane also failed to return.

On the morning of November 3, General Vandegrift learned that five Japanese destroyers had landed many troops east of Koli Point. The marines also later discovered what had happened to the bombers that had taken off to intercept the Japanese—they had fallen victim to the bad weather, and all had crashed in a dreadful storm that hit the islands that night.

When the general learned of the new landings, he sent the message to Colonel Carlson and his Raiders. They would not be brought out. They were to stay at Aola Bay, and two more companies would join them.

Major John Mather of the Australian Army was attached to the battalion, and he brought native scouts who knew the island.

Every night the Japanese landed more troops, for Admiral Yamamoto's plan was completed on November 6. The navy would land the 38th Army Infantry Division and the 8th Special Naval Landing Force with heavy weapons and supplies. This would be largely accomplished by November 12. On the night of November 12, two battleships would bombard Henderson Field. On the night of the 13th the last of the troops would be landed, and a strong force of cruisers would bombard the airfield. For this operation the 2nd Japanese Fleet was split into two sections, one built around the carriers *Hiyo* and *Junyo* and the other around two battleships, the *Hiei* and the *Kirishima*, and an entire division of heavy cruisers.

Independently, Admiral Yamamoto sent the 8th Fleet to escort the transports and protect the troops' landing. Yamamoto then had 2 carriers, 4 battleships, 7 heavy cruisers, 4 light cruisers, and 30 destroyers to move 11 transports and 14,500 infantrymen to Guadalcanal.

As the Japanese landed night after night, and the Marine Raiders moved across the island, hacking their way through the jungle, General Vandegrift's offensive continued. The troops attacked toward Kokumbona. West of Point Cruz they killed 350 Japanese in one position.

On the coast, the 7th Marines saw the Japanese landing east of Koli Point and attacked the next morning, but were driven back.

The new Japanese troops had tanks and heavy artillery ashore, and they knew how to use them. At this point General Vandegrift was concentrating his forces west of the Malimbu River, trying to come to grips with the enemy in a major engagement.

On November 4, the Americans unloaded troops and supplies by daylight, then moved the transports across to the safety of Tulagi for the night. As usual the Japanese destroyers came in after dark to unload their own troops and supplies. On the night of the 4th, four American cruisers and six destroyers lay in Indispensable Strait, ready to strike enemy targets. That night was dark, the air searches were not successful, and the American task force remained in position.

On Guadalcanal, the marines continued to attack west of the Matanikau River. They fought and killed 350 Japanese west of Point Cruz and captured 30 machine guns and several field pieces.

On November 5 the two reinforcing companies of Raiders and army garrison troops were landed at Aola Bay by American destroyers. Colonel Carlson waited fretfully for new orders. They came on November 5. General Vandegrift informed Carlson that Japanese troops had landed a new infantry regiment at Kamimbo and Tassafaronga. Carlson was to march his Raiders across Guadalcanal and attack the regiment. At dawn on November 6 they set out. Each man had food for only four days, because their whole operation as originally planned was to have been a short-term project. By this time the army troops should have been at Aola Point, and the Raiders should have been drinking beer in Espiritu Santo. Instead they were deep in the jungle foraging for food from the first day. Carlson had the solution to the problem: If they wanted to eat, they had to find the Japanese and take the food away from them.

Carlson was up front in the column, carrying a full pack, doing everything he asked his men to do. The route would take them to the villages of Gegende, Reko, Tasimboko, Tina, and Binu. These places had been selected, because intelligence reports indicated there were Japanese there, and because they were close to the coast. Every four days the troops back at Aola were to send a landing boat to a point determined by radio, and Carlson would pick up the supplies they unloaded. Until then they lived on rice, tea, raisins, chocolate, and a little sugar and salt.

On November 7, the F4Fs found four Japanese destroyers on their way north after delivering troops of the 38th Japanese Division to

Guadalcanal. They strafed the ships and dropped 100-pound bombs on them, scoring some hits but not stopping the ships. Three planes were shot down.

Very early in the morning a dive bomber on antisubmarine patrol sighted a submarine half a mile off Cape Esperance and dropped depth charges. An oil slick came to the surface, and the pilot thought he had sunk the submarine. But oil slicks could be most deceptive, and sometimes a submarine captain deliberately released some oil just to give the impression to an attacker that the submarine had been destroyed. The submarine's survival was proven later that morning when it torpedoed the transport *Majaba*. That ship had been carrying ammunition, but fortunately for the Americans the explosives had all been unloaded. The *Majaba* was beached at the mouth of the Tenaru River.

These days, Admiral Halsey was moving his ships around rapidly. He was trying to come to grips with the Japanese destroyers and covering cruisers that kept running down The Slot every night to deliver troops while he also tried to maintain a strong protective force of cruisers and destroyers to accompany his own transports that brought the 8th Marines and their supplies to Guadalcanal.

On November 8 the Americans continued to advance, and the Japanese fell back, but the day's action was not spectacular. At night, on the sea, there was more activity. A number of PT boats had been brought down to Tulagi, and every night they set out to find the Japanese destroyers that came down The Slot. Three PT boats encountered two destroyers in The Slot that night between Savo Island and Cape Esperance. They fired five torpedoes and claimed one hit on a destroyer. One PT boat returned with a five-inch shell hole in its hull, but no men were hurt.

The Japanese were having their troubles. The air battles of Y-Day had so depleted the 11th Air Fleet that there were not enough Zero fighters left at Rabaul to cover the destroyers on their runs down The Slot. The little field at Buin was virtually deserted. The air strength that did exist consisted of a number of seaplane fighters at the eastern end of Bougainville, but most of these had been shot down by the F4Fs in the first week of November.

On November 7 the main body of the 38th Japanese Army Division arrived at the Shortland base. Five destroyers were sent to Guadalcanal carrying 600 troops and Lieutenant General Tadayoshi

Sano. At midafternoon on their way south they were attacked by F4Fs, dive bombers, and torpedo planes but were not hurt. At night, as they came to Guadalcanal, they were attacked by four PT boats, but again drove them off and landed their troops.

The Japanese submarines still moved around the island without much fear. On November 8 one submarine torpedoed the transport *Edgar Allen Poe*, and then came to the surface and shelled the ship. The *Poe* did not sink, but was taken under tow for Nouméa. But by now the Americans were learning how to combat submarines, and they had formed "hunter-killer" groups, which consisted of destroyers and destroyer escorts working in close cooperation with bombing planes. One such group was sent to the area where the *Poe* had been torpedoed.

In the Guadalcanal jungle, the Raiders reached Gegende but found no Japanese there. They went on to the second point, Reko. A native scout named Poi was leading the column when suddenly a volley of rifle fire broke out from the jungle alongside the trail. Poi fell, shot through both arms. The Raiders stopped and began circling to surround the enemy. One Raider saw five Japanese soldiers in a little clearing. They turned and fired at the Raider and then ran for the jungle. Two were slow and the marines shot them down; the others escaped.

On November 9, the Carlson column reached Binu, where new orders awaited them. A Japanese force had landed near the Metapona River and had been trapped in a pocket by marine and army units. Carlson was to remain at Binu and send scouts to determine the size and composition of the Japanese unit.

On November 10 Carlson sent a patrol to the lines of the 2nd Battalion of the 7th Marines, and learned from them that the Japanese were boxed in as reported. It was always safer to check out the information one received from higher authority. That day, the other two companies of the Raider Battalion arrived at Binu, doubling Carlson's strength.

On the 10th General Vandegrift sensed the increasing Japanese resistance, although the marines' advances on the west flank of their drive and on the east cleared Japanese positions near Tetere. The Japanese land-based air force was still suffering from previous attrition. The Cactus Air Force planes shot down one Zero that day, but the real action came when the daily evening search planes sighted five destroyers 210 miles north of Guadalcanal, obviously coming down to land more troops after dark. A force of 17 fighters and 8 dive bombers attacked the destroyers but could do no better than "near misses" whose effect was not really known. The minesweeper *Southard* attacked and sank the Japanese submarine *I-172* off San Cristobal Island.

There was very little activity the next day anywhere on Guadalcanal. It was a miserable day, cold and rainy, and at Binu the Raiders gathered around their fires and joked.

"Hey Mac, you know what day this is?"

"Yeah, the sixth day we've been in this f——g jungle."

"It's Armistice Day, that's what it is. The day to celebrate the War to End All Wars."

"Hah. What a joke. Out here in this f——g jungle, eating gooey rice and drinking *tea*."

In the air there was not even that much respite. From the carriers, Admiral Yamamoto sent 10 dive bombers and 12 Zeros to attack Henderson Field. The F4Fs went up and shot down several planes; they claimed 5 Zeros and 1 bomber with 2 Zeros and 1 bomber as "probables."

On November 12, the American advance stalled in the face of a strong Japanese counterattack. Colonel Carlson sent out four patrols to various points to make contact with other U.S. units and the Japanese. At ten o'clock in the morning, Company E called Carlson at Binu. The company had gone out to explore a trail cut earlier by Sergeant Vouza's native scouts. The company radioman reported they had made contact with the 7th Marines and learned that a large Japanese force had escaped a marine trap the night before and probably was moving toward Binu. Ten minutes later Company C called Carlson. They had found Japanese soldiers in force, armed with machine guns, mortars and 20-mm cannon three miles southwest of Binu. They could use some help.

Carlson moved his three other companies around to attack and surround the Japanese. At 11 o'clock, Company E spotted two companies of Japanese troops crossing the Metapona River. From various reports, Carlson deduced that the Japanese had split their force and were preparing to make a surprise attack on the rear of the 7th Marines. C Company ran into a Japanese bivouac in the woods on the edge of a broad field. The Japanese reacted quickly to the appearance of the first marine and soon had the company pinned down in the field under machine gun, mortar, and 20-mm cannon fire. The company brought up its own mortars and retreated under their covering fire. When Colonel Carlson arrived at the scene at 4:30 in the afternoon, he found his whole company disorganized. He sent C Company into reserve and brought in E Company to fight the Japanese. He radioed for air support, and just at dusk two American dive bombers appeared and dropped bombs in the woods. As darkness fell, the Japanese moved out. Carlson suspected that they might, and sent a patrol across the field. When the Raiders reached the woods and found the enemy gone, Carlson then moved the whole force back to Binu, arriving at 11 o'clock.

That night Colonel Carlson made some changes in his command, relieving the commanders of C and D Companies and promoting men in the field.

On the afternoon of November 12, the 11th Air Fleet made its move. Twenty-five torpedo bombers, supported by eight Zero fighters, attacked the American ships bringing supplies to Guadalcanal. The marine, navy, and army pilots of the Cactus Air Force were ready, and 20 F4Fs and 8 P-39s engaged the Japanese and drove them off, shooting down a claimed 16 bombers and 5 fighters, with a loss of 3 F4Fs and one P-39.

On the morning of the 12th, American planes raided Shortland Island at dawn and bombed the transport ships lying in harbor there but caused no damage. At six o'clock that night the 11 Japanese army transports moved south to the edge of Lunga Roads and waited. That night the battleships *Hiei* and *Kirishima* were to open Admiral Yamamoto's new drive to capture Guadalcanal with a bombardment of Henderson Field. They were already on their way to Guadalcanal escorted by two divisions of destroyers.

Three American attack cargo ships lay in Lunga Roads that day, unloading. They had been brought safely down to Guadalcanal by Admiral Scott's task force. A second group of transports under Admiral Turner was on its way to Lunga, guarded by Admiral Daniel Callaghan's task force of cruisers and destroyers. The *Enterprise* was still under repair at Nouméa so she could not help in this difficult time when Japanese and Americans were vying to see who could land the most men on Guadalcanal. But her escort force, including two battleships and four destroyers, was detached and went to sea under Rear Admiral "Ching" Lee.

That afternoon of November 12, American and Japanese warships were milling around in Guadalcanal waters, each trying to keep track of the other, each trying to defend its own landings and break up the enemy's. Admiral Turner's information suggested that the Japanese had 2 battleships, 4 heavy cruisers, 2 light cruisers, and 12 destroyers coming down to Guadalcanal. To defend the American transports, Admiral Callaghan had only 2 heavy cruisers, 2 light cruisers, and 8 destroyers. But they would have to do the job if it was to be done at all. By evening it was apparent that the night of November 12 would be the night of crisis.

17

THE BATTLE CALLED GUADALCANAL

REAR Admiral Koki Abe was in command of the Japanese force sent down to Guadalcanal on November 12 to bombard Henderson Field. Early in the afternoon Admiral Abe had ordered his ships to assume the double half-ring formation the Japanese used to fight off air attack. Five destroyers were spread into an arc five miles ahead of the cruiser *Nagara*. Six other destroyers took the same position relative to the cruiser but closer in. The battleships *Hiei* and *Kirishima* came up behind about a mile apart. As the afternoon wore on, the weather changed from sunny to overcast and then to rain. Admiral Abe ordered a float plane catapulted from the *Hiei*, but after an hour it had not sent back any message. They moved along at 18 knots, into the teeth of a tropical storm. The rain soon came down so hard that it was difficult for the officers on the bridge of one ship to see the closest vessel. Many of the ship commanders thought Admiral Abe must soon order them to slow down for safety's sake. But Admiral Abe drove them on at 18 knots. They must maintain the speed, he said, to be sure they reached Guadalcanal and began their mission on time.

Finally the scout plane reported. "More than a dozen enemy warships off Lunga."

These were Admiral Callaghan's ships, and just then they were in a long column. The destroyers *Cushing, Laffey, Sterett,* and *O'Bannon* led. Next came the cruisers *Atlanta, San Francisco, Portland, Helena,* and *Juneau.* Behind them came the destroyers *Aaron Ward, Barton, Monssen* and *Fletcher.* This disposition had been adopted because it had been successful for Admiral Scott at the battle of Cape Esperance. Admiral Callaghan and his staff did not know that the basic reason for Scott's success was purely accidental, the crossing of the enemy T when neither force was aware of the other. On the night of November 12 the ship with the most effective radar was the *San Francisco,* the flagship, but she was tucked in the middle of the column, and the destroyers out front had the worst radar of all.

At ten o'clock that night, the transport ships off Lunga were sent over to Tulagi for protection, and Admiral Callaghan moved up through Lengo Channel into Iron Bottom Sound. He was moving toward the rainsquall that hid Admiral Abe's ships, although at that hour the American ships were still steaming under clear, starry skies. But as they headed north the weather worsened rapidly.

At ten o'clock Admiral Abe was in his chartroom, checking the work of the navigators. He had a message from the army on Guadalcanal: "Weather now very bad here." He knew that already, because the pilot of the *Hiei*'s scout seaplane had announced that he was going to land at Bougainville rather than try to find his ship in the storm below.

The storm was going to cause some trouble for the bombardment force if they continued in it, so Admiral Abe decided to get out. He ordered a simultaneous 180 degree turn by all ships. Then he slowed them to 12 knots. That ought to get them clear and let the southbound squall run on. They could follow it and carry out the bombardment with the high explosive, quick-fused shells they had brought to use this night.

At 11:40 the rainsquall passed by, and a few moments later, Admiral Abe ordered the ships to turn 180 degrees again, resuming their original run toward Guadalcanal but now under clear skies. There was a difference. The fast run through the storm had caused the ships to separate into two major groups. Thus they ran down until they reached Savo Island. On his flag bridge, Admiral Abe studied the latest messages. The army on Guadalcanal reported that the weather had cleared, and no enemy ships could be seen off Lunga. Bougainville base reported that it was sending several float planes to act as observers.

Admiral Abe was tortured by indecision. He was only 12 miles offshore. If he was to carry out the bombardment mission, the guns should be loaded with the high explosive one-ton shells that were filled with antipersonnel bombs and incendiary charges. If he was to engage other warships, his force should be loading with armor-piercing shells.

At 1:24 a radar operator aboard the American cruiser *Helena* caught an unusual blip on his screen. It showed up as a trace or long line with another behind it. The operator was experienced enough to recognize two columns of ships, one behind the other, and he sent out the report.

Three minutes later Admiral Callaghan ordered his column of ships to change course, to head directly toward the enemy. At 1:30 the *Helena* announced that the enemy was on their port bow, 9 miles away, steaming at a speed of 23 knots. Added to the American speed of 18 knots, that meant the two forces were heading for collision at a rate of more than 40 knots.

The Americans at long distance had the advantage of their radar, and thus they saw the Japanese before the Japanese saw them. But for some reason Admiral Callaghan did not order the ships to open fire or to fire torpedoes as they came within range. Aboard the *San Francisco*, Admiral Callaghan was forever calling for ranges and courses, but he gave no orders.

At 1:42 Admiral Abe's indecision was ended. A message came from the destroyer *Yudachi*:

"Enemy sighted."

A moment later came the call from the *Hiei*'s masthead lookout that he had sighted four warships five degrees to starboard, about six miles away.

The admiral ordered the bombardment ammunition put down and replaced with armor-piercing shells. Again he agonized. Should he turn away from the enemy while the change was made? He decided against it.

Had Admiral Callaghan ordered his ships to open fire when they came within range, the battle could easily have been over in a few minutes, because the Japanese battleships and cruisers were in no condition to return fire as they changed types of ammunition. But Admiral Callaghan came on, without firing, and eight precious minutes were gained by Admiral Abe to change over his ammunition.

One of the American difficulties was that by moving in a straight line, the U.S. ships could only fire forward. That could have been changed immediately by an order from Admiral Callaghan, turning 90 degrees right or left and bringing the batteries to bear. Once again, that way, Admiral Callaghan would have crossed the T. But he did not. It was 1:45 before Callaghan gave the order to stand by to open fire.

At that point the two forces had virtually overrun each other. Aboard the *Yudachi* the crew was astounded to see an American destroyer suddenly bearing down on them from the darkness. They did not fire, but only because they were not yet finished with the transfer of ammunition. The Americans were equally confused, and Lt. Comdr. Edward N. Parker, captain of the *Cushing,* turned left when he sighted the *Yudachi.* He thus narrowly avoided a collision with the enemy ship, but also led the American line in a confusing maneuver that had the U.S. ships nearly piling up on one another as they turned sharply to 315°.

The *Hiei* searchlight began probing the night. Suddenly, it fell on the bridge of the American cruiser *Atlanta* two and a half miles away. The port wing of the *Atlanta*'s bridge was suddenly lighted up as brightly as if it were noon.

The gunnery officer of the *Atlanta* waited no longer for an order. "Commence firing. Counter-illuminate," he shouted.

The range was not quite a mile. The *Atlanta* began to fire. Half a minute later the *Hiei* returned the fire, at almost point blank range. One shell landed on the bridge of the *Atlanta,* killing Admiral Scott and all but one other man on the bridge. Just then came the command from the flagship to open fire.

So close was the *Hiei* to at least four American destroyers that the American five-inch guns were effective. Some of the shells went over the ship and threatened the destroyer *Amatsukaze* on the other side.

The *Atlanta* was hit many times by shells from the *Hiei,* but she was finished by the Japanese destroyers, which began launching torpedoes with their usual efficiency. One or more of them hit the *Atlanta* and stopped her cold in the water. She was out of the fight.

The destroyer *Cushing* fired six torpedoes at the *Hiei*, but all of them missed, another sign of the great difference between Japanese and American night fighting techniques, and of the superiority of Japanese destroyer crews as torpedo artists. The *Laffey*, coming alongside the *Hiei*, also fired torpedoes, and these bounced off the battleship's sides. But at close quarters the *Laffey*'s machine gunners raked the *Hiei*'s bridge, killing Captain Suzuki and several men and wounding Admiral Abe. The *Cushing* and the *Laffey* were quickly reduced to wreckage by the big guns of the battleship.

The third and fourth ships in the American column were the *Sterett* and the *O'Bannon*.

The captain of the *Sterett* replied to Admiral Callaghan's order that odd numbered ships fire to starboard by swinging her guns around. As he did this, the main battery director picked up a Japanese cruiser through his binoculars. She was 4,500 yards away.

The word came from the flagship.

"Get the big ones first. Commence firing. Commence firing. Give 'em Hell, boys!"

The *Sterett*'s five-inch battery began firing at the cruiser. The shells began hitting.

Lieutenant McWhorter, the torpedo officer, was trying to get his torpedo director located on the target. He could see the target through his glasses, but the operator could not pick it up through the director. Even when McWhorter pointed the target out and gave the man a true bearing, he could not find it. McWhorter jumped up and took over the director himself, but he could not see the target through the finder.

The *O'Bannon* came speeding up the starboard side of the *Sterett* and got between the *Sterett* and the Japanese cruiser so the *Sterett* looked for other targets. Just then a Japanese salvo hit the *Sterett* portside aft, and disabled her steering.

Commander Jesse Coward, the captain of the *Sterett* turned toward the *Hiei*. Lieutenant Commander Gould, the executive officer, leaped through the pilot house and shouted at McWhorter, "Battleship close aboard on the port side. Dead in the water."

It was a battleship, but it was not dead in the water. McWhorter sped to the port side of the ship and set up the mathematical solution to the firing: Target angle 075, speed 6 knots. Torpedoman

Solloway trained the director on the target. The range was just over a mile.

"Permission to let these fish go," shouted McWhorter to the captain.

"Yes, fire when ready," shouted Commander Coward. "Commence firing. Commence firing."

Then came the series of muffled explosions and the hollow ring of the brass tubes as the torpedoes leaped out and splashed into the water on their way to the battleship.

The destroyer's five-inch guns had turned and were firing on the battleship's superstructure. It seemed an endless time to Lieutenant McWhorter, but finally two explosions erupted at the battleship's waterline. A spray of water leaped high in the air, a spray glowing red that looked to McWhorter like the lighted fountain of an amusement park. Torpedoman Calhoun, who was working the director at that point, said he saw some Japanese jumping over the side of the ship to escape the heat of the fires.

A pair of shells hit the destroyer's foremast and destroyed the radar and identification lights. Star shells began to burst around the destroyer, and from the *Sterett* it seemed to be a general dogfight, all ships mixed up, so that it was hard to tell friend from enemy.

To port of the *Sterett*, a searchlight from a Japanese ship went on, illuminating another Japanese ship just off her bow. The *Sterett*'s torpedo tubes could not be brought to bear in time. Another Japanese searchlight illuminated a destroyer crossing the *Sterett*'s bow port to starboard, range 800 yards.

Captain Coward, whose night vision left something to be desired, asked Lieutenant McWhorter, who was on the bridge, "Is that one of ours?"

"No sir. It's a Jap. See those wavy stacks. . . ."

McWhorter was already on the run for the starboard torpedo director, and a bearing. He did not ask the captain's permission this time.

"Commence firing. Commence firing."

A torpedoman turned the switches.

"Fire one. . . ."

"Fire two. . . ."

The Japanese ship swung around on a course paralleling the *Sterett*'s. A salvo from the American ship's five-inch guns struck the

Japanese ship's bridge, ripping it open from pilothouse to waterline. The hole glowed with fire, and the destroyer took a list to port.

There was no use wasting another torpedo on her, Torpedo Officer McWhorter decided. When the torpedoes struck, they lifted the destroyer out of the water.

"Oh you poor son of a bitch," came a shout from somewhere up forward aboard the *Sterett*. And then the Japanese ship was afire from end to end, and she shuddered and plunged to the bottom.

The *Sterett* passed the dying destroyer abeam, not more than 600 yards off. The burning ship lit up the area, and in the flames McWhorter could see other burning ships, some of them American. And the fire illuminated the *Sterett* for some Japanese marksman, for a heavy-calibre salvo hit the destroyer's No. 3 gun and the ammunition handling room below. A ball of fire 30 feet in diameter rose to the top of the gun mount. McWhorter heard terrifying screams from the gun crew and saw two men, their clothes on fire, tumbling backward out of the gun mount to the deck.

Captain Coward rang up FULL SPEED AHEAD, and then STOP. By this jackrabbit hopping, he confused the Japanese marksmen, and the proof of it was projectiles splashing fore and aft of the ship.

The cruiser *Nagara* suddenly put two parachute flares up, and by their light the last six ships of the American column were clearly outlined. Captain Tameichi Hara of the *Amatsukaze* made ready to fire torpedoes. On this Japanese ship that task was regarded as too important to leave to a junior officer, and he made the calculations himself. Hara waited until his torpedo officer was impatient. They moved closer to the enemy, until they were less than two miles apart, and then Hara gave the order.

"Ready torpedoes. Fire."

Eight torpedoes rushed out of their tubes. Just then, the destroyer *Yudachi* nearly collided with the American destroyer *Aaron Ward*, which turned sharply to avoid a crash. The U.S. destroyer *Barton*, just behind the *Aaron Ward*, had to come to a virtual stop to avoid hitting her sister ship. The change worked perfectly for Commander Hara; two pillars of flame shot up from the side of the *Barton*. She broke in two and sank in seconds. The *Aaron Ward* got in the way of the *Kirishima*'s guns and was blasted; she sank later.

Commander Hara turned, looking for new game. Back to the west he could see the *Hiei*, wreathed in flames. He headed toward her, then in a minute saw gun flashes to port that illuminated a four-masted ship, an American cruiser. It was the cruiser *Juneau,* and Hara attacked her.

"Torpedoes ready," he shouted. "Target 70 degrees to port."

"Torpedoes ready."

"Hold it. The target is moving. Four torpedoes this time. Steady. . . . FIRE!"

The four torpedoes left their tubes, and three minutes later a torpedo struck the cruiser *Juneau* and sent up a spout of water.

The battleship *Kirishima* stood off about half a mile from the *Hiei* and fired at any American ships she saw. None seemed to fire at her until late in the battle, for she was hit only once by an eight-inch shell from a cruiser.

The American flagship *San Francisco* began firing on an enemy ship, but then was illuminated by a Japanese searchlight, and the *Kirishima* began firing on her. For some reason or other, Admiral Callaghan then ordered a "cease fire," and the *San Francisco* stopped shooting—but her enemies did not. A destroyer came down the side and fired on the bridge. So did two other ships. In a minute so many shells hit that bridge that they virtually wiped it out, and killed Admiral Callaghan and Capt. Cassin Young.

The cruiser *Portland* began firing on the Japanese, and, in turn, an enemy ship fired on her, hitting once with a shell that wounded the executive officer. Five minutes after opening fire, Capt. Laurance DuBose received the "cease fire" order but did not believe it. The *Portland* stopped firing for a few moments, then started again since so many ships were firing at her. Then a torpedo struck, smashed her so hard that a chunk of metal protruded from her side, and caused her to turn in circles. As she came around, the *Hiei* came in sight, and the *Portland* put more shells into the battleship.

The American cruiser *Helena* was very lucky that night. She began firing in line and fired on many enemy ships, but she was scarcely hurt; only a small shell from a destroyer passed through her superstructure and did minimal damage.

The *Juneau* was last in the American column of cruisers. She opened fire but, unfortunately, on the *Helena.* She stopped at Admiral Callaghan's orders, and just then a torpedo from *Amatsukaze* smashed into her side, broke her keel, and put her out of action. The *Juneau* was dead in the water.

After the destroyer *Barton* sank, the *Monssen,* which was right behind her, fired a torpedo salvo of five "fish" at the *Kirishima*. All missed. Star shells began lighting up the ship, and the captain, who for some reason believed the star shells were American, switched on his lights and made a perfect target for another Japanese destroyer and the *Nagara*. In two minutes the *Monssen* was burning and out of the fight. The destroyer *Fletcher* was last in the American line, and when her captain saw the *Barton* blow up and the *Monssen* burning, he turned away from the battle to get out of the line of fire, intending to come in and launch his torpedoes from a new approach.

But when the *Hiei* turned away and the *Kirishima* followed, the Japanese destroyers and cruisers broke off the attack and steamed north with their battleships. The fight was over 15 minutes after it began.

The Japanese retired northward, except for the destroyer *Akatsuki*, which had sunk. Five miles south of Savo Island the destroyer *Yudachi* suddenly erupted in flame and smoke. An internal explosion, perhaps triggered by an apparently dud shell blown up by some minor fire, shook her and in a minute she was stopped dead. The destroyers *Murasame*, *Amatsukaze*, *Samidare*, and *Ikazuchi* were all damaged, but not too seriously. *Samidare* stopped to take the survivors off *Yudachi*, and the Japanese went on.

As the light of morning came, the waters of Guadalcanal were full of smoke and several burning vessels could still be seen. Down south, close to Lunga Point, was the *Atlanta*, which was kept afloat only by constant work of the pumps. She was taken in tow that morning by the tug *Bobolink*. Under tow, she was attacked by one two-engined Betty bomber. The crew of *Atlanta* opened up their remaining guns to fire on the plane and drove it away. As they moved toward Kukum, the crew fired with rifles at every head that appeared in the water, until the captain pointed out that they might well be killing American survivors instead of Japanese.

Finally at two in the afternoon, the *Atlanta* was anchored off Kukum, but it soon became apparent that she could not be kept afloat long, and there were no drydocks in Guadalcanal. So that night the *Atlanta* was scuttled in deep water three miles off Lunga Point.

The *Portland* had lost her steering in the fight, and not much could be done with her until the afternoon, when the *Bobolink* came back from the *Atlanta* tow and took on *Portland*. She was brought into Tulagi Harbor early on the morning of November 14.

The *Helena, San Francisco, Juneau, O'Bannon, Sterett,* and *Fletcher* set out for the safety of the New Hebrides on November 13. It was a sorry procession, *San Francisco* with her upper works shot away, and the others limping, with scores of wounds among them. But they could make 18 knots, and they moved through a quiet sea toward safety. The *Sterett's* firepower was down to two guns. She had taken 11 hits and survived. The *O'Bannon's* sound gear was disabled, among other damage, and the cruisers seemed like floating wreckage. But they moved on under the *Helena's* captain, G. C. Hoover, who was made the tactical officer in charge by the deaths of two admirals that night before. The *O'Bannon* went ahead to send a message to Admiral Fitch asking for air cover; Captain Hoover had seen a message announcing the presence of two Japanese carriers (they were not nearby). None of the ships was in condition to be alert for attack; most of the men aboard were concerned about survival, the treatment of the wounded, and the repair of emergency facilities.

Around noon, Lieutenant McWhorter went on the bridge of the *Sterett* for a condition red air alert that did not materialize. He was watching the destroyer's signalman using his signal lightbox to send a message to the *Juneau.* Suddenly he saw an enormous explosion next to the *Juneau,* and the whole ship was hidden by a sphere of flame. The signalman aboard the *Juneau* was thrown high into the air, and McWhorter saw the man tumbling around in a hail of debris. Then the smoke obscured the view, and when it cleared, there was no more *Juneau* but a column of smoke rising 1,000 feet in the sky. She had gone down with her 700 men. No one in the convoy thought there could be a survivor, and they steamed on to get away from the submarine *I-26* that had delivered the fatal torpedo to the ship's magazine. But the next morning a search plane sighted 100 men still alive in the water. It took the rescuers too long to reach them, and when a PBY finally arrived, the number of survivors was down to six. A destroyer picked up a single survivor on a raft a week later. Three men paddled a raft to a small island whose name they did not even know, where friendly natives saved them. That was the end of one light cruiser.

The failure of the rescue attempt was one of the grimmer stories of the American war effort. Perhaps the stricken ships of Captain Hoover's convoy could be forgiven for steaming on, rather than searching for the submarine, driving it down with depth charges, and looking for survivors. But as so often happened at this phase of the war, the communications system failed miserably. A B-17 came over the damaged flotilla and the ships made contact and asked the air crew to relay a rescue request to Admiral Halsey. It never arrived at Halsey's headquarters.

Back in The Slot, the destroyers *Cushing* and *Monssen* continued to burn. Late on the afternoon of November 13 they sank. The *Aaron Ward*, dead in the water, was spotted in the morning by the *Hiei*, which lay just north of Savo Island, guarded by three Japanese destroyers. The *Hiei* began firing on the *Aaron Ward* and continued until the search planes of the Cactus Air Force came over and attacked her. Then she stopped. She would be too busy thereafter to pay any attention to one crippled American destroyer. The *Aaron Ward* sat in the water until afternoon, when a tug hooked up and towed her toward safety.

The cruiser *Portland*, which could steam only in circles, found the crippled Japanese destroyer *Yudachi* that morning and sank her before she was towed off.

The *Hiei*'s ordeal, serious as it had been during the night, had only begun. At six o'clock in the morning the first strike of dive bombers left Henderson Field. They scored one hit amidships and a near miss. An hour later a group of four marine torpedo bombers appeared and delivered the first torpedo attack ever made by marine pilots. They put one torpedo into the *Hiei*. Just after 10 A.M. six more dive bombers appeared and dropped their bombs, but scored nothing closer than a near miss. Six F4Fs strafed the ship a few minutes later, and the marine torpedo planes came back and put another torpedo into the battleship.

The 11th Air Fleet had been able to send down a number of Zero fighters to cover the *Hiei*, and they engaged in air fights with the American planes. The F4Fs claimed to have shot down seven Zeros.

Late in the morning, nine torpedo bombers from the carrier *Enterprise* arrived on the scene, and they exploded three more torpedoes against the *Hiei*. The 11th Bombardment Group of the U.S. Army Air Force sent 14 B-17s to bomb the ship. They dropped 56 500-pound bombs, and one of them hit the battleship. It was then 11 o'clock in the morning.

A few minutes later more planes arrived from Henderson Field.

Six dive bombers attacked and scored three more hits with 1,000-pound bombs. Six torpedo planes attacked, and two of their torpedoes exploded against the ship.

The *Hiei* was still floating, still fighting, although at least half her antiaircraft guns were out, and the inaccuracy of the gunners attested to the casualties she must have taken.

At 2:35 the *Enterprise* torpedo bombers were back again, having landed at Henderson Field and rearmed. They put three more torpedoes into the *Hiei*.

Just before sunset the marine dive bombers were back again too, and they made one near miss on a destroyer in the *Hiei* screen.

That night the *Hiei* lay low in the water. Her captain and her admiral were wounded. Four hundred and fifty of her crew had been killed. Admiral Yamamoto ordered the destroyer *Kirishima* to take the *Hiei* in tow and bring her back to Truk. But Admiral Abe and Captain Nishida flatly disregarded the direct order and scuttled the *Hiei*. She was sunk that night, and the survivors set off north toward Truk in the destroyers. When Admiral Yamamoto learned of the scuttling of the battleship, he was furious and called a court of inquiry. Admiral Abe and Captain Nishida were both ordered to "retire," which meant go home to live in Japan in ignominy for the rest of their lives.

So the battle the Japanese called the Third Battle of the Solomon Sea and the Americans called the Naval Battle of Guadalcanal came to an end. Admiral Abe had failed in his primary mission, which was to pulverize Henderson Field. He had paid for that dearly the next day in the sinking of his flagship, a loss which would not have been accomplished without the efforts of planes from Henderson Field. The Japanese combined plan to smash Henderson Field, and then take it with troops of the 38th Division was upset.

As for the Americans, they had taken a dreadful beating in destruction and damage of ships: four destroyers sunk or scuttled, two cruisers sunk, three cruisers disabled, and two destroyers disabled.

Admiral Yamamoto was not content with anger at Admiral Abe for his failures; the chief of the Combined Fleet was determined that his plan would not fail. In the early morning hours when the *Hiei* was still afloat, Yamamoto ordered Admiral Kondo, who was then 500 miles east of Rabaul, to rescue the *Hiei* and then go on to bombard Henderson Field on the night of November 14.

18

THE END OF THE BATTLE

ADMIRAL Tanaka and his eleven destroyers had been scheduled to bring the six army troop transports and five cargo ships to Guadalcanal on the night of November 12 under cover of the shelling of the Abe squadron. But when the shelling was abandoned in favor of battle, Yamamoto gave orders that Admiral Tanaka was to turn back to Shortland, and he did. The move was postponed until November 14, which was to give Admiral Kondo time to soften up Henderson Field.

On the night of November 13, "Louie the Louse" appeared over Guadalcanal. It was 1:30 in the morning, and as the men around the airfield listened to the droning of his hateful engine, they knew what was coming next. The green flares appeared over the field, and the heavy cruisers *Suzuya* and *Maya* stood offshore and fired 1,000 rounds of eight-inch ammunition. These shells were the special thin-skinned projectiles the Japanese had developed for antipersonnel bombardment, filled with fragmentation bombs and incendiaries. This morning the shells missed the installations on the bomber strip at Henderson Field, but did much damage in the "cow pasture." Two F4Fs were set afire by the incendiaries, and 15 others were damaged by the fragmentation shrapnel.

The Japanese cruisers were nagged that night by a pair of Ameri-

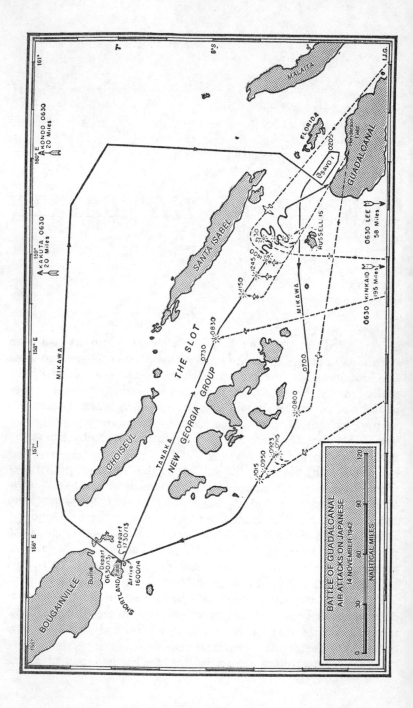

BATTLE OF GUADALCANAL
AIR ATTACKS ON JAPANESE
14 NOVEMBER 1942

NAUTICAL MILES

can PT boats that came out from Tulagi and attacked repeatedly, no matter how much they were discouraged by fire from the cruisers' smaller guns and machine guns. They did not sway the course of events, however, and the cruisers retired at the appointed hour.

When morning came it was apparent that the cruisers had not done very well. The regular morning search by the dive bombers went off on schedule, and at 6:30 reported back by radio that they had found a force of four cruisers and three destroyers 150 miles west of Guadalcanal. These were the ships of Admiral Mikawa: the *Chokai, Kinugasa, Suzuya,* and *Maya,* all heavy cruisers, the light cruisers *Isuzu* and *Tenryu,* and six destroyers. The search planes had undercounted.

The first U.S. strike was launched at 7:15 and included five dive bombers and six torpedo bombers. The dive bombers attacked the *Maya* and hit her on the port side, starting fires. The torpedo bombers attacked the *Kinugasa* and put four torpedoes into the big cruiser. She was burning heavily as the American planes left the area.

Just at this time, search planes from the carrier *Enterprise* also discovered the Mikawa force. Two search planes circled the Japanese ships as they waited for an air strike. Every fifteen minutes they sent messages about the Japanese movements. They stayed up there until they began to run low on gas. Then they attacked the cruiser that was leaving a noticeable oil slick behind it (*Kinugasa*), and each plane's bomb struck, setting new fires. The bombers then headed for Henderson Field nearly out of gas.

A few minutes later two more American bomber pilots from the *Enterprise* discovered the Mikawa ships and attacked. They were green pilots who had not even thought about sending a report. One of them survived the attack; the other did not. Neither did any damage.

At about 10:30, 16 more planes from the *Enterprise* encountered the Japanese ships and dove on them with bombs. They did serious damage to the cruiser *Isuzu* and more to the *Kinugasa.* Later that morning the *Kinugasa* sank.

Early on November 14, the Japanese transports sailed with their destroyer escorts out in front and on both sides of the formation. Admiral Tanaka led them in his flagship *Hayashio* at 11 knots. At dawn on the 14th the flotilla was attacked by American B-17s and carrier bombers. The attackers did no damage, and three were shot down.

In midmorning when the large dive bomber force of the *Enter-prise* was sinking the *Kinugasa*, Admiral Tanaka saw the planes from his flagship as they flew by to the southwest. The weather was spotty, heavy cloud interspersed with clear sky, and perhaps the American bombers did not see the transports. More probably the pilots pre-ferred to attack warships rather than transports.

The results of the American air attacks were soon relayed to Admi-ral Tanaka. He had expected the support of the Mikawa ships to cover the landing of the 38th Division. But Mikawa was going back to Shortland. With one ship sunk and three damaged, he could not carry out his mission satisfactorily.

Four days earlier Tanaka had word of the concentration of Ameri-can naval forces in the Guadalcanal area, including the movement of the American carrier force, and he expected trouble. But nothing quite like what he was to get.

Admiral Halsey was out to get those transports and cripple the Japanese attempt to reinforce the troops on the islands. To do so he had sent Admiral Kinkaid with the *Enterprise,* and they had helped smash Mikawa's group. Halsey had also detached Admiral Lee's two battleships and four destroyers and sent them to the transports and sink them. Altogether, the Japanese supply force consisted of 11 army transports and cargo ships. They had all the heavy equipment of the 38th Army Division aboard.

At 11 o'clock 19 dive bombers and 7 torpedo bombers from Hen-derson Field found the transports. As the planes came into view Ad-miral Tanaka ordered the destroyers to raise a smokescreen and the transports to take evasive action, but the pilots were not confused. One group of dive bombers selected one column of ships and a sec-ond group took another column. The *Sado Maru,* which was carry-ing troops and the staff of the 38th Division, was crippled by bombs. The bombers put two 1,000-pound bombs into another transport. The worst damage was done by the torpedo bombers, which sank the *Canberra Maru* and the *Niagara Maru.* (The Japanese custom of naming ships after foreign cities and geographical points indicates Ja-pan's prewar preoccupation with foreign trade.) After the American planes had left, Admiral Tanaka supervised the rescue of survivors from the two sunken transports, and dispatched the *Sado Maru* with the destroyers *Amagiri* and *Mochizuki* back to Shortland.

Later that morning of November 14, Tanaka's ships were attacked by Cactus Air Force bombers, which sank the *Brisbane Maru*. A little later, more bombers came over and attacked; this time they scored several hits on the remaining transports and cargo ships but did not sink any. B-17s from Espiritu Santo repeated the performance. Early in the afternoon, the *Enterprise* launched her last dive bombers for another attack, and then retired south, having told the bomber pilots to land on Henderson Field.

By this time Admiral Tanaka had called for and secured air cover. Another bombing attack from Henderson came over the ships and was jumped by Zeros, but eight F4Fs attacked the Zeros and kept them away from the bombers, which sank the *Shinanogawa Maru* and the *Arizona Maru*.

To Admiral Tanaka, the day was endless. An hour after those last two transports were sunk, more American bombers appeared, B-17s and dive bombers. They attacked without success, but then just before dark more bombers came in, and this time they sank the *Naku Maru*. The destroyer *Suzukaze* took off the survivors of the 7,000-ton transport, and then she sank, just as the sun was setting. As she went down, the transport train was again under American attack, but in the growing dusk no hits were scored.

So the day's work was done. The Japanese had set out with 11 transports and cargo ships filled with men and supplies. By nightfall, six of the ships had been sunk and one was limping back to Shortland. About 400 of the troops had been killed in the attacks, but 5,000 had been rescued by Tanaka's destroyers. Those destroyers were still picking up survivors at nightfall.

Admiral Tanaka and his men were nearly exhausted. His lasting memories of that day were the sight of bombs wobbling down from B-17s; dive bombers screaming toward the ships, pulling up, and launching bombs, with every one either hitting a ship and starting a fire or splashing and sending a column of water mast high; and the sharp list that meant another ship was going down.

He might have turned back, but his orders were explicit, and he had rescued almost all the troops, who were now aboard the destroyers. They must be delivered to Guadalcanal. So as darkness fell, Admiral Tanaka left the rescue destroyers behind, regrouped his flagship and the three remaining destroyers of Division 15 around the four transports and at 13 knots turned toward Guadalcanal, knowing that he could not arrive at the appointed hour, but would come to the island almost at sunup on November 15.

On the afternoon of November 14, Admiral Tanaka received a message that shook his resolve. A Japanese search plane reported that four enemy cruisers and four destroyers were steaming at high speed east of Guadalcanal. He knew they must be after his ships, and he hesitated. The 8th Fleet was supposed to cover his arrival at Guadalcanal, but Admiral Mikawa was far away and not coming back. Admiral Kondo's 2nd Fleet was also supposed to be in the area for safety's sake, but there was no indication that those ships would appear. Admiral Tanaka weighed his options, but not for long. A message came from Admiral Yamamoto: Tanaka was to head at best possible speed for Guadalcanal.

That message was followed by one that made Tanaka more hopeful. Admiral Kondo was reported to be coming at full speed to attack those American ships east of Guadalcanal. Tanaka's relief force sped on. Late in the afternoon, he was further heartened by the sight of the destroyers left behind to rescue the troops of the sunken transports. They had increased speed and now joined up. Just before midnight, the relief force came up with Admiral Kondo's ships, which now assumed the guardian role, five miles away.

Early on the evening of November 14, Admiral Lee with his battleships *Washington* and *South Dakota* and four destroyers, was moving around the western end of Guadalcanal, about nine miles from the shore. The Americans suffered from one serious problem: lack of training. The four destroyers with Lee were not a division; they were ships from four different destroyer divisions, and they had no division commander aboard. They had been chosen for this task, because they had more fuel than any other available destroyers.

As Admiral Lee's ships moved west of Savo Island, the men could see the burning transports on the horizon. Admiral Lee ordered a course change that would take him down The Slot. He wanted to reach Admiral Kondo's force as quickly as possible. Lee didn't know where Admiral Kondo was, and the coastwatchers on Guadalcanal couldn't tell him. Kondo was very close.

As Kondo approached Savo Island, he sent the light cruiser *Sendai* and three destroyers out ahead as a screen. At 10:10 that night, the *Sendai* was ten miles northeast of Savo Island, when her lookouts sighted Admiral Lee's ships five miles off the port bow, traveling southeast. Admiral Shintaro Hashimoto was the officer in charge of the *Sendai* scouts, and he detached the destroyers *Ayanami* and *Uranami* to go around the western side of Savo and if possible attack the battleships. He also sent a quick report to Admiral Kondo, who then detached the cruiser *Nagara* and four destroyers and sent them west of Savo Island, while his force held course for a few minutes and then turned south, a battleship, two cruisers, and two destroyers.

At 11 o'clock the radar operators aboard the *Washington* found a blip on the screen and began tracking it. The blip was the Japanese cruiser *Sendai*, which was nine miles away. The *Washington* tracked the *Sendai* until she was six miles away and then fired nine 16-inch shells at her. The *Sendai* was not hit, but she immediately put up a smoke screen and retired at high speed northward, followed by the destroyer *Shikinami*.

The Japanese destroyers *Ayanami* and *Uranami* were moving along the south shore of Savo Island when they were sighted by the American destroyers *Benham, Preston,* and *Walke*. The *Walke* fired first, with her five-inch guns. The *Benham* and the *Preston* followed. The *Gwin*, which was last in line, sighted the *Nagara* and opened fire on that cruiser. The Japanese ships responded and put shells into the *Gwin*'s engine room and one on the fantail, which did enough damage that she moved around on the safe side of the battleship *Washington* for protection.

The Japanese, as usual, were proficient with their torpedo attacks, while the Americans were not. The destroyer *Walke* was hit by many shells and began to slow, trying to get away her torpedoes. The *Benham* was firing at all targets that presented themselves. The *Preston* fired at the *Nagara*, which fired back. The *Preston*'s shells did not hurt the cruiser, but the *Nagara*'s shells knocked out both firerooms and the after stack. Soon she was a wreck amidships. Then along came the Japanese torpedoes. The *Walke*'s forecastle was blown off. The *Benham*'s bow was blown off.

The *South Dakota* chose this time to confound her crew with an electrical failure, and her effectiveness was reduced to almost nothing.

At 11:30 three separate groups were fighting in the channel between Savo Island and Guadalcanal. The Japanese destroyer *Ayanami* had been badly damaged by American shells. Five minutes later all four American destroyers were out of action and the *South Da-*

kota was at least temporarily so. The *Walke* sank just after this, and her depth charges exploded beneath her survivors, cutting their number drastically. The *Benham*, limping along, went through the survivors, but was too badly hurt to help. The *Preston* was ablaze internally, and she sank a few minutes later. The *Gwin* came through that water moments afterward and was further damaged by the *Preston*'s exploding depth charges. The *Washington*, unhurt, was speeding into battle. Her sailors stood by the rails and threw life rafts to the men in the sea as she hurried on. The *South Dakota* regained power at 11:45 but was immediately beset by more trouble. A blast of one of her guns set fire to airplanes on the fantail catapults. The next salvo blew the planes overboard.

The *South Dakota* was then the object of more than 30 Japanese torpedoes. Somehow they all missed. But a few moments later she came under the enemy searchlights, and the whole Japanese bombardment force fired on her. She was taking serious punishment.

Admiral Lee had been tracking a large target for some time but feared it might be the *South Dakota* and so refrained from opening fire. Then the Japanese turned on their searchlights, and he saw that it was an enemy battleship. The *Washington* began to fire on the *Kirishima*.

The Japanese ships concentrated on the *South Dakota* with guns and torpedoes. The *Washington* fired rapidly, and soon the *Kirishima* was wrecked, her steering gone, her upper works destroyed and blazing. The *South Dakota* and the *Washington* also fired on the *Atago* and *Takao*, guided by the enemy searchlights, but soon the *South Dakota* was out of it, her radar knocked out, one main battery turret damaged, and many casualties. She moved out of the fight.

Just after midnight on November 15, Admiral Lee turned north, and the Japanese hastened to respond. Their task was to save the transports, and the *Washington* was going for them. In the next hour Admiral Lee moved west to draw the Japanese warships away from his cripples. The *Gwin* escorted the bowless *Benham* to Espiritu Santo. The *Benham* never made it. She was abandoned later and sunk by gunfire.

Admiral Lee had concluded that the Japanese had turned their transports around, and so he headed south and was joined by the *South Dakota*. Admiral Kondo abandoned his plan of bombardment and scuttled the *Kirishima* northwest of Savo Island, then headed north. The destroyer *Ayanami* had been badly damaged, and she too was scuttled that day.

While the battle proceeded, Admiral Tanaka turned his force of transports and destroyers around. He instructed his three escorting destroyers, those unencumbered by survivors, to join the battle, but by the time they moved it was all over. Two of them fired torpedoes at the *Washington*, but then she was past. He turned back to complete his mission: the landing of the reinforcements at Guadalcanal. He headed for Tassafaronga. The plan had called for him to land the troops from the transports between midnight and two o'clock in the morning, which would give the soldiers plenty of time to get ashore and inland and the ships a chance to get away from The Slot before morning came with the expected onslaught of American bombers.

Petty Officer Tsuji was a member of the Imperial Japanese Navy serving aboard the army transport *Yamaura Maru,* one of the transports assigned to move the 38th Division's troops and heavy equipment to Guadalcanal. To Tsuji and his best friend, Petty Officer Rakusen, the voyage began as had so many others. They and their army transport had participated in the invasions of Malaya, Burma, and the Dutch East Indies in earlier and more prosperous times for the Japanese Army. But as the ship loaded in Java, there was no way of knowing that this voyage was going to be any different from the others. Even as the ship stopped at the Shortlands to join the convoy led by Admiral Tanaka, Tsuji and his companions remained confident. The 38th Division was just another unit of army troops, off to another victory, it seemed.

Admiral Tanaka knew that the plan was no good at this point; it was far too late. So he decided to run the transports aground. It was unprecedented to voluntarily destroy four transports, so he consulted higher authority. Admiral Mikawa said absolutely not; Admiral Kondo said go ahead and do it, and so Tanaka did. The convoy came down just as dawn was breaking and Tanaka issued the orders. The transport captains ran their ships into the beach, and when Admiral Tanaka saw them grinding ashore, he turned and took his destroyers to The Slot as fast as possible, hoping to avoid the American air search of the morning and the expected bombings.

But as the ships came down The Slot just before dawn on November 15, they were harried by Allied bombers, and some of the vessels were hit. On the lower deck of an army transport, the seamen were hardly party to Admiral Tanaka's plans, but as the ships neared Guadalcanal, the admiral's decision had to be made known. Run aground? It was unheard of in the ever-victorious Japanese Army. But that was what was to happen, and suddenly the six transports were off Koli Point, and the unthinkable was on them: American dive bombers and fighters were zooming all around the ships, and torpedo planes were coming in low to drop their "fish."

When Tsuji and his friend saw that the captain of their ship was, indeed, heading straight in to the beach, they stopped in their tracks and began to pray "as if the hour of our death were arranged," Tsuji wrote in his diary.

As Tsuji prayed he heard and saw the bombs falling around his ship, and he saw the waterspouts as the bombs struck just off the bow, and the explosion, the surge of fire and smoke, the mangled steel and bodies thrust upward on the transport next to his own as they sped for the beach.

Aboard *Yamaura Maru* the shrapnel from high explosive bombs made a pattern on the deck that reminded Tsuji of rice grains on a threshing floor.

It was all very unreal. For no reason, Tsuji thought of his last leave in Tokyo, just weeks before, as the ships had put in at Tokyo Bay for oil and provisions. His prayer to Kannon, the Goddess of Mercy, finished, Tsuji gave himself to the memory as he waited for the ship to beach. He spoke to Rakusen of his thoughts, and they laughed nervously together.

"You remember how you paid for everything in Tokyo because I was broke," Tsuji said.

"And how sick I got on sake in that joint in the Ginza," Rakusen laughed.

"Next time it's my turn, right?"

"Of course."

They both knew it was a brave lie. There would be no next time. Ever.

Then the ship crashed on the beach, and the captain ordered.

"All ashore. All men ashore."

They began climbing down the cargo nets they had thrown over the side. A few brave souls manned hoists as the bombers rode above them, and a few vehicles were taken ashore. But mostly it was men, their rifles, and a few precious bags of rice that went over the sides, into the gentle surf and up onto the beach into the trees beyond, there to wait for orders.

They came soon enough. There was only one place to go: up the mountain trail built by the Pioneer Forces, through the jungle, to the main encampment of the Japanese command. Slowly, in their canvas shoes and wet fatigue uniforms, surrounded by soldiers, the sailors began the long hike.

They climbed all day, and into the night. As darkness fell, Tsuji noticed a sort of incandescence in the jungle along the trail. Perhaps it was the presence of Kannon. Perhaps it was caused by rotting vegetation, but it impressed him deeply and made him think of home and his native village so far away and also of the month of May with its bright promise. It was autumn in Japan, the leaves were turning and the ground would be crisp. Not like this sodden, dark jungle in its heat.

Finally, before dawn, they came to the naval unit's station. In the inimitable style of the Japanese forces, they had been sent to the naval station, although they were not in any marine or naval troop, because they were seamen, not soldiers.

Tsuji found himself at a construction camp, the Pioneers' headquarters. Here he would live, and here he would watch his companions join the dead in their shallow graves beneath the small crude stone markers that showed where they slept.

As morning came Tsuji arose from his blanket on the ground and looked around him. He was sleeping in the Pioneer cemetery. As the light came streaming in from the east, he saw colors very much like those of autumn at home—yellow and red leaves on the trees, and then below him on the steep hillside, a river of green forest, like the pines of his own Honshu mountains.

Dawn brought out the American planes from Henderson Field.

Before six o'clock on the morning of November 15 the American airmen looked down on the grounded *Kinugawa Maru, Yamatsuki Maru, Hirokawa Maru,* and *Yamaura Maru.* From Bougainville and the Shortlands Admiral Kusaka put up as many fighters as he could to try to protect those transports on the beach. The first American bombing raid scored hits on two of the transports. The second, half an hour later, hit more of them, and a third bombing raid at 7 in the morning found supplies on the beach and bombed them. Five more attacks were made on the Japanese ships, and they burned. Admiral Kusaka sent more Zeros that day, but the F4Fs engaged them over Savo Island and claimed to have shot down seven planes while losing one.

As darkness fell on November 15, back at Nouméa Admiral Halsey could claim a clearcut victory. The Japanese had set out to land 10,000 men on Guadalcanal, plus the heavy equipment, big guns, and ammunition of an entire infantry division. Of the total, only 2,000 had actually gotten ashore, with 1,500 bags of rice, which would supply them for four days, and 260 rounds for mountain guns, the ammunition dump that was to be destroyed by bombers that same day.

The cost to the Japanese had been 2 battleships, 1 heavy cruiser, 3 destroyers, 11 transports, and about 50 airplanes, plus 6 damaged warships.

The Americans, on the other hand, had safely landed the 8th Marine Regiment from 4 transports, which had then retired. They had lost 2 cruisers and 7 destroyers and suffered serious damage to 3 cruisers and lighter damage to 1 battleship. There was no doubt that it was a costly battle to both sides, but there was no doubt either that the Americans had the best of it, and the outcome would vitally affect the struggle for Guadalcanal.

19

TASSAFARONGA

COLONEL Carlson's Raiders had been in constant contact with the Japanese for a week. On November 12, as the Battle of Guadalcanal developed at sea, he occupied the village of Asamana and discovered that the Japanese had laid out a bivouac area there for at least a battalion and had carefully marked the assembly points of various units with signs stuck to the trees. That day and the next, Carlson's men ambushed the Japanese time after time. On November 13 Carlson moved his troops up to Asamana and from there sent out patrols that ambushed a number of small Japanese units. The 7th Marines and the army troops had worked out a plan to ambush a large Japanese unit, but the enemy got wind of it and the force swam the Malimbiu River, and made its way up into the hills on the west. So the Raiders, having marched across the island, found there was nothing more for them to do on that mission, and Carlson went to Vandegrift's headquarters for a new assignment.

On November 13 the marines captured a number of landing craft and 15 tons of rice. The latter hurt, for the Japanese were extremely short of supplies. Indeed, because of the logistical problems, the landing of the 38th Division without its tanks, big guns, ammunition, and supplies threatened to become a liability.

The Americans faced a similar problem. On November 16 Admiral Turner assigned several transports to deliver more troops of the Americal Division to Guadalcanal and to take in supplies. The marines and army troops were critically short of food, ammunition, aviation gas, bombs, and torpedoes at Henderson Field. On the ground, the marines harried the Japanese almost constantly. The Japanese had broken into many small groups and worked their way back into the jungle. General Kawaguchi's personal gear was captured by the Raiders near Asamana, but not General Kawaguchi. Several of the forces that had been landed by Admiral Tanaka were regarded by the Americans as of little danger, because those Japanese had been so thoroughly disorganized and deprived of their supplies. Every day the marines patrolled, and if they found Japanese activity, they called for artillery or for air support, and both responded as needed. The control of Henderson Field was making all the difference in the world, as Admiral Yamamoto had surmised weeks before.

When Colonel Carlson came up to the 1st Division command post and asked for a new job, General Vandegrift gave him one. He and the Raiders were to track down and destroy Pistol Pete, the group of Japanese howitzers that fired several times each day on Henderson Field. They were also to find the trail the Japanese had used to get from the Lunga River to the Matanikau River and set up an ambush.

By November 18, General Vandegrift was preparing for another major attack, moving troops across the Matanikau River west of Point Cruz. The Cactus Air Force found relatively light air opposition, just a few Zeros in the air, and three of these were shot down by Army P-38s, brand new twin-engined fighter planes for the Pacific air forces that had enormous speed and diving capability and immense firepower. These planes had considerable advantage over the Zeros except in tight maneuvers. The search planes from Henderson Field found no Japanese shipping in The Slot or anywhere near it. The Cactus Air Force was called upon for a few air support missions that day.

On November 21 the Americans were moving, but slowly and against stubborn Japanese resistance. For the next five days operations were limited; a few Japanese were routed along the trails and killed; machine guns were captured and a few supplies destroyed. But the Americans were not coming to grips with the enemy. A few Japanese bombers came over, mostly in ones and twos, but instead of striking straight for Henderson Field as they had for months, they bombed the marines in their camps, inflicting a few casualties. The Imperial General Staff and Admiral Yamamoto had given up the hope of taking Henderson Field through air and sea action. The cost had been prohibitive. The Imperial General Staff still indicated its complete commitment to the capture of Guadalcanal, but if it was to be done, it was going to be accomplished by the army.

Finding the Japanese was a major problem. From the islanders on Guadalcanal, the marines learned that there were about 3,000 troops at Rekata Bay on the northwest coast of Santa Isabel Island. Were they assembling there to move down to Guadalcanal? A group of 50 Japanese on a barge were reported at Rendova near New Georgia. Were they headed for Guadalcanal? The marines suspected a new effort at supply of the Japanese on a piecemeal basis.

They were quite right. Admiral Yamamoto and the 17th Army Command at Rabaul were thoroughly distressed by the presence of 10,000 Japanese troops on Guadalcanal with diminishing resources and no method of supply. They could not supply the troops from the air, because the Cactus Air Force was too formidable. They could not supply them by transport; the events of November 14 and 15 had proved that.

During the third week of November, various methods of supply were attempted. The Americans were not particularly aware of Japanese naval activity off Guadalcanal, but it existed nonetheless. At the Shortland base, Tanaka's men sterilized old oil drums and filled them with medical supplies and rice. The drums were roped together. They were loaded aboard a destroyer, and that destroyer made a high-speed passage to Guadalcanal, arrived at night, pushed the drums overboard close to shore, announced by radio that they were there, and sped back to Shortland to gain safety and to repeat the performance. This system had already been tried at New Guinea, where the Japanese forces around Lae were also cut off and starving.

Another method of supply, particularly at New Guinea, but transferred to Guadalcanal as well, was by submarine. The submarines were loaded with food and medicines and then surfaced just offshore late at night to deliver the supplies to Japanese landing boats. There was nothing new in this method. The Germans had used it in World War I. The Americans had used it at Corregidor and at Guadalcanal in those first desperate days.

By the end of November, the Japanese on Guadalcanal let it be known that these supply methods were totally inadequate. Japanese headquarters announced that by the end of the month the food would be completely consumed. Actually, all rice and other staples were gone before the end of the month, and the men had begun foraging and eating wild plants and animals to survive. The sick lists grew longer every day.

Admiral Yamamoto, when approached by the army, was aghast to learn of the condition of the troops. Aboard the *Yamato* there was plenty. When an army representative visited the flagship to plead for more supplies for the soldiers on Guadalcanal he was served a dish made of sea bream, a fish dear to the hearts of Japanese, and then broiled sea bream and chilled beer from home. They served Scotch whisky and English cigarettes.

There was no way that such delicacies could find their way to the campfires of Guadalcanal. Rice would be enough. On November 27, Admiral Tanaka was ordered to begin the regular resupply of the soldiers with all the means at his disposal. Four destroyers moved into Shortland from Rabaul, loaded with drums of food and medical supplies. The first effort to make the run through The Slot would be on November 30 and would employ eight destroyers. Two of them would be heavily armed, but the other six would sacrifice armament to accommodate more supplies. Most of their torpedoes were unloaded and replaced by drums of food and medicine. Only one torpedo remained for each tube. The quantity of ammunition for the guns was sharply reduced.

On November 29 the flagship *Naganami*, accompanied by the destroyer *Takanami*, and six supply destroyers set out with Admiral Tanaka in command. The ships sailed south during the night. Tanaka hoped to avoid detection by the Americans.

The American air searches were no better than usual, and they did not find the Tanaka force. This deficiency was certainly not due to any shortage of planes. Henderson Field had been heavily reinforced in recent days and now housed 124 planes, including 8 B-17s. The Seabees were extending the bomber strip and laying Marston matting for a mile. The two fighter strips were also being matted so there would be no trouble with mud. The whole American effort had turned around, and while one could not say yet that it was cursed with oversupply, the ability of Admiral Turner to resupply the marines and the airfield was proved. Further, the *Jamestown*, a motor torpedo boat tender had been brought down to Tulagi, and 15 PT boats were operating out of those waters. Eight U.S. destroyers were assigned to regular transport escort duty between the Solomons and Espiritu Santo and Nouméa.

Where the United States was short was in carriers. The *Saratoga* was on her way back under Admiral Ramsey, and *Enterprise* had a new commander. After his desertion of the *Hornet* in her time of need, Admiral Kinkaid had been moved to command of a five cruiser task force and was replaced by one of the "Young Turk" rear admirals who had just been promoted. Rear Admiral Frederick C. Sherman was an airman through and through, not a retreaded battleship commander as had been most of the task force leaders in the early days of the war.

The Americans had the battleships *Washington* and *North Carolina* and soon would have the *Indiana*. The battleships *Maryland* and *Colorado* were in the Fijis and could come up on command. Further, there had been an enormous change in outlook of the respective high commands. Admiral Yamamoto was sobered by defeat in the efforts to land men on Guadalcanal, and the dreadful attrition to his carriers, battleships, and destroyers. In terms of fleet actions he had more than held his own; the Japanese had proved themselves superior in the management of battle, and the only serious defeats suffered by the Imperial Navy had been Admiral Goto's unlucky meeting with Admiral Scott, who won the engagement despite his personal confusion as to the course of events, Admiral Abe's disastrous foray, and Admiral Kondo's error at the last naval battle. Yamamoto had another problem. The Japanese Navy's system of pilot training had always been sharply restricted to the best men. When the war began, the Japanese naval pilots were as good as any in the world, as a team far superior to the Americans. But in the battle of attrition beginning with Midway, the trained pilots had been going down one by one, and Japan's training system had not caught up. So Yamamoto was now getting pilots fresh out of training who too often took their new planes out and were shot down on that first vital mission. Yamamoto was beset by other problems, such as supply and the inability of the 11th Air Fleet and the carrier force to stand up against the enormous number of planes that the Americans were throwing into the battle. With the arrival of the P-38s the disparity of fighters grew even greater. The Zero had the advantage of long-range, fleetness, and maneuverability. More and more, however, the stronger armament and superior fire power of the American aircraft was tilting the battle. The same had to be said for the Betty, the bomber-of-all-work that at the beginning of the war had been the finest and most numerous in the Pacific. But the Betty was not totally outstripped by the B-17s and the B-24 four-engined bombers that were starting to come in. So Yamamoto's course was to keep the Combined Fleet out of major action and preserve the carriers. He was under further wraps from the Imperial General Staff. He had thought seriously of committing the *Yamato* to the battle for Guadalcanal, and that 70,000-ton battleship might have made an enormous difference in the battle for Henderson Field. But Tokyo had indicated that, because of her enormous fuel consumption, the best thing the *Yamato* could do was sit still. The fleet's daily consumption of fuel had gone far beyond prewar expectations, and now amounted to 10,000 tons. The reserves at the Kure naval base had been reduced to 65,000 tons, which was obviously a dangerously low level, and the American submarine menace grew worse each week as the U.S. submarines sank more tankers. So he kept the *Yamato* at Truk, out of action. He still thought of the war in terms of one more decisive victory and then the supreme effort to get to the peace table. Since he could not control the army's activity, in his sphere the battle had to be naval, and he was holding his forces for that day.

Admiral Halsey was prosecuting the war in the South Pacific with great vigor. He had only one absolute for his officers: fight. If they fought and lost, even if they made errors in judgment, he would not complain. If they showed the slightest timidity, he would have them out of his command. If they proved totally inept, he would break them as quick as look at them. One day when a new destroyer commander showed up in Nouméa, Halsey laid that all out for him. Quite probably, if Admiral Callaghan had survived the battle of Guadalcanal, Admiral King would have demanded his head for carelessness and bad planning, but Admiral Halsey would have protected him.

"Go get 'em" was one of Halsey's fondest phrases, and every ship commander in the South Pacific knew it. Even before Halsey began to get the materials necessary to win the battle, he showed that indomitable spirit. In November, as the materials began to flow, largely in response to a direct order from President Roosevelt that Guadalcanal should be held, Halsey became ever more confident and ever more effective. He was determined to protect the American position on Guadalcanal, but not in the old way. His ships would be used in task forces and would stay out of the dangerous waters of The Slot except when on a mission.

One such mission was that given to Admiral Kinkaid's task force of cruisers. Kinkaid was told to counter any and all night landing attempts by the Japanese. The cruisers were to be brought to a point south of Guadalcanal, and when reports came that the Japanese were launching a resupply mission, they were to move up to stop it.

Three days after Admiral Kinkaid was moved to his new cruiser command, he was snatched back from the South Pacific by Admiral King to take command of the American naval force that was planning to wipe the Japanese out of the Aleutian Islands. The Japanese had landed there successfully during the Midway battle, but had not made any efforts to advance. There had been a few naval encounters, mostly to the advantage of the Japanese. Now Admiral King had seen the availability of resources, and he wanted the Japanese threat destroyed.

So as Admiral Tanaka prepared for his first major resupply mission since the unfortunate attempt to deliver the 38th Division and its supplies, the command of the five cruiser force was turned over to Rear Admiral Carleton H. Wright, who had been a cruiser task force commander for Nimitz in the Pacific since July.

Kinkaid was an excellent battle commander of surface ships. Before he left the South Pacific he had drawn a battle plan for the task force. No more would the Americans move their ships in a straight line, without regard for the effective use of their most important intelligence weapon: radar. The cruisers had been divided into two groups, making sure that each group had the newest search radar aboard at least one ship. The four destroyers of the task force would operate as one group, under a division commander, and accordingly could be expected to make much more effective use of their torpedoes. The cruisers' float planes would be employed as the Japanese had employed theirs, for night search and flare illumination of the battle area. The Americans would not use searchlight, so if any searchlights came on, they could be sure they were enemy. Recognition lights, whose use had cost at least three ships in the Guadalcanal battles, would be used only when the ship commander was *certain* he was being fired on by an American ship.

Fifteen minutes after Tanaka sailed, on the evening of November 29, Admiral Wright received a message from Admiral Halsey to get going: the Japanese were sending a force of destroyers and transports to land troops and supplies at Guadalcanal that would arrive on the night of November 30. Once again Admiral Nimitz's radio intelligence team had made good use of their mastery of parts of the Japanese naval code. At 11 o'clock that night the task force sailed on the 600-mile journey to Guadalcanal. The ships traveled at high speed, 28 knots.

On the morning of November 30, Admiral Tanaka turned east from Bougainville to confuse the Americans about his purpose. He was upset about the presence of an American plane that seemed to be shadowing him that morning. His ploy worked perfectly, for the pilot never reported his findings.

Not quite as effective as Nimitz's radio intelligence was the report made by Coastwatcher Mason. On the morning of November 30, from his vantage point, he counted the masts of the Japanese ships in Buin Harbor and notified Guadalcanal that 12 destroyers were missing. So Guadalcanal knew someone was on the move, but where they were heading and why was still a mystery.

On his trip toward The Slot, Admiral Tanaka had word from a Japanese reconnaissance plane of an American force of twelve destroyers and nine transports apparently heading for Guadalcanal. He did not want to meet them; his mission was to supply, not to fight, but he prepared for action anyway, and the ships went to ready stations.

As the sun set the weather took a turn for the worse. It began to rain, and the stars were blotted out. Tanaka slowed down. But the squall passed over, and the visibility improved. Tanaka speeded up.

The American force came out of Indispensable Strait early in the evening of November 30. There they encountered three American transports and five destroyers heading back toward Espiritu Santo. Halsey ordered two of those destroyers to join Admiral Wright, and they took positions at the end of the cruiser column.

At 11 o'clock the American task force was in Iron Bottom Sound, heading for Savo Island. Admiral Tanaka's ships were just passing west of Savo and turning southeast.

Marines at the Guadalcanal battlefront keep up with the news from home
in September 1942.

Native policemen aided Captain Martin Clemens of the
Solomon Islands Defense Forces, an Australian, who stayed on
Guadalcanal throughout the Japanese occupation. Coast-
watchers also gave American troops on Guadalcanal warning of
Japanese ships and planes coming down The Slot.

American troops move out to clear the island of Japanese.

Four marines wade up the main street of their camp during the rainy season on Guadalcanal.

Japanese barges and tank lighters sunk in the Lunga River.

Japanese troopship, *Kyusyu Maru*, damaged during the Naval Battle of Guadalcanal, November 13-15, 1942, lies sunk by the stern off Guadalcanal beach.

e USS *San Francisco* after November 13, 1942, engagement off
Savo Island.

USS *Pensacola* in Espiritu Santo Harbor, showing stern and portside damage caused by a Japanese torpedo. The cruiser was one of those hit during engagements of November 13-15, 1942, off Guadalcanal.

Beached Japanese transports burning on Guadalcanal during the Second Battle of the Solomons, on November 16, 1942.

B-17s were used extensively against the Japanese during the contest for Guadalcanal.

This vivid streak marks the end of one of the Japanese planes which attacked a U.S. task force January 29, 1943 off Rennell Island, severely damaging the heavy cruiser USS *Chicago.*

The USS *Chicago* riding low in the water a few hours before she went to the bottom off Rennell Island.

The Kinkaid plan had called for two destroyers to move ahead of the main American flotilla, but somehow this had not been done, and so the Americans were deprived of advance knowledge of the enemy. Just after 11 o'clock the American radar picked up a strange blip.

This time the Americans were alert. Admiral Wright did not lose a moment in ordering a 40 degree turn that put the American ships in the column formation he wanted. Then, the single blip dissolved like an amoeba into a number of smaller ones, ships in formation, heading southeast toward Guadalcanal.

In fact, Admiral Tanaka had already given orders for the supply destroyers to be ready to dump their drums, because the current and tide would take them ashore at the Japanese end of the island. The ships had slowed to 12 knots, and were about a mile offshore. But before Tanaka gave the "execute" order, three enemy planes began circling the Japanese ships. These were the observation float planes that Admiral Wright had sent off earlier from his ships to land at Tulagi in order to take off again as his force neared the island.

The Japanese had been throwing up green flares all this time, and Admiral Tanaka hoped the Americans had not sighted them. They had not because the float planes had been late in arriving. But that matter became totally unimportant seconds later when a lookout reported "enemy ships bearing 100 degrees." Next came another report. "Seven enemy destroyers."

The Japanese ships had already broken battle formation, but now Tanaka ordered them to put down the drums and assume their battle stations. There was no time to try to reassemble the usual Japanese battle formation.

At 11:15 the American destroyer commander asked permission of his admiral to break off from the line and make an independent torpedo attack. Admiral Wright hesitated and second-guessed the destroyerman. He thought the range was too far.

The moment of battle is scarcely the time for an admiral to begin quizzing his subordinates about their knowledge, but Admiral Wright did just that; five precious minutes passed, and the Japanese ships moved away from the Americans and past them. The moment was gone. When the admiral finally gave the commander the go sign, the destroyers launched 20 torpedoes at the Japanese ships, but the range and angle were all wrong, and $200,000 worth of American weaponry went to the bottom of the sea without doing any damage.

Finally, the American float planes gained enough altitude to begin their work. Their problem had been the glassy, windless surface of Tulagi Bay that for precious minutes had kept them from getting the aerodynamic lift they needed to break the suction and take the planes off the water. They began dropping flares around the Japanese ships, which accomplished the purpose of lighting up Tanaka's destroyers without using telltale searchlights.

The moment that Admiral Tanaka saw the first American cruiser he gave his battle order: "Close and attack." The Japanese did, although for a change they were at a slight disadvantage because of the glare of the American flares. Still their shooting was good. The destroyer *Takanami* was the first to approach the Americans and the first to fire. Her opening salvo struck an American ship, and her next five salvos also struck other ships. But by that time *Takanami* was in desperate trouble. The concentrated fire of the cruiser *Minneapolis*, the cruiser *New Orleans*, and several other ships fired on her repeatedly, until she was aflame and her guns had been destroyed. Apparently, all the American ships were concentrating their fire on this one target.

The flagship *Naganami* was also in action. Her searchlight swept toward the Americans and caught an American cruiser. The light stopped and lingered on the cruiser's bridge. The *Naganami* was running in the opposite direction, so she swung around and paralleled the cruiser course, firing her guns and readying her torpedoes. At a range of three miles she launched eight torpedoes. Just before 11:30 two of them struck the cruiser *Minneapolis*, Admiral Wright's flagship, sending such huge columns of water over the ship that the eight-inch guns were silenced for a few moments. The guns regained power, but then the general power system failed, and the *Minneapolis* was out of the fight, her captain concerned with the problems of keeping the damaged ship afloat.

Another of *Naganami*'s torpedoes struck the cruiser *New Orleans*, which was trying to avoid a collision with the wavering *Minneapolis*, and blew up two forward magazines. The ship broke in two, and the whole bow section slipped along the port side of what was left.

The *New Orleans*'s after guns, the *Pensacola*, and other American ships fired on the *Naganami*. A number of near misses gouged holes in her, but she did not take a single direct hit, perhaps because she was travelling at top speed of 45 knots.

The Japanese destroyers *Oyashio* and *Kuroshio* fired ten torpedoes at American ships. One of them struck the cruiser *Pensacola* below the mainmast. She lost power and began to list, and her captain took her out of the fight and headed for Tulagi. Meanwhile, the American destroyers were again launching torpedoes, and the Japanese destroyer *Suzukaze* was so busy turning to avoid them that she did not launch any of her own.

The American heavy cruiser *Northampton* turned to avoid the three damaged vessels ahead of her, and kept firing, but two of *Oyashio*'s torpedoes struck her and opened her up as a can opener rips through a tin of beans. She listed to port, slowed, and finally stopped.

The American ships became thoroughly confused, and some were firing on each other. Two of the destroyers had to leave the scene to avoid gunfire from crippled cruisers.

Altogether the action lasted almost half an hour, and then both sides began taking stock. Admiral Wright in the stricken *Minneapolis* gave up his command to Admiral Tisdale in the *Honolulu*, which went around Savo Island to try to find the Japanese. All he found was a "destroyer landing troops on the beach at Guadalcanal" that turned out to be one of the wrecked transports that Tanaka had run aground two weeks earlier. She steamed around Savo Island once more and found nothing.

Admiral Tanaka pulled clear of the battle and called up the *Takanami*. She did not answer. He sent the *Oyashio* and *Kuroshio* back to find her and to see what help they could give. They did find her south of Cape Esperance, dead in the water. At about that time the *Honolulu* appeared, and the two Japanese destroyers fled, leaving the *Takanami* survivors in the water. Some of them made their way by small boat and raft to Guadalcanal where they joined the troops, but 26 Japanese sailors and the ship's log were rescued by the Americans.

Apparently, the *Honolulu* never saw the *Takanami* or the two undamaged Japanese destroyers, and later Admiral Morison wrote that the *Takanami* had sunk during the heat of the action with all hands.

In any event Admiral Tanaka had lost a ship. He assembled all the others around the flagship, and to his surprise discovered that not one of the other Japanese destroyers had suffered even a single direct hit. But they had fired all their torpedoes, and the supply destroyers did not have sufficient ammunition to engage in further action. To do so would not have been in accord with Japanese navy doctrine anyhow, since the torpedoes were gone and the Japanese placed a much higher value on the destroyers as torpedo platforms than did the Americans at that time.

The battle the Japanese called the Night Battle of Lunga and the Americans called the Battle of Tassafaronga was over. Admiral Tanaka had not fulfilled his supply mission, but had inflicted one of the most stunning defeats of the war in terms of relative strengths of forces employed. With nothing but destroyers, he had sunk the cruiser *Northampton* (she was abandoned that night) and caused serious damage to three other American cruisers, while losing a single destroyer. The *Minneapolis* and the *New Orleans* had to be sent back to the United States for repairs and were out of action for nearly a year. The *Pensacola* had to go back to Pearl Harbor, and she also was out of action until October, 1943.

In postmortem, the American admirals tried to figure out what had gone wrong. They had many explanations: surprise, the lack of military training with this task force, the numerical inferiority of the American destroyers. But the truth was that the Americans conducted a sloppy battle. The float planes did not do their job. The destroyers did not do theirs. The marksmanship of the cruiser gunners, who fired hundreds of salvos, was dismal. In the final analysis, it added up to a well-known story: In night fighting tactics the Japanese were far superior to the Americans. They had already had much more practice, and Admiral Tanaka's destroyers worked as a team, but that was not the real answer. The Japanese had a better conceptual use of the destroyers in night actions than the Americans and were thus much more effective in fighting. The Americans could take some pride in improvement of their damage control methods—they saved three of the cruisers. But the end result was a stunning victory for the Japanese.

20

STRAIGHT DOWN
THE SLOT

WHEN Admiral Yamamoto learned that Admiral Tanaka had not delivered the supplies to Guadalcanal that night, he was furious again, and the fact that Tanaka had scored a major sea victory over the Americans did not help. Yamamoto knew better than any other Japanese commander that the Americans had an enormous capability to construct ships, and it was already showing in the battle for Guadalcanal. Time, as he saw, was not on his side, and every day's failure to deliver the supplies meant more wastage of the troops starving on the island.

Tanaka reasoned that night that many American destroyers were still unhurt; without weapons himself, he had no desire to run the gauntlet. Only later did he realize that the Americans were thoroughly disorganized, that most of the destroyers were engaged in rescue operations, and that if he had gone back to deliver the supplies, he probably would have been successful and could have steamed away without another fight.

Admiral Yamamoto's displeasure was quickly felt. Admiral Tanaka had tried hard and would try again to carry out a mission that at best was improbable, the small scale and piecemeal resupply of a large fighting force trapped on an island, with the enemy in control of the air and the sea by day.

On December 1 Admiral Tanaka was back at Shortland, and in the next two days the destroyers *Arashi* and *Nowaki* and *Yugure* were assigned by Admiral Yamamoto to join the supply fleet. On December 3, in his flagship *Naganami* accompanied by ten destroyers, he sailed again. Seven of the destroyers were loaded with supplies, and the other three were the escort.

In the morning, the ships sighted a group of B-17s, but the planes were obviously bent on other business, for they did not attack. Late in the afternoon, as the Japanese force was steaming under air protection from 12 Zero float planes from Buin, a group of American fighters, bombers, and torpedo bombers attacked. Each side lost several aircraft, and the destroyer *Makinami* was damaged by a near miss from a bomb. Several men were killed and wounded, but the ship's capacity was not seriously impaired, and the relief force steamed on. The American pilots returned to Henderson Field to report that they had put two 1,000-pound bombs into one ship, one into another, and that two other destroyers had been hit by U.S. torpedoes. It was a wildly optimistic evaluation of the real performance.

When Admiral Tanaka reached Savo Island, he turned the ships to the Guadalcanal coast, and at midnight the seven supply destroyers began dumping their drums overboard. They had time to take to small boats, haul the rope ends into shore, return to the destroyers, hoist the boats, and pull away. The only opposition that night came from several PT boats, which were kept away by the three escort destroyers as the supply ships did their job.

The supply mission, however, was not a success, through no fault of Admiral Tanaka, but because of the aggressiveness of General Vandegrift's troops ashore and the weakness of the Japanese troops. The Americans were patrolling and engaging the Japanese constantly and effectively prevented a large force from reaching the shore the next day to retrieve most of the drums. The men who did come were too exhausted to pull in many drums. Only 300 of the 1,500 came into Japanese hands. The rest washed out to sea or were sunk by the machine gun fire of Cactus Air Force planes the next day.

Back in Buin on December 4 Admiral Tanaka made preparations for the next run. That evening Admiral Mikawa arrived at Buin in his flagship, and Admiral Tanaka was ordered to report on the battle of November 30 and the supply operations. Tanaka took this opportunity to unleash his true feelings that the whole supply operation was an enormous waste of Japan's resources and could never succeed. The situation must grow worse, not better, as a consequence of the American buildup of power. He felt that the complete demoralization of the Japanese troops on Guadalcanal and of the fleet could be the only outcome. He recommended that the troops be evacuated immediately from Guadalcanal and that the strong base wanted by the High Command be built at Shortland.

This discussion was not at all what Mikawa and Yamamoto wanted to hear. The Imperial General Staff had *demanded* the capture of Guadalcanal at all costs. Plans were being made in Tokyo to assign an *entire army* to the capture, but until they could be carried out, Yamamoto had to take responsibility for supply of the 15,000 men on Guadalcanal.

Yamamoto's buildup of the supply force showed how vital he held the supply mission: In the next three days Admiral Tanaka received four more destroyers, the *Urakaze, Tanikaze, Ariake* and the spanking new 2,500-ton *Teruzuki.* She became Tanaka's flagship.

On December 7 the admiral undertook his third drum supply run. This time he elected to send the ships up under a divisional commander, Captain Torajiro Sato. The Cactus Air Force was out in strength and attacked the supply group. That night Captain Sato reported that the American bombers had dropped a bomb that blew in the side of the destroyer *Nowaki.* She had to be detached and sent back to Buin under tow of the *Naganami* escorted by two other destroyers. When Admiral Tanaka received that message, he set out in his new flagship for the scene. But before he could arrive, he had bad news: The destroyer team had approached Guadalcanal, harried by American planes all the way, and then had been subjected to a concentrated attack by American PT boats. This was the first time the PT boats were operating in a new fashion. They had the services that night of several float planes from the damaged cruisers (which had been left behind at Tulagi). The float planes found the Japanese supply destroyers and dropped flares, and the PT boats attacked, firing torpedoes, moving in close, and strafing the Japanese destroyers. The harassment caused many casualties and persuaded Captain Sato to turn around and go back to Buin without delivering his supplies. When Admiral Tanaka learned of the decision in mid-ocean, he concurred.

The American pressure grew stronger every day. On December 8 the destroyer group returned to Buin, just in time for an air raid on the Shortland anchorage by B-17s. Two tankers were badly damaged, but the destroyers remained intact.

Admiral Tanaka was ordered to mount his fourth attempt to re-supply Guadalcanal, knowing that the troops there must be close to starvation, since they had not had effective supply for a month.

Meanwhile, the Imperial General Staff had a new idea. Let the submarine force assist more in the resupply of Guadalcanal. A group of submarines, most of them of the 2,000-ton I-boat class, was sent to Buin. They were loaded with supplies and one by one were dis-patched for Guadalcanal to land at Makino Point on the western end of the island. This entire operation, mounted under Rear Admi-ral Hisao Mito at Rabaul, was separate from Tanaka's. The sub-mariners, who hated the duty and were persuaded only by the revela-tion that the troops in Guadalcanal were reduced to eating grass, called it the Mole Operation. The first run, made early in December, was successful. Lieutenant Commander Yahachi Tanabe took the *I-176* to Guadalcanal and unloaded the first supplies the troops had seen for days.

But the second mission was not a success. On December 7, the *I-3* left Buin loaded with provisions. Two nights later *PT 59* attacked as she surfaced off Cape Esperance. The PT boat hit her with two tor-pedoes and the submarine blew up, leaving only one ensign to swim ashore to Guadalcanal to report.

The submarine supply system continued, and by and large it was more successful than supply by destroyer. Most of the assigned sub-marines got through, but still the amount of supplies they could deliver constituted no more than a drop in the bucket for 15,000 sur-vivors on Guadalcanal.

On December 11, Admiral Tanaka led the fourth supply mission himself. The ships were attacked from the air, but the planes were driven off. Eleven destroyers headed for Guadalcanal. At midnight just south of Savo Island they were attacked by a swarm of PT boats. Seven destroyers dropped 1,200 drums of supplies and began to with-draw. The PT boats attacked. Two of them managed to put tor-pedoes into the *Teruzuki* and the ship caught fire and lost way. The fire reached a magazine, and the destroyer blew up. Admiral Tanaka, on the bridge, was knocked unconscious. When he came to, the ship was sinking, and the *Naganami* was alongside taking off survivors. He moved his flag to that vessel, but no sooner had he gone aboard than she and the *Arashi* both took off at high speed, leaving many survivors on the sinking ship, because the PT boats were attacking again. The two destroyers dropped lifeboats as they went, and some survivors managed to get to Guadalcanal and the Japanese lines.

On December 12, Admiral Tanaka returned to Buin. He learned that Admiral Yamamoto had finally decided that the cost of this method of resupply was too expensive, and had suspended the destroyer runs to Guadalcanal. Tanaka was ordered to report to Rabaul and begin taking supplies and troops to build a base on New Georgia, whose position had become newly important in the failure of the 17th Army to mount the expected offensive at New Guinea and to retake Guadalcanal.

Admiral Tanaka did not know it, but his recommendation had been the basis for a decision by Admiral Yamamoto and the Imperial General Staff that Guadalcanal must be evacuated.

The men spoke of fighting and victory. But as the days passed, the enormity of their situation came in upon them like a cloud. The planes overhead bore white stars not red suns. The sounds of the artillery that pounded the mountains were not Japanese sounds. But the enemy, even though his presence was ever around them, was not the major factor in their lives. They could see, in the eyes and lips of their officers, the truth: They were abandoned on this island. Tsuji, better than most, *knew* how desperate their situation must be. To purposely run a ship aground had never been heard of in Japan. And not one ship, but six—six ships loaded with men and guns, tanks and trucks, and rice and tinned food for half an army—had been run aground. And so little of the food had been saved. Even the bags of rice that Tsuji and his fellow seamen had saved and landed aboard the trucks ("Tokyo Taxis," they called them) were found to be half spoiled by the seawater.

The rice, Tsuji found, was gone too soon. His group had not brought enough supplies to help the others. Instead, in less than a week, they were eating into the slender supply of the Pioneers. And in three weeks all the rice was gone, and they were foraging for food. Not many of them knew how at first, but they learned, or they starved. And some learned *and* starved. The numbers of graves continued to increase until Tsuji and the others, weary as they were, began to build a shrine. As they built, many of the unit lay down and did not get up. And their headstones joined the circle around the clearing. Among those who would die were Petty Officer Tsuji and his friend.

By this time the 15,000 troops on Guadalcanal were really beginning to succumb to starvation. They were unable to mount any sort of offensive. Back on November 30, the day of the Battle of Tassafaronga, Carlson's Raider Battalion had ambushed a hundred Japanese soldiers in a bivouac area on the south bank of the Lunga River. They caught the Japanese with their rifles stacked and killed nearly all of them before they could recover from the surprise. Mombula, the 1,500-foot mountain that stood above Henderson Field, was still in Japanese hands, as was the western tip of the island. Carlson's troops took Mombula and then went back to the marine lines, their task completed. For the marines, the long slugging match was nearly over.

On December 9, General Vandegrift was relieved of command of the Guadalcanal forces, replaced by Army Major General Alexander Patch, because, as Admiral Halsey saw, the Army would be taking over the fighting on Guadalcanal. Shortly afterwards the marines began to move out.

The Japanese plans for evacuation were settled at high level conferences first in Tokyo and then in Rabaul. General Hitashi Imamura of the 8th Area Army came down from Java to take charge. Admiral Yamamoto's staff officers and the army representatives worked out the details. On January 14, the Japanese sent 9 destroyers to Guadalcanal to carry 600 new troops who were to be the rear guard of the evacuation. On the return trip the destroyers were jumped by planes of the Cactus Air Force, and four destroyers were damaged by bombs or near misses. The brave little force of American PT boats sent out 13 boats that night to patrol, and two of them got involved with the destroyers. They attacked, but the destroyers outmaneuvered them, and one of the boats was run aground on a reef off Florida Island.

Beginning in December there was a remarkable change in the attitude of the American command. No longer was every mission of the Cactus Air Force reported in the war diaries. No longer was the question of gasoline supply raised, or the worry about Japanese reinforcement.

The crisis that had persisted from August through November had ended. The Americans had never won a clearcut victory at sea, nor on the ground, except the defensive actions that saved Henderson Field twice. But they had won a decisive victory in the air, and the Japanese 11th Air Fleet seemed completely unable to respond further. Nor was there any reason, for the enormous effort of the Japanese pilots in September, October, and November had been hinged to the basic plan of retaking Henderson Field. That objective had been abandoned; the Americans sensed it and the Japanese knew it. The battle now was for the Japanese rescue of the forces they had committed to the island. Admiral Halsey's efforts were no longer aimed at buttressing the position of the land forces and air forces so they could "hold": Most of his time was spent planning new action.

As if to underline this change, the beginning of the KE Operation, as the Japanese called the evacuation, went unnoticed in the American dispatches, and the damages to the destroyers seemed almost routine.

Every day there were reports of fighting, and that meant men killed and wounded on both sides. On December 15 Halsey reported to Admiral Nimitz on the events of the previous 24 hours: Guadalcanal's ground forces had been patrolling again, and they had killed 25 Japanese soldiers. Six marines were wounded. Munda on New Georgia was bombed three times in the attempt to slow down the construction of the new Japanese base in the Solomons. Also around New Georgia, the Cactus Air Force had shot down 3 float Zeros out of a force 12. One B-17 was lost in the bombing raid but the crew was rescued. Six destroyers approaching Munda were attacked by nine American dive bombers. (That was Admiral Tanaka bringing the first of the New Georgia garrison force.)

Actually, the attention of the Americans was largely diverted to New Georgia. General Patch's army troops and the remaining marines were working their way south to cut off the remaining Japanese on Guadalcanal, but the airways were filled with messages about troop transports and teletype machines and the comings and goings of hundreds of ships. The old "shoestring" of August had been replaced by a towing hauser, and it showed.

The preoccupation with administrative detail in this period indicated the growing resources at Admiral Halsey's command and his efforts to clear out the northwestern Solomon Islands as quickly as possible. The heavy ships of the fleet were on the lookout for Japanese capital vessels. The submarines were working to interdict supplies, particularly oil from Truk and Rabaul. The defenses of Guadalcanal were strengthened and port facilities at Tulagi improved. Now the destroyers that accompanied the American transports had little trouble. The force of PT boats had increased, too.

In January, Guadalcanal was occupied by the rest of the Army's Americal Division and the 25th Division. The 1st Division of marines was in Australia. After a rest period in New Zealand, the 1st Raider Battalion and the 2nd Parachute Battalion, the men who had fought so hard to hold on in those fierce months from August through November, were returning to Nouméa.

The army troops set out to clear Guadalcanal. In December, General Patch was waiting for reinforcements, so he concentrated on smoothing out the American perimeter and lopping off any Japanese intrusions such as that at Point Cruz, a hangover from the early days of the campaign. Occasionally, the Japanese made a successful raid, as on one December night when a party got through the lines onto Henderson Field and wrecked a plane and a truck. At the end of December, General Patch ordered an advance against the Japanese on Mount Austen, overlooking Henderson Field. As was so often the case, American intelligence underestimated the number of enemy troops there or their strength in arms, and paid a heavy price for a frontal assault. Colonel Oka, the Japanese area commander, was there with two infantry battalions and a regiment of mountain artillery. There were 500 men manning a line of pillboxes against the American advance. It took frontal attacks by the 132nd Regiment, plus fire support from destroyers and a heavy concentration of army artillery fire to take the strongpoint.

In January, General Patch's command was reorganized as the XXIV Corps. It included the 25th Army Division and the 2nd Marine Division. The Americans had 50,000 men on the island.

The Japanese position was hopeless. Unit after unit was cut off, and instead of surrendering, most of those troops elected to make one last brave charge in the name of their emperor, with the full knowledge that they would be killed. The whole Guadalcanal operation became a Japanese army problem, with the navy concerning itself only with the actual evacuation that was planned. General Hitoshi Imamura was in charge as head of the 8th Area Army.

With his diminishing resources, Admiral Yamamoto attempted to halt the growing strength of the Americans at Guadalcanal. The supply of twin-engined Betty bombers was very short, so he used Kawanishi flying boats, which were even larger and more ungainly as attack craft than the American PBYs. The bombs they carried were too small, and the pilot training was too slight for them to have much effect. Writing of it later, Admiral Morison, the Navy's historian, termed the attempt "stupid and ineffective," which seems a bit harsh under the circumstances.

On January 10, General Patch had all the troops he felt he needed, and he began the drive to destroy the Japanese army presence on Guadalcanal. No one in the American organization knew how many Japanese were on the island. Japanese records show that 31,500 men of the army and navy had been landed on the island by January. But even the Japanese could not say how many were still alive by January 10, for men died every day of starvation and disease. These losses were far more serious than those inflicted in combat. And among those left alive many were so weak that their performance in battle was brief and ineffectual; they fought bravely, inflicted casualties, and died the heroic deaths they sought. The futility of it is apparent nearly four decades later, but at the time, General Imamura's approach was to rescue as many men as possible so that they might fight again from other Solomon Islands and recapture Guadalcanal.

For a week in mid-January Colonel Oka's force held out on the height called Gifu by the Japanese. A few soldiers responded to pleas that they surrender, but the majority refused. One platoon talked the matter over, and the men decided they were too weak even to surrender, so they waited for death. It came to them in the form of a heavy shelling by big American guns.

The American attack was so well coordinated that no Japanese on the island could fail to realize what was happening. American planes dominated the skies. Occasionally, a Japanese Zero or a bomber came over, but almost invariably it would be shot down. American ships dominated the seas, day and night. If there were not many warships around, it was because they were not needed and were employed elsewhere. The American artillery dominated the land battle, and the American tanks, trucks, and jeeps made the going easier than it had been before, although in the jungle they still had to depend on airdrops and Melanesian carriers for supply.

The Japanese fought what must be credited as a brilliant rear-guard action, considering the state of their supply and the daily bombardment from the air and from a force of destroyers operating out of the Tulagi area. The destroyers *Nicholas, O'Bannon, Radford,* and *De-Haven* were assigned to bombard enemy positions and did so, often putting out 1,000 rounds of five-inch ammunition per day against selected targets. The effect was devastating.

The Americans drove the Japanese along the coast from the central Japanese position at Kokumbona west of Point Cruz. The American engineers built roads as they went, which solved the later problems of supply. There were so many troops involved that large flanking operations were the rule. But the Americans had to fight for every foot of the ground. They reached the Bonegi River, below Tassafaronga, which had been the central point of Japanese resupply. The 600 troops of the covering force made a stand here, covering General Hyukatake's rear as he prepared to evacuate the survivors. The 13,000 survivors by this time were a motley group. There were a few men left from the original Guadalcanal garrison and the Pioneer Forces that had built the airfield. There were men from the 2nd Army Division and a handful of Colonel Ichiki's troops and General Kawaguchi's reinforcements. There were men from the 38th Division, fliers from the 11th Air Fleet who had been shot down and parachuted into Guadalcanal or the sea, and sailors who had escaped their sinking ships. Admiral Yamamoto and General Imamura wanted them back and were prepared to make heroic gestures to get them.

By the end of January, Guadalcanal was so secure in American eyes that when Secretary of the Navy Frank Knox came to the South Pacific, he was brought to the island by Admiral Nimitz and Admiral Halsey. Guadalcanal, once the desperate worry of even President Roosevelt, was something of a showplace, although not yet "secured." From the American viewpoint the Pacific offensive had begun.

Late in January, Admiral Halsey's naval action moved up to the New Georgia area, bombarding the Japanese at points where they were constructing air bases. The Japanese tried to stop these raids by counterraids conducted by the 11th Air Fleet. But the fleet's strength these days was no match for the combined U.S. Army, Navy, and Marine aviation from Admiral Halsey's command and General Mac-Arthur's. At the end of the month Admiral Kusaka did send several groups of Betty bombers and Zero fighters to Guadalcanal. Times had changed; the new pilots on one raid failed to find Henderson Field. The next raid that came over was costly to the 11th Air Fleet; the Americans sent up the F4Fs and shot down a dozen Zeros at the price of four American planes. The ratio was typical of the new Japanese problem; there were too many American planes in the sky and too many American ships in the sea. Since January 14, Admiral Yamamoto had not even tried to resupply the troops on Guadalcanal. Air and sea strength to be committed at Guadalcanal was being saved for the evacuation effort.

21

THE LAST SEA FIGHT

IN the third week of January Admiral Halsey's intelligence reports indicated a Japanese buildup in the rest of the Solomon Islands. The effort did not seem so much aimed at retaking Guadalcanal, as moving the scene of battle elsewhere under conditions more advantageous to the Japanese. One report said the Japanese were looking to invade Canton Island, and to establish even more powerful bases in the southern Solomons. The intensified air activity from the 11th Air Fleet, after weeks of quiet, indicated the same thing.

At this point Admiral Halsey could put forward five task forces, one of battleships and destroyers, one of light cruisers and destroyers, two of aircraft carriers that included cruisers and destroyers, and one of heavy cruisers, light cruisers, destroyers, and—something new for the South Pacific air force operations—auxiliary or "jeep" carriers. These had begun coming off the ways in large numbers to meet the submarine threat in the Atlantic and to augment the growing American carrier forces. Finally, Admiral Fitch's land-based air force had doubled in size.

Each of these types of task force was capable of meeting different sorts of Japanese threats. Task Force 18, which was the cruiser and "jeep carrier" force, set out in response to those last Japanese air raids attempted against Henderson Field. During the previous weeks, Admiral Nimitz had conferred with Halsey about American plans and assessment of Japanese moves. Nimitz thought the Japanese might well be making a new attempt to reinforce Guadalcanal. He was concerned about the Japanese submarines that still operated freely in the whole area. The intelligence estimates were correct in one sense—the enemy had made big plans concerning Guadalcanal. But so complete was the Japanese upper echelon secrecy that the Americans had no clue to the real situation: that General Imamura and Admiral Yamamoto were planning the total evacuation of Guadalcanal. Pending that move, Admiral Yamamoto was keeping his ships at Truk and Rabaul, rather than expending the precious fuel that had in the past few weeks become a critical factor in the naval war. Admiral Yamamoto had foreseen this problem since the beginning of the war. He had been unable to strike that decisive victory that would send the Americans to the conference table, and now Japan was beginning to feel the might that the American economy could bring to bear—the staggering production of ships and planes and the transportation resources to move hundreds of thousands of fighting men to the fronts.

Back in Washington, Admiral King was growing increasingly restless with the delay in securing Guadalcanal. The rest of the 25th Army Division was to move into Guadalcanal, and the 2nd Marine Division and the 8th Marine Regiment were to come out. The troops would be transferred in four big troop transports, and they would be protected by all those task forces that Admiral Halsey had at hand. Halsey was hoping that Admiral Yamamoto would send out the Combined Fleet to contest the changeover at Guadalcanal, and this time he was ready for it.

Rear Admiral Robert C. Giffen was the commander of the cruiser task force. It consisted of 3 heavy cruisers, the *Wichita*, *Chicago*, and *Louisville*, 3 light cruisers, the *Montpelier*, *Cleveland*, and *Columbia*, and 8 destroyers. The new addition, the auxiliary carriers, consisted of the *Chenango*, with 11 fighters and 9 bombers, and the *Suwannee*, carrying 18 fighters and 15 torpedo bombers.

From the beginning, the American force was badly managed. The "jeep carriers" were new to most of the "battleship admirals" and Admiral Giffen regarded his aircraft defenses as more nuisance than assistance. The trouble was that these carriers could only travel at 18 knots, which held back the fast cruisers. Later the surface ship commanders would learn to use auxiliary carriers by sending them out in front where their slow speed and maneuvers back and forth to find the face of the wind for launching planes would not distress the task force. But Admiral Giffen had no experience in these matters, so the whole force slowed to accommodate the carriers, and the ship commanders grumbled.

On the evening of January 27 the task force left Efate Island to move toward Guadalcanal with the transports. The ships steamed northwest, conducting training exercises as they went. The *Wichita* had just come from North Africa with the two auxiliary carriers, and neither Admiral Giffen nor his crew were familiar with the South Pacific or with the Japanese way of conducting warfare.

Admiral Halsey had told Admiral Giffen that he was to meet that division of destroyers operating off Guadalcanal at a point southwest of the island on the night of January 30. On January 29 the navigator pointed out that unless something changed they would never make it. Those carriers were holding back the whole task force. So Admiral Giffen left the two auxiliary carriers in the company of a pair of destroyers and steamed on without his built-in air cover.

During the afternoon of January 29 the radar operators of the task force were thoroughly confused by many blips that appeared on their screens, but some of them were proved to be friendly craft whose IFF (Identification Friend or Foe) units were not working properly.

At 2 in the afternoon the carrier *Chenango* was ordered to launch planes to chase away or shoot down shadowing enemy planes. Five minutes later the *Chenango* launched fighters and bombers for combat air control and carrier protection. Two of the bombers were equipped with the newest plane radar. The *Suwanee* launched four fighters and three bombers as combat air patrol over the cruisers and over the antisubmarine planes. All planes were landed before nightfall.

So as darkness fell over the cruiser force on the night of January 29 there was no air cover, nor was any requested from Henderson Field.

The Japanese had not been asleep. Many of the planes that snooped the cruisers that afternoon were Japanese, so in the middle of the afternoon Admiral Kusaka ordered an air strike of Betty bombers, to be made after dark.

Admiral Giffen was a careful commander. He ordered complete

radio silence, which prevented the Japanese from monitoring his radio frequencies and using the transmissions to find the ships. It was an excellent tactic—for the war that ended in 1918. For the war of January 1943, it was less than optimal, since the Japanese planes had been shadowing the cruisers all afternoon, and the Japanese submarines in the area had been reporting on their positions. The real effect of Admiral Giffen's radio silence was to prevent the task force from sending planes to check on the blips that came up on the radar screen.

At the 11th Air Fleet bases in Rabaul and at Buka, 31 twin-engined bombers took off. The Japanese had been working on a new attack technique, to strike just after darkness fell, when the enemy would be hampered by poor visibility. The Americans were totally unprepared for such an attack. As usual, the ships had all gone to General Quarters at sundown, but once that ended they had decreased their vigilance.

The cruisers were fifty miles north of Rennell Island, very close to the point where they were supposed to meet the extra destroyers. They were travelling in two columns. Half an hour after sunset the bombers arrived in the area; Admiral Giffen's radar sets showed them 60 miles to the west. Still, he did not prepare for an attack, and the task force steamed along, relaxing for the night.

The Japanese torpedo bombers circled around so they would not be silhouetted against the pink light of the last of the day in the western sky. Then they split into two groups, to attack both columns from the dark side.

The first attackers came in. One torpedo bomber launched a torpedo against the destroyer *Waller*; it missed. The pilots zoomed in low and strafed the destroyer and the cruiser *Wichita* and then pulled up in a climbing turn. Another plane attacked the *Louisville*, and her captain avoided torpedoing by a sharp turn to port.

It seemed that the attack was over, particularly after the antiaircraft guns shot down a low zooming plane that had strafed. Admiral Giffen did not falter. He did not even zigzag, but moved straight on toward his rendezvous.

The torpedo bombers came in again, now that they had found their quarry and the darkness was almost complete. First several planes flew over the formation of ships, dropping flares that lit them brightly. Red and green float flares drifted to the surface and outlined the course of the ships; the flares became targets for the ships' gunners who now kept their eyes on the water, not in the air.

A few moments later the Japanese bombers came in again. One dropped a torpedo which hit the *Louisville*. This was one of the few times so far in the war that a Japanese torpedo did not detonate. That indicated the state of training of the pilot. He had dropped too soon, and the torpedo had not had time to arm itself.

The antiaircraft guns barked, but the Japanese continued to harry the formation, attacking the *Chicago*, the other cruisers, and the destroyers. The antiaircraft gunners fired accurately and brought down several planes. One blew up astern of the *Waller*, and another hit so close to the *Chicago* that her decks were blackened by burning aviation gas. The light from the two planes was better than any flare, and in that light another torpedo plane came down and put a "fish" into the side of the *Chicago*. Then a second torpedo hit.

At eight o'clock the attack was over. The other ships had been scarred, but the *Chicago* had suffered serious wounds. She was taken in tow by the *Louisville* and headed back for Espiritu Santo. Admiral Giffen's concern for punctuality at the rendezvous point seemed unimportant now.

During the night, the task force was vigilant, and a Black Cat night fighter came from Espiritu Santo to hover; in the morning the two jeep carriers put up combat air patrol. But the Japanese continued their watching, and dawn found more Japanese planes in the area. The task force split up that morning with the undamaged cruisers going back to Efate and the *Chicago* tow changed over to the tug *Navajo*, which had come out for the task. *Chicago* was screened by six destroyers, but no one thought about air cover. The combat air patrol circled around the ships as they travelled at four knots, but did not watch for the enemy further out.

Just before four o'clock in the afternoon, the Japanese struck the *Chicago* again when she was just 40 miles from the big carrier *Enterprise*. They were after the carrier, but the combat air patrol of the *Enterprise* was alert, and there were too many planes for comfort, so the Japanese bombers decided to strike the crippled ship instead. Sneaking through cloud cover they approached the *Chicago* before the fighter patrol from the *Enterprise* found them, and nine Betty bombers launched torpedoes against the slow convoy. Four torpedoes smashed into the *Chicago*'s side. One other struck the destroyer *La*

Vallette. Soon the *Chicago* sank in 12,000 feet of water, although most of her crew were saved. The *La Vallette* was damaged, but she could be towed to safety and was. Most of the Japanese bombers were shot down, but they had won another encounter with the American Navy and had shown their perfection of two techniques of torpedo attack that were to be used again and again in the months to come.

When Halsey had the facts of the encounter, he was extremely angry at the ineptness of his cruiser commander. Once again, the American lack of experience was showing. There was, however, one bright spot: The American transports delivering the army troops and collecting the marines from Guadalcanal were forgotten by the Japanese in their excitement at attacking the naval vessels. So the transports landed and embarked again without any trouble at all.

22

MIRACLE IN THE SLOT

IN January, General Patch conducted a number of operations against the Japanese, further diminishing General Hyukatake's fighting strength. But by this time, fighting was not the primary mission of the Japanese Army on Guadalcanal; survival was. The following poem by one of the survivors of the Japanese force indicates the state to which they were reduced by the end of 1942:

No matter how far we walk
We don't know where we're going
Trudging along under dark jungle growth.

When will this march end?

Hide during the day
Move at night
Deep in the lush Guadalcanal jungle.

Our rice is gone
Eating roots and grass
Along the ridges and cliffs

Leaves hide the trail. We lose our way
Stumble and get up, fall and get up.

Covered with mud from our falls
Blood oozes from our wounds
No cloth to bind our cuts
Flies swarm to the scabs
No strength to brush them away
Fall down and cannot move
How many times I've thought of suicide.

At the end of January the commander of the U.S. XXIV Corps decided that it was time to begin mopping up the enemy, and he sent a battalion of the 132nd Infantry Regiment to the southwest coast of the island. The major purpose of this operation was to stop the reinforcement of the Japanese troops west of Cape Esperance. So little was known of Japanese activity that General Patch was not sure how many enemy supply missions had been made since he came to the island in December.

The Americans moved from the Lunga area in five LSTs, protected by four destroyers and many planes from the Cactus Air Force. This activity was noted by the Japanese on the island, who feared that their KE Operation had been unearthed by the enemy, and the word went to Rabaul where Admiral Kusaka strained his resources to mount a counterstrike. Half the troops had been unloaded, and three LSTs and two destroyers were taking the landing craft back to the American side of the island when the Rabaul air force planes attacked. For some reason all the air cover had remained with the still loaded LSTs on the west side of the island, so when the formation of Japanese dive bombers appeared and the coastwatchers had the warning, there were no planes immediately available to protect the empty LSTs and their escort. The dive bombers attacked and sank the destroyer *DeHaven*. The antiaircraft guns brought down at least one Japanese bomber, but most of them flew home safely.

To the Japanese, the American plan to move into the western side of the Guadalcanal appeared to be an attempt to stop their evacuation. To the Americans, a report on February 2 of 20 Japanese destroyers steaming down The Slot appeared to be another attempt to reinforce the Japanese garrison, and the Americans reacted as swiftly as had the Japanese. Actually, one cruiser and those 20 destroyers were the first evacuation ships, and the Japanese wanted nothing more than to be left alone that night.

The destroyers came down The Slot that evening, and at 5 P.M. the Cactus Air Force put into the air 24 bombers and 17 fighters to stop them. In the past, those night runs of the destroyers had usually been covered only by a few float planes if there were air cover at all. But on this night, Admiral Yamamoto had given orders that the best air defense possible must be presented above the evacuation force, and the American planes, apparently not as careful as they might have been, were jumped by 30 Zeros. The bombers tried bravely to stop the force. They did put a bomb into the destroyer *Makinami* but it didn't sink her, and the Zeros drove off the American planes before they could do more damage. The destroyers and one light cruiser continued on to Guadalcanal.

Admiral Halsey had a new weapon to use against the Japanese, and this was the night that the Americans chose to use it: the naval mine. Three of the old four-stack destroyers were converted to mine-layers and they dropped 300 mines off Cape Esperance. The speeding Japanese force came into the mine field. As they approached, the American PT boats came darting out from the shore, to try to deliver their torpedoes. The Japanese respected the PT boats as dangerous and did not make the mistake of disregarding them at any time. That night they concentrated their efforts and sank the *PT-111* and put so many salvoes around the *PT-48* that her captain beached her on Savo Island. The *PT-115* was also beached after making an abortive attack and taking heavy Japanese fire that nearly swamped her. The *PT-37* was hit by a shell that penetrated the plywood hull and blew up a gas tank. The whole boat went up in splinters, killing all but one of the crew. The *PT-47* drew the wrath of the destroyers and barely managed to escape by heading into a squall near Savo Island.

The PT boats were harried not only by the destroyers that night, but by an air cover of Japanese fighters and bombers that was accompanying the relief force. The *PT-124* made its attack and fled to safety. But another boat following just after her, the *PT-123*, was bombed by a Japanese plane and blown out of the water.

As the ships approached the shore, the destroyer *Makigumo* ran afoul of one of Halsey's mines, and the damage was so serious that although the *Yugumo* took the *Makigumo* in tow, the tow had to be abandoned and the ship scuttled.

By midnight the ships were just offshore, and the loading operations began. The destroyers and the cruiser loaded men all night long, and as dawn approached, they upped anchor and headed back up The Slot, to be met soon by covering Japanese aircraft. Just after sunrise the Cactus Air Force put up its bombers to search and intercept, but this time the Japanese were able to protect the retiring ships. They reached Shortland with their 5,000 evacuees the next day.

So covert was this evacuation operation, and so successful, that the Americans even on February 3 had no inkling of it. They still believed that the destroyers had been bringing supplies and perhaps more troops for the Japanese Army on Guadalcanal. Even when the American troops captured a strongpoint near Tassafaronga on February 2 and found it abandoned, they did not understand its import. The Japanese had left so hurriedly they had not destroyed the radio station there, or ten pieces of artillery, or some shops. But American intelligence was bemused by the past and suggested that the existence of this material suggested a new Japanese attempt to take the island.

Not all the Japanese were waiting at Guadalcanal for the next evacuation convoy. Many were moved by barge from the tip of the island to the Russell Islands, but the coastwatchers and the American observation planes that saw the shuttling of the barges were unable to differentiate between empty and loaded boats, and the impression grew that troops were being moved in for a new offensive. Consequently, Admiral Halsey prepared for another major naval action, and moved his two carrier task forces closer to Guadalcanal. Admiral Marc Mitscher had replaced Admiral Fitch as commander of the land-based air forces, and he was warned to be prepared for a major assault. General MacArthur was requested to hit Rabaul and the northern Solomons harder with his B-17s. Every American effort was devoted to watchful waiting for the new three-pronged Japanese attack that would subject Henderson Field to another siege.

On February 3 the Japanese evacuation force massed again at Buin. For some reason, neither the air searchers nor the coastwatchers paid much attention as the single cruiser and 20 destroyers headed for Guadalcanal. There was, as always these days, the air gauntlet to be run, but Admiral Kusaka was proving that in desperate circumstances he could provide adequate air support, and the 65 American planes that appeared in the sky were met by even more Zeros. The smoke trails of falling aircraft resembled fireworks in an amusement park on the Fourth of July, but the Japanese air cover achieved what it set out to do, although at high cost: All the destroyers got through, although the *Shiranuhi* and the *Maikaze* were damaged. That night the PT boats did not come out in force; they had been too badly mauled by the Japanese destroyers two nights earlier. The American fighters and bombers tried to mount an assault, but night fighting was still not their strong point, and the Japanese had planes over Henderson Field all night long, dropping flares, bombing and strafing, to keep the Cactus Air Force down.

In the morning, the ships were gone, this time carrying 4,000 men to safety. The Japanese took a different route to their base this time, and the morning search of Cactus Air Force bombers did not find them. The searchers did note about three dozen empty landing barges floating in the water off Cape Esperance, and they so reported when they landed. But the message never got to an intelligence officer who might be considering the Japanese overall strategy, and no one put two and two together. As of February 5, the Americans were still waiting for the other shoe to drop, for Admiral Yamamoto to launch a new strike by the Combined Fleet. The air power that the enemy had assembled for this period was impressive and gave further credence to the idea that an attack was in the offing.

On February 6 Admiral Yamamoto launched the final rescue mission, and it was the easiest of all, for the weather seriously hampered the American air strikes. The bombers damaged the destroyers *Isokaze* and *Hamakaze* but not enough to turn them back from the mission. That night the 18 destroyers rescued the last 1,800 men on Guadalcanal, and 2 other destroyers picked up the survivors who had moved to the Russell Islands.

Even on the morning of February 8 the Americans still had no inkling of the plan that the Japanese had devised, attempted, and completed with virtually no losses of ships or men. There had been heavy losses in aircraft on both sides, but that was the price that had to be paid.

The Americans were ready to strike hard. On the morning of February 8 they reached the Cape Esperance beaches, ready for a desperate battle and found only empty quarters, vacated campfires, abandoned supplies, and empty landing boats drifting in the water offshore. They finally got the idea: The Japanese, at least in this area of the island, were gone.

That day the American troops moved forward, still cautiously, waiting for the snap of rifles and the popping of machine guns, but these sounds were not heard. At 4:30 in the afternoon, on the Tenamba River, one finger of the pincers they had planned met the other without having seen a Japanese soldier all day long. Then it was conclusive. General Patch sent a message to Admiral Halsey, announcing the "total and complete defeat of Japanese forces on Guadalcanal." It was bravado and exaggeration, but it was true nonetheless. Admiral Yamamoto and General Imamura had combined forces to carry out one of the most remarkable military movements in the history of warfare, and yet it was still defeat. The Japanese had occupied Guadalcanal in order to advance their striking power against Australia and the United States. For the first time the Americans had struck back, not in a desperate defensive action as Midway was, but in a genuine offensive.

In the beginning, the American effort had been slipshod, and it very nearly failed from inadequate resources and inadequate military command. But as the weeks—not months but weeks—rolled on, the Americans seemed to catch on more each day. The magnificent effort of the pilots of the Cactus Air Force in the first three months saved the island in spite of the bad judgment of the senior commanders. With the coming of Halsey, defeatism and conservatism were replaced with a fighting spirit, and from that point onward the course of the battle changed quickly.

In the air, the Americans won the battle on two levels. First, the original band of pilots performed as valiantly as any men in the air ever had, during a period as desperate as the Battle of Britain. That takes nothing away from the bravery of the Japanese, who for the first half of the battle suffered from a 1,000-mile round trip in order to fight. In the second half of the battle, when the Japanese had bases closer to Guadalcanal, the Americans were bringing in more and more planes, while the pipeline from Japan was slowly shrinking.

On the ground, the Americans and Japanese were about even in numbers after that first period in which the Americans missed their chance to take over the whole island. But if they had taken it just then, without supply, perhaps General Vandegrift could not have held it. The marines performed brilliantly at Bloody Ridge and again in the second major assault against Henderson Field. The Japanese, hampered after October by ever more serious shortages of supplies, could do nothing but wait for reinforcement, and they waited successfully, but they left 24,000 men dead on that island as compared to the American loss of about 3,000.

On the sea, the battles of Guadalcanal for the most part showed a superiority of naval performance by the Japanese. The Americans were hurt by the poor quality of their torpedoes, and by the poor quality of their training. Destroyers played a crucial role in the Japanese victories. The performance of the Japanese destroyermen was no less than brilliant. They were led by Admiral Raizo Tanaka, whose abilities were better appreciated by Admiral Nimitz than they were by Admiral Yamamoto and the Imperial General Staff. Admiral Tanaka had one failing from the Japanese point of view: He spoke his mind directly on the problem of resupplying the Japanese forces on Guadalcanal, and he had the misfortune to be precisely right about a serious blunder in policy. From the South Pacific he was transferred first to Singapore and then to Burma, where he spent the rest of the war in desk jobs.

In terms of ships lost, the numbers were precisely the same: 24 Japanese ships and 24 American. The Americans lost two carriers, but the Japanese lost two battleships, and so it all evened out in terms of tactical success. But in a strategic sense, Guadalcanal was a disaster for the Japanese Navy; the Americans could afford to lose those ships. The United States was already engaged in a massive shipbuilding program that Japan could not hope to match.

Above all, however, Guadalcanal was the beginning of the confirmation of Admiral Yamamoto's prediction that the tide would turn. There would be more months of false hopes in Tokyo, in Rabaul, and in Truk. Admiral Yamamoto would fall a victim to his archenemy Admiral Nimitz. A few months after the evacuation of Guadalcanal, Nimitz's radio intelligence operators would learn of Admiral Yamamoto's coming visit to Rabaul by plane; and would be presented with an itinerary. They would take the intelligence to Admiral Nimitz and suggest that Yamamoto be assassinated by an American air ambush. Nimitz would approve and it would be done.

A flight of P-38 fighter planes would intercept Yamamoto's two

Betty bombers out of Rabaul; and he would be shot down and die in the wreck. Japan and the Imperial Navy would never quite recover from the shock of it; but it would be just a reflection of what was happening to Japan in the war. The American juggernaut was able in the fall of 1942 to turn its productive capacity to the Pacific, the North African campaign having been launched successfully. And that change above all others, coming at the time of the desperate struggle for Guadalcanal, constituted the turning of the tide.

Notes

1. The Best Laid Plans . . .

THIS chapter begins with material based on the Yamamoto biography and Ienaga's book on the Pacific war. I also used *Australia in the War of 1939–45*, Series One, "Army," Volume V, Southwest Pacific Area, First Year, by Dudley McCarthy. This book, published by the Australian War Memorial at Canberra, was useful for a disinterested view of the American conduct in the early months of the Pacific war and the Australian point of view about the South Pacific.

The material about Admiral King and the American command is from research done for my *How They Won the War in the Pacific*. The material about Admiral Ghormley is from Dyer's book and Ghormley's own story as it appears in manuscript in the Operational Archives of the Navy. The material about Admiral Fletcher is from the same sources and from my *How They Won the War in the Pacific*.

2. The Landings

THE opening of this chapter relies on the Australian war history, the Japanese history of Rabaul air operations, and the Yamamoto biography. The account of the carrier operations is from their action reports of the period, and *The Cactus Air Force*. The account of the landings is from Tregaskis' *Guadalcanal Diary* on the American side and the BKS Volume 1 of the Japanese naval history of the struggle. (See page 289 of Bibliography for complete name of BKS.) Also I used my own *Raider Battalion* (Pinnacle Books, 1980) for the account of the Raiders and parachute troops on Tulagi, and the U.S. Marine Corps history of the Guadalcanal Operation. Saburo Sakai's account lent much color. The action reports of the carrier squadrons lent more. The quotation about the calm that prevailed on the *Canberra* on the day of the invasion is from the Australian war history. The notes about the superiority of the Zero as a fighting machine come from various reports in the Navy Operational Archives of the period. All the way up from the squadron level to that of the Joint Chiefs of Staff, operations were always second-guessed to see what went wrong and what had to be improved in material and performance. Guadalcanal brought a new appreciation of the Japanese warplanes and started the study of how best to fight them.

Hara's *Destroyer Captain* was useful in this chapter. So were the BKS Volumes 1 and 2 on naval operations. The COMSOPAC war diary was used here, as was Morison, *The Cactus Air Force*, and Dyer's book on Admiral Turner. The most interesting part of the Savo Island battle from an analytical point of view was the continued failure of the American air search operations. Throughout the sea war the Japanese showed themselves far superior to the Americans in this regard. Even as late as the Battle of the Marianas in July 1944, the Japanese had advance knowledge of American positions through air search while the Americans—then as at Guadalcanal—relied very heavily on Admiral Nimitz's code breakers at Pearl Harbor for such basic information. The Japanese superiority at the Marianas in this regard is more understandable because the Americans were operating from the carriers while the Japanese had land-based air search there. But at Guadalcanal there were plenty of land-based searchers in the McCain-Fitch and MacArthur commands. The problem was that the searches and reporting were never properly coordinated during the campaign.

3. Like Wolves on the Fold . . .

FOR this chapter I depended on Hara's *Destroyer Captain,* Dull's history of the Japanese fleet operations, and BKS naval volumes. For the American story I used the COMSOPAC war diary, the reports of Admiral Turner and various action reports of vessels. It was apparent that at this point in naval history the American mastery of night techniques was abysmal while that of the Japanese was superior. The Americans were not prepared for battle and most of the ship commanders were not constitutionally prepared for surprise, which the surviving captains would be—later in the war. American gunnery, as this battle showed, needed improvement desperately. But it seemed to me that the most serious failures were at the top. There was no lack of valor by the American officers and men who manned the ships, but it was no joke to see an enemy ship and then be told by a queasy captain not to open fire, or be restrained by a queasy admiral so worried about his aircraft carriers that he would not let them attack the enemy.

4. Counterattack

THE principal sources for the information about the Japanese plans at Guadalcanal were the Yamamoto biography, the Hara story, and the Sakai autobiography. The sources for the material about the Marines were the COMSOPAC war diary, Morison, Tregaskis, *The Cactus Air Force,* and Dyer. The Matsunaga flight over Guadalcanal was pieced together from information in Tregaskis and the Yamamoto biography. Parts of the story of the Ichiki battalion are told in the Hara book, parts in the Tregaskis book, and some in the Marine history of operations and the COMSOPAC war diary.

5. The Lost Opportunity

THE question of the Marine movements came from the book on Nimitz and his admirals and from Admiral Ghormley's informal reminiscences on his period of command in the South Pacific. The Rabaul air force book by Masatake Okumiya provided some detail; so did *The Cactus Air Force*. The differences between Admiral Nimitz and his subordinates show clearly in the dispatches. The American stories of air battle are from the squadron reports and *The Cactus Air Force*.

The material about the movement of the Combined Fleet is from Hara and Dull. The material about the Tokyo Express is from the Tanaka article in *The Japanese Navy in World War II*. Admiral Fletcher's usual timidity is reflected in his action report on the battle. The tale of the *Ryujo* was told by Captain Hara, whose destroyer was escorting the carrier. The story of the American carriers in action is from Morison and the carrier action reports for the battle.

6. The Slugging Match

THE *Cactus Air Force*, the Okumiya book, and Admiral Tanaka's article provided much of the material for the opening pages of this chapter. Captain Hara told part of the story of the Kawaguchi brigade. My own previous research for the book on Nimitz and his admirals was another major source here, particularly for the story of Undersecretary of the Navy Forrestal. The story of the *I-26* is from *I-Boat Captain* and from Hara and from Morison. A study of the action reports of the task force shows how little attention was paid to antisubmarine warfare and how ineffective the destroyers were when they knew a Japanese submarine was in the vicinity.

7. Sweating It Out

THE *Coastwatchers* is the source for the material in the beginning of this chapter, augmented by the Australian war history. *The Cactus Air Force* is the source for detail on operations at Henderson Field. The King-Nimitz meetings come from the Navy Department records of those meetings. The story of the gloomy meeting aboard Admiral Ghormley's flagship is from *How They Won the War in the Pacific* and the Dyer biography of Admiral Turner.

The source for the material on Yamamoto's planning is the biography of the admiral, augmented by the Hara book; the Okumiya book gives details. The story of "Red Mike" Edson and his Raiders on Savo Island is from my own *Raider Battalion,* which came from research in the naval archives and at the U.S. Naval Academy. I also used Morison for this part. Morison and the action reports, plus the Tregaskis book, were principal sources for the stories of the *Little* and the *Gregory.* One of the oddments of the Guadalcanal story is that all during the campaign neither side knew much about the strength of the other, and they never did learn. General Hyukatake would certainly never have tried to retake the island with a battalion and then a regiment and finally a brigade had he known that General Vandegrift had a division and a half on the island. The material about the pilots came from *The Cactus Air Force* and from other materials in the Marine Corps and Navy files about Captain Marion Carl, who was the cousin of a childhood friend of mine (same name) in Portland, Oregon. Early in my studies of the Pacific War I became interested in his remarkable career on Guadalcanal (and I don't think that it is an exaggeration to call it a career). Admiral Ghormley's defeatism is evident in the dispatches and in his personal memoirs of the time.

8. Bloody Ridge

THE story of Bloody Ridge is one of the most stirring in the annals of the U.S. Marine Corps. The Marine Corps official history tells it very well. Morison tells it only briefly, for it is not the focus of his book. I dealt with it at some length in my *Raider Battalion*. I tried here to correlate the Marine, Marine Air, and Naval Air material. *The Cactus Air Force* was extremely useful in this; so was Tregaskis' *Guadalcanal Diary*. The running story of Admiral Ghormley's digging of his own professional grave is in the messages.

9. The Sinking of the *Wasp*

I am indebted to Commander Orita and Mr. Harrington for strightening me out several years ago on the real role of the Japanese submarines in World War II. At Guadalcanal, as the Hara book shows better than any others, the submarines were immensely useful to the Japanese. Most of the time the Americans had no idea that half a dozen and more subs were operating in the waters south of Guadalcanal, watching American ship and plane movements. Several of the submarines had an extra advantage, a float plane that could be launched and recovered.

As Admiral Turner began his determined supply effort for the beleaguered Marines on Guadalcanal, he knew what dangers he faced. That is made quite clear in the Dyer book. I got another dimension for this period from Lieutenant Commander McWhorter's book about the destroyer *Sterett*. The reactions to the Japanese defeat at Bloody Ridge come from the Hara book and the Yamamoto biography. The story of I-19's remarkable feat in sinking the *Wasp* and damaging two other ships with one spread of torpedoes is told in Hara and in *I-Boat Captain*. The mystery of the malfunction of American torpedoes is one of the oddest of the war, because it was apparent from the earliest days of the Philippine campaign that there was something wrong. But tradition and belief in the infallibility of the system died hard, and it is not pressing hindsight to say that the commanders in the field seemed bent on disregarding the evidence about torpedoes. The real problem is that they would pay no attention to the action reports of the men who used them.

10. The Judgment of Admirals

CAPTAIN Hara, in particular, has been critical of Admiral Yamamoto's failure to follow up the actions of the fleet in September. No one could be critical of Admiral Turner's bravery in moving into Guadalcanal without adequate protection. Even if he had lost the gamble, Admiral King would scarcely have faulted him for that, a thought that never seemed to cross the minds of the more timid commanders. King, and Nimitz too, could be forgiving of failure and even of error, unless it was error in judgment, and particularly faintness of heart, of which there was so much in the American command just then.

The Japanese suffered at this time from a different malaise: overconfidence. The Imperial Army had become so accustomed to victory over the years of the China war and then the lightninglike strokes of 1941 and 1942 that the generals simply had not taken the time to study the military machines of other countries. They had also hypnotized themselves into believing that the Japanese fighting man was worth two of any other nation's. In reality, no fighting man is worth two of any other nation; military preparedness and effectiveness are matters of leadership and training. The Japanese were long on both suits and the Americans were just then short, but the Imperial Army helped the Americans by underestimating them and by showing a strategic stupidity in refusing to see what the effect of the Guadalcanal invasion must be on the Japanese plans for New Guinea and points south.

The Japanese war histories, army and navy, so diverge that it is sometimes hard to believe they are talking about the same war. And that same attitude comes through in reading the Yamamoto biography and other works about the Japanese war effort. This inability to cooperate on the higher levels was one of the worst problems the Japanese faced at Guadalcanal.

In those days of September, if the Japanese had decided to send two divisions of troops into Guadalcanal (as they eventually did) they might have wiped out the Americans in a hurry.

The detail of Nimitz's discussions, ponderings, and trip to the South Pacific to see for himself what was going wrong comes from my own study of the admiral and his commanders for *How They Won the War in the Pacific*.

11. Cape Esperance

THE Okumiya book tells laconically of the difficulties of the Rabaul air force in this period when the tide was turning in the air over Henderson Field. There was a new hope in the hearts of the Americans and it showed in the COMSOPAC war diary and the messages. The Marines were beginning to move again although the Japanese opposition was fierce. The Japanese confusion about the date for the great battle was typical of the problem of the divided commands and the communications failures between army and navy. The deadly results of the battle of the Matanikau triangle were another illustration of the Japanese Army's error in underestimating the enemy's strength and will to fight. Those who believe that Admiral Yamamoto was "copping out" ought to consider that he built a new fighter base at Buin for the prime purpose of staging planes to attack Guadalcanal. He certainly would not have done so had he not been giving his major effort to the naval phase of the re-capture of the island. Here again the strange dichotomy of the Japanese military organization created difficulties for the admiral. While the Americans had all sorts of support from the air forces of General MacArthur, all the Japanese air effort was the responsibility of the Japanese Navy, and there were not enough planes to go around. Meanwhile, the Japanese Army was still taking half the aircraft production to stock up its stores in the Philippines and other areas where it had large land armies.

For the battle itself I used the accounts of Morison and Dull and Hara, and the official reports and endorsements of the various commands. Since Admiral Scott's victory was the first the Americans had achieved at Guadalcanal on the sea, it was regarded within the command as brilliant, when in fact it was totally accidental. The "lesson" of maintaining a long skirmish line was repeated later, and disastrously, by Admiral Callaghan.

12. X-Day

THE story of X-Day, its postponements and reverses, comes largely from the Japanese sources. The official Japanese naval history deals in euphemisms with the whole affair, never quite explaining why X-Day became Y-Day and what happened to the latter. But by using the Army and the Navy documents and Morison and the COMSOPAC war diary it all becomes evident. *The Cactus Air Force* account of General Geiger's efforts was also important here. The COMSOPAC war diary gives a feeling for the bleakness of October 10, when it appeared that the Japanese were about to land six transports full of troops and there was nothing that General Vandegrift could do about it. Both Miller and Morison make use of the story of General Geiger's demanding that fuel caches be found. Right up to the last, Nimitz tried to cajole Admiral Ghormley into fighting spirit, but he did not succeed; and finally it all came to a head in the desperation of October 15.

13. Halsey Enters

THE coming of Halsey to Guadalcanal turned the war around. Some high officers later said that Halsey was worth a division of marines. Probably this was not an overstatement, given the situation at that time. What was needed was the sort of spirit that would make every man in the theater of operations give his maximum effort. On Guadalcanal every man was doing just that. But not so much could be said for the rear echelon people who were half-convinced that the struggle was lost. Halsey came in like a breath of spring after a hard winter, showing an optimism he could not really have felt, given the circumstances, but never letting on that he doubted the outcome. There was something about his arrival that electrified the command and it was far more than simple slogans like "Kill Japs." It was the knowledge that at last the Guadalcanal effort had a fighting leader. He came that way and he remained. At the heart of it was the widespread belief that somehow Halsey would win the victory. Right behind him, of course, came a vast increase in ships and guns and planes, but at the moment they were not at Guadalcanal or anywhere near it. Halsey had no more to work with than Ghormley had been given, but Halsey used it where Ghormley had let it lie.

With Halsey there was no room for Navy politics or defeatism. Oddly, he was one of the old "battleship admirals" who had successfully converted his thinking to modern carrier warfare, something he had already shown by his willingness, alone among the carrier admirals of the Pacific in the first year (except Fitch), to risk his carrier against the enemy. At Nouméa he kept that approach. One day Arleigh Burke, then a captain and a destroyer squadron commander, checked in at Halsey's office by request. Burke had just sent one of his destroyers down to Sydney without clearing it with Halsey, and the "old man" was apparently furious. As Burke came into the office in the old Japanese consulate the staff expected that the destroyerman would be on his way back to Pearl Harbor that afternoon by PBY.

When Burke entered the office he snapped to attention before the desk and stayed there. Halsey gave him a pained look.

"Captain Burke. Why did you send that ship to Sydney? For repairs I suppose? I don't know whether I made it clear that we are in critical circumstances and no ship is to move out of the area without my express permission. Well?" He speared Burke with a steely eye.

"Not for repairs, sir. I sent the destroyer down to Sydney for booze. We are out of whiskey and the men are out of beer."

Halsey laughed. "All right, Burke. That I consider to be a legitimate reason. But let me tell you if you had said you had sent her for repairs I'd have had your ass."

So Captain Burke went out of the admiral's office floating on air, the staff was confounded, and the story spread through the fleet like fire in a gasoline barge. This happened after the battle for Guadalcanal, when the fighting was raging for the Northern Solomons. But the same sort of story was told time and again at critical periods. Admiral Halsey would forgive men any sort of disciplinary breach (short of murder) if they would fight for him. And they did.

14. Y-Day

AGAIN, the Japanese official sources were primary to this account of the delayed attempt to take Henderson Field. The COMSOPAC war diary and Morison were also vital, as was *The Cactus Air Force*. I also used the Hara book and Dull.

15. Santa Cruz

CAPTAIN Hara's account, the Dull history, and the official Japanese BKS were the main sources for the Japanese material here. The story of Admiral Kinkaid's operations comes from the Task Force Action Report and the COMSOPAC war diary. The sinking of the *Hornet* was probably quite unnecessary, occasioned by Admiral Kinkaid's flight to save the *Enterprise* since it was the last U.S. carrier in the South Pacific. In fact, it was not used immediately, so its loss may not have been quite so vital as Admiral Kinkaid believed. But it seems obvious that it would not have been lost, because Admiral Mikawa and Admiral Kondo shared Admiral Kinkaid's timidity, and instead of coming to "mop up" as Yamamoto wanted, they made a half-hearted effort and thus the *Enterprise* was never in danger. On the other hand, the saving of the *Hornet*, considering the damage she had suffered, would have meant that she would have gone home for a major repair job. In that instance she probably would not have affected the future course of the war much one way or the other, because a year later, when that repair job might have been expected to be done, the U.S. Navy had plenty of carriers in the Pacific. The real damage done here was to the morale of the naval aviators and the men of the *Hornet*, who felt they had been betrayed.

16. Buildup

THE COMSOPAC war diary was essential to this chapter. Once again radio intelligence played a major role in Halsey's success in stopping the Japanese by informing him of enemy troop and supply movement to Guadalcanal. The radio intelligence system was so accurate and so useful that it made up for many of the American deficiencies at this stage of the Pacific War. Another important source here was my research on Carlson's Raiders, who were employed originally to make the Aola Bay landing and then sent across the island to outflank the Japanese.

17. The Battle Called Guadalcanal

THE Dull history and Morison were essential to this chapter as well as the action reports of the ships and the war diaries of the command. Hara and Tanaka were also helpful. McWhorter's story of the U.S. destroyer *Sterett* provided a personal dimension for the battle as seen by an American participant. Okunami's *Rabaul Air Force* gave some indication of the Japanese air activity.

18. The End of the Battle

ADMIRAL Tanaka's own story was vital to this chapter, as was the COMSOPAC war diary and the action reports of the ships involved on the U.S. side.

19. Tassafaronga

THE story of Carlson's Raiders comes from my own research into that outfit, their various reports, Carlson's autobiography, and the records of the U.S. Marine Corps. The material about Japanese supply methods comes from *I-Boat Captain*, Hara, Tanaka, and BKS. The story of American participation in the naval battle is from Morison, the ship's records, and Halsey's reports.

20. Straight Down The Slot

THE reactions of Admiral Yamamoto come from Hara and a reading between the lines of Tanaka. Tanaka's advice to his superiors comes from his own story. The COMSOPAC war diary for this period is most interesting because it shows how the whole American approach to the war had changed almost overnight, with the commitment of more troops and more ships and planes to the South Pacific following President Roosevelt's autumn dictum to his admirals and generals that the Guadalcanal operation must not be allowed to fail. Somehow in the preoccupation with success the Americans lost sight of the Japanese on the island; they never did have very good intelligence about the land operations, and in December and January it was abysmal. Since the Japanese were by this time incapable of any offensive effort the American intelligence-gathering weakness was relatively unimportant, except that it allowed the Japanese to withdraw successfully, which obviously saved many lives on both sides.

21. The Last Sea Fight

THE message files and the COMSOPAC war diary were essential to this chapter. The story of Admiral Giffen's fumblings in the South Pacific is told by Morison in his usual low-key way so as not to infuriate his audience, which was the naval establishment. But the facts are there; it is only the emphasis that is lacking; and every author must make his own interpolations of naval language. What was apparent in the reports was that Admiral Giffen simply did not know how to handle auxiliary carriers, but for that matter neither did most other American task force commanders at that time. The small carriers were still very much experimental, and that was true nine months later during the Gilberts invasion, when once again lack of vigilance in antisubmarine warfare cost the Americans dearly and caused the loss of one of the auxiliary carriers, *Liscome Bay*. The action off Rennell Island also showed another facet of the Pacific war: The Americans had an enormous amount to learn about modern naval warfare and the Japanese at that time were far more competent. That is not as belittling of the American effort as it might seem; after all, the Japanese had been on a war footing since 1936, and they ought to have been skillful. The Japanese navy pilots who had shown so much capability during the first months of the war had all been trained against live targets in China and some of them were veterans of the Panay bombing incident. Six years of the most intensive war training *ought* to produce expertise and it had, just as three years of war had made the British expert in antisubmarine warfare and the Germans just as expert in the use of submarines. What the whole naval aspect of the Guadalcanal campaign showed was that there is no substitute for experience and the later developments of the Pacific war proved the point. Admiral McCain, who got his combat experience as land-based air commander at Guadalcanal, later commanded the carrier task forces very capably. So did Admiral Marc Mitscher, who finally succeeded to McCain's Guadalcanal command. Captain Forrest Sherman, who had the *Wasp* shot out from under him, became Admiral Nimitz's chief of staff, and never lost that aggressiveness that led him to try to persuade Admiral Fletcher to fight.

Captain Arleigh Burke, who performed so ably in destroyers, became Mitscher's chief of staff and in a period of Mitscher's illness ran the carrier task force. Admiral Willis Lee, who commanded the tiny battleship force of two at Guadalcanal, was advanced to lead the fast battleship force of later times. Admiral Turner became the chief of all Pacific amphibious invasions and, of course, Admiral Halsey went on to command the Third Fleet and to earn further distinction in the American war against Japan.

22. Miracle in The Slot

A whole book could be written about the tribulations of the Japanese soldiers and sailors on Guadalcanal in the fall of 1942 and early weeks of 1943. In Japan such books have been written and have been best-sellers, in spite of the grim and sometimes grisly nature of the subject. The Japanese effort of those months is the story of deprivation. It is also a story of character, for under the circumstances it would have been remarkably easy for the Japanese units to have become mobs, with no source of supply or even inspiration. They did not. They remained tightly disciplined until the evacuation and when that move was made every living Japanese on Guadalcanal was removed. As the war turned out it counted for little that the Japanese high command was able to mount so vast an operation without the Americans even suspecting what was happening until the effort was concluded. One has to go back to ancient history to find such successful deception and the Greeks and Romans did not have the advantage of air observation and radio.

But lest it be thought that the end of the Guadalcanal campaign was anticlimactic the reverse is really true. The Japanese did not evacuate the Solomons. Instead they chose to move out of a most difficult position, and to defend the islands of the Northern Solomons which were far more accessible to their warships and their air forces. That is another story.

BIBLIOGRAPHY

THE primary sources for this book on the battles of Guadalcanal are the official records of the United States and Japanese navies, and the records of the Japanese Army as they pertain to Guadalcanal. The Operational Archives of the Navy Department provided the war diaries, action reports, battle experience narratives and other papers on which the book draws. The Japanese records, reconstructed by the Japanese Self Defense Agency a number of years after the war, are understandably incomplete since many units were completely wiped out during the battle. In places—such as the story of the Tulagi battle on August 7 and 8—the Japanese have had to rely on the American reports. I also used Samuel Eliot Morison's authoritative *History of U.S. Naval Operations in World War II*, Volume 5—Guadalcanal. The authoritative source for the Japanese side is the Boeicho Kenshujo Senshishitsu Senshi Sosho (War History of the Imperial Defense Forces War Room) which contains about 100 volumes dealing with every aspect of the long Pacific war, from the Japanese point of view, although without bias as to the turns of events. I used the three volumes dealing with the Imperial Army's venture in Guadalcanal and the two volumes that deal with the Navy's part. The Army record is more extensive because it concerns all that happened in the entire South Pacific area.

Other books consulted include Paul S. Dull's *A Battle History of the Imperial Japanese Navy* (Naval Institute Press, Annapolis, 1978). This book contains some confusing errors, such as the author's statement that at the Battle of Tassafaronga Admiral Tanaka delivered his drums of supplies. In a postwar interview with Captain Tameichi Hara, Admiral Tanaka said he did *not* deliver the supplies that night, and that omission accounted for Admiral Yamamoto's growing antipathy to Tanaka that finally ended in his being shipped off to naval "Siberia" as commander of an unimportant base in Burma. In spite of a number of such problems in dealing with this book, it is valuable because of the author's careful search of Japanese records.

Captain Hara's book, *Japanese Destroyer Captain* (Ballantine, New York, 1961) is a first-hand account of certain operations that concerned Guadalcanal. It gives considerable insight into the actions and many facts that do not appear in official histories. Captain Hara, however, suffered at the time from a backlash that also disturbed a number of other Japanese officers: the feeling that Admiral Yamamoto was highly overrated and could in large part be blamed for Japan's defeats. I find this attitude wrongheaded, particularly in view of Admiral Yamamoto's prewar predictions as to what would happen if Japan attacked the United States. But in the 1960s Japan was suffering fits of iconoclasm, and Yamamoto had been too important a hero to the Japanese people not to be pulled down, too.

Richard Tregaskis' *Guadalcanal Diary* (Random House, New York, 1943) was extremely useful for color about the early days of the desperate fight for Guadalcanal. It was a surprise to me to find that the book was as fresh and interesting when I consulted it again in 1980 as it had been in the war years when it was a best-seller. Tregaskis gives the feeling of what it was like to be a marine on Guadalcanal in that time of uncertainty; the factual errors are only those that were common at the time, and they do not disturb the narrative.

I also used *Stand and Fight*, the story of a destroyer in battle, an unpublished manuscript in the Navy files, written by Lieutenant Commander Thomas McWhorter. It contains certain inaccuracies and incorrect conjectures but it is valuable for the feeling it gives of destroyer actions in the South Pacific at the time of Guadalcanal and particularly those of the Battle of Tassafaronga.

In 1971 the U.S. Naval Institute published *The Japanese Navy in World War II*, for which all students of the Pacific war must be grateful. A number of Japanese officers who were directly concerned had written articles for the Institute's *Proceedings*, assisted by some Americans (particularly Raymond O'Connor, Roger Pineau, and Clark Kawakami, all of whom have been involved in various translations and books about the Japanese in World War II). I used Toshikazu Ohmae's *The Battle of Savo Island* and Raizo Tanaka's *The Struggle for Guadalcanal*. The latter gives the best account of Admiral Tanaka's Tokyo Express yet written, although it is understated, in the Japanese style.

Hiroyuki Agawa's *The Reluctant Admiral: Yamamoto and the Imperial Navy* (Kodansha International, 1979) is a full-scale biography of the

late commander of the Combined Fleet. As far as Yamamoto's character
is concerned it is excellent. As far as Guadalcanal operations are concerned it is disappointing, because the information is scanty and scattered and the Admiral's thoughts and plans are never delineated. The
Japanese Self Defense Agency's history is far more revealing.

Saburo Ienaga's *The Pacific War* (Random House, New York, 1978)
is an excellent study of the whole war from a leftist standpoint. I was
cautioned against it by at least one American scholar of Japanese history;
but I found it quite valuable, especially for the poem on page 265–66,
which sums up the desperation of the Japanese troops who thought they
were marooned on Guadalcanal. The poem is from Kashichi Yoshida's
Gadarakanaru-Sen Shishu (Guadalcanal Battle Poems).

Zenji Orita's *I-Boat Captain* (with Joseph D. Harrington) is valuable
to anyone dealing with any aspect of Japanese submarine operations. It
does not have much about the Japanese submarine supply system for
Guadalcanal but there was not much of it, and Comdr. Orita was not
directly involved.

From the Dull, Orita, and Hara books one gets a clear, matter-of-fact
picture of the successful Japanese submarine operations at this time,
which were so deadly largely because of ineffectual American antisubmarine tactics.

A feeling for the Japanese airmen's life at the time of Guadalcanal is
given very well in Saburo Sakai's *Samurai*, with Martin Caidin and Fred
Saito. (I used the Bantam edition of 1978.) Sakai was one of Japan's
most successful naval aviators. His story of the fight against the Americans on the first day of the Guadalcanal invasion tells how seriously the
Japanese Zeros and their pilots outclassed the Americans in the beginning. Nevertheless Sakai was seriously wounded in that fight and barely
made it back the 550 miles to Rabaul in his battered Zero. He was almost immediately invalided back to Japan for recuperation.

Another source for the story of the 11th Air Fleet is *Rabauru Kaigun
Kokutai* (The Japanese Naval Air Force at Rabaul), by Masatake Okumiya (Tokyo, 1976). This book is more mundane; as Mr. Dull said of
the *Boeicho Kenshujo Senshishitsu* series, it is Germanic in its style of
history: exhaustive, and giving every detail including operational orders
as they were issued. But wading through and finding the action accounts
is not difficult. Many times they do not agree with the American accounts, and perhaps because of the loss of records—perhaps for other
reasons—the detail about operational and battle loses is very scanty.

I dealt with the roles of the major American commanders during the
period of the battles for Guadalcanal in my *How They Won the War in
the Pacific: Nimitz and His Admirals* (Weybright and Talley, New York,

1970). I restudied the whole matter for this book and came to the conclusion that Vice Admiral Frank Jack Fletcher's conduct of operations
during the period was one of the major reasons for the initial difficulties.
This matter has been glossed over during the years, although Admiral
Morison dealt with it in his official history in a very restrained fashion, as
befitted an "inside" account. One of the problems of the naval air force
in this period was that the carriers were commanded by officers who were
not aviators themselves, who seemed not to understand the primary purpose of the carrier as a weapon of attack and who probably distrusted the
carriers as much as they seemed to distrust the judgment of those around
them.

I also relied for command assessments and other information on Vice
Admiral George C. Dyer's *The Amphibians Came to Conquer*, Vol. 1,
the biography of Admiral Richmond Kelly Turner, amphibious commander at Guadalcanal. Admiral Dyer has several insights into the command structure and shows how much Admiral Turner did and how little
faith Admiral Ghormley had in the whole Guadalcanal operation.

The activity of the Australian Coast Watchers was extremely important in those desperate days when the marines were struggling to control
the air and to save Henderson Field from bombing and bombardment.
That tale is told by Commander Eric Feldt, Royal Australian Navy, in
The Coast Watchers. (I used the Bantam edition of 1979.)

The most complete account of the activities of aircraft and men of all
services who gathered on Guadalcanal in August and September of 1942
is given in *The Cactus Air Force* by Thomas G. Miller, Jr., and I relied
on that heavily for the story of the American side of air operations.

For the day to day picture of what was happening on the American
side I used the *War Diary of the South Pacific Command* extensively. It
is impersonal—it does not even register the change of command from
Ghormley to Halsey—but it gives an excellent picture of the concerns of
the American command, running the gamut from survival in those dark
days of August and September to almost nonchalance in the beginning of
1943. From that document one can gain a glimmer of the reason that
the Japanese were able to conduct that miraculous withdrawal of 11,000
men with so little incident. The attention of Admiral Halsey and his subordinates was basically elsewhere; they had begun to prosecute the offensive against the Japanese in the South Pacific.

INDEX